LETTING GOD

LETTING GOD

CHRISTIAN MEDITATIONS FOR RECOVERING PERSONS

A. PHILIP PARHAM

HarperSanFrancisco
A Division of HarperCollins*Publishers*

LETTING GOD: *Christian Meditations for Recovering Persons.*
Copyright © 1987 by A. Philip Parham. All rights reserved.
Printed in the United States of America. No part of this book
may be used or reproduced in any manner whatsoever without
written permission except in the case of brief quotations
embodied in critical articles and reviews. For information
address HarperCollins Publishers Inc., 10 East 53rd Street,
New York, NY 10022.

HarperCollins books may be purchased for educational,
business, or sales promotional use. For information please
write: Special Markets Department, HarperCollins Publishers
Inc., 10 East 53rd Street, New York, NY 10022.

HarperCollins Web Site: http://www.harpercollins.com
HarperCollins®, ☕®, and HarperSanFrancisco™ are
trademarks of HarperCollins Publishers Inc.

Library of Congress Cataloging-in-Publication Data
Parham, A. Philip.
    Letting God.

    Includes indexes.
    1. Alcoholics—Prayer books and devotions—English.
2. Devotional calendars. I. Title.
BV4596.A48P37   1987   242'.66   86–45835
ISBN 0–06–250669–2 (pbk.)

06 07   BANTA 28 27 26 25

Acknowledgments

This book reflects the lives of many people. I have received godly wisdom from the pain and recovery of more people than I can possibly acknowledge, as well as from countless Twelve Step meetings. At the retreats I attend and conduct, I find myriad spiritual treasures, in the form of stories, jokes, anecdotes, and quotable sayings. Many appear throughout this book; I thank all the originators. I have long since forgotten their names, but not their faces. I thank God on their behalf, who, in Christ, was always in their company — and still is.

I am particularly indebted to several special people. To John Beebe, priest and friend, I am grateful for more than the cheer he gave me in my writing. Father John filled my cup with hundreds of illustrations from his sermons. I have used many of these gems with his permission and blessing.

To Keith Miller, I am honored by his foreword to this book, and above all, I am grateful for his graceful and unconditional love as a Christian friend in recovery. Keith's wonderful books have fed me in the past, and his personal companionship has been an added gift. His prayers and presence in the midst of my own pain have ministered Christ's health and wholeness to me.

To James Colaianni, fellow Christian and theologian, my admiration and thanksgiving for his permission to use portions of his published works by Voicings Publications. I am indebted to James for the many stories and pertinent illustrations that have informed and enriched my words on recovery and Christianity.

I received unique help for my August meditations on the Twenty-third Psalm from observations about shepherds and sheep in Palestine adapted from *God's Psychiatry* by Charles L. Allen, copyright © 1953 by Fleming H. Revell Company, renewed 1981 by Charles L. Allen and used by permission of Fleming H. Revell Company.

For all my friends in the National Episcopal Coalition on Alcohol and Drugs, in my Al-Anon fellowship and in my Codependents Anonymous groups, I praise God for their experience, strength, and hope, which have now become mine as well.

Above all, I give thanks to God for my family. To my wife, Ruth, for her superb skill as a typist and for her direct, sweet spirit — I stand in awe. I dedicate this book to my daughters Susan, Sharon, and Sandy, with all my love, respect, and blessings.

I predict that *Letting God* will be used by thousands of people and for a long time. This is a book that fills a void in the world of daily devotional literature. The sudden proliferation of Twelve Step programs in recent years (based on the principles of Alcoholics Anonymous) has brought hundreds of Christians into contact with a different spiritual approach to recovery from addictive and compulsive behaviors. And although such people are extremely grateful to God for their recovery, the daily devotional books relating to Twelve Step programs assiduously avoid any mention of Jesus Christ or specific biblical references. This means that Christians have no literary "place" to go to get nurtured through Christ regarding the specific issues of their recovery.

But this is exactly what Phil Parham has provided in *Letting God*: a sensitive and well-prepared daily devotional book that is unashamedly Christian and yet deals specifically and sometimes poignantly with the difficult spiritual issues surrounding Twelve Step recovery.

This book can be helpful to recovering Christians or to non-Christians in Twelve Step programs who are open to the idea of a Higher Power as revealed in Jesus Christ. I am personally grateful to Phil for writing this book, and I commend it to other people who are trying to find and do God's will one day at a time.

Keith Miller
Austin, Texas

Preface

"Letting God" is a shorthand version of the slogan of Alcoholics Anonymous "Let go and let God." These daily Scripture readings, meditations, and prayers provide Christian reinforcement to this important slogan. In the last fifty years the success of Alcoholics Anonymous has enabled the development of hundreds of other programs of recovery based on the Twelve Steps and the slogans. The best known are Al-Anon, Alateen, Adult Children of Alcoholics, Overeaters Anonymous, Narcotics Anonymous, Gamblers Anonymous, and Emotions Anonymous. This book is for Christians who are involved in any or all of these groups.

The book is addressed to Christians in recovery programs; it is not for all Christians. If you do not regard addiction and compulsive behavior as diseases and are convinced that these conditions result from sin, you will not find your opinions echoed here. If you are also sure that people with addictions are the victims of their own weakness, mental illness, or stubbornness, then this book will not reinforce your beliefs. But if you believe in the power of God in Christ to heal, and you can set aside your judgment about the causes of addiction, then you will find sustenance in *Letting God*.

These pages are all about God. "Letting God" testifies to the release of tension, the surrender to trust, and being at ease instead of in "dis-ease." What is offered each day is relaxation and peace in Christ. You will be called to turn over control of your steering wheel. You will be urged to relax your power and control and open your door to the priceless gift of serenity in our Lord and Savior. You will be presented with Scripture, stories, short essays, and even humor as the way to let God take over. I have learned in thirty years of experience with alcoholics and other addicts and twenty-five years as a Christian pastor that living the gospel truth *and* Twelve-Step recovery creates a hallowed and holy life. This holiness is not sainthood but a serene state of being, achieved as we cease our striving, halt our stressful effort, and fall into the arms of our Higher Power, Jesus Christ.

"Letting God" is the key to most all experiences of sacredness and spirituality. The surrender to the divine within and without, the acknowledgment of the humanity of the Holy and the holiness of the human, is to "Let go and let God." As we allow God to be God, without trying to fix or manipulate his reality in heaven or earth, we welcome his healing love. We let love flow. We use no force, no struggle, no strain, no competition, no trying harder, no willpower, but simple giving up and giving in to his higher power. We admit and accept our weakness and God's strength. If we do not make this unconditional surrender to God, our own spirituality will lie dormant and lifeless. Our selfish will becomes our god, and we run rampant toward our own self-destruction, screaming to the end, "I can do it myself!"

But when we take that first step of surrender and admit our out-of-control powerlessness, we become open to God's own miracle in Christ. We learn how wonderful and blessed it is to receive and accept, to be vulnerable and defenseless before God. To become like softly turned soil, like good, yielding dirt ready for the seed of life, is to encourage recovery to take root. We stop declaring our own independence. We become as little children: we abandon our own unmanageable control and allow love to manage and control us. When we let go and let God, we give up our natural compulsion for power, to be right, to be managing directors, to be our own master. We release the hurt little inner child deep within each of us, starving for affection and attention, and collapse into the everlasting arms of our Savior.

I believe firmly that by surrendering to God as he is known in the gospel of Jesus Christ *and at the same time* surrendering to Twelve-Step recovery, we surrender to the same healing love of God. A Christian and a person in recovery are not in conflict; they are companions and friends. A recovering Christian works a program and lives a faith that produces and glorifies the same God of faith, hope, and love. Going to meetings and going to church are the same pilgrim's road. When we "let God" we are already walking the "King's highway." As Christians, we know that the way of the cross is no easy road. We also know that such surrender is frightening, as "it is a fearful thing to fall into the hands of the living God." (Hebrews 10:31) But it is only when "into his hands we commit our spirits" (Luke 23:46) that we may live. Recovery and salvation are the same. Our life depends on God.

May these pages draw you even closer to this truth.

A. Philip Parham
Easter 1987

1. We admitted we were powerless over alcohol—that our lives had become unmanageable.
2. Came to believe that a Power greater than ourselves could restore us to sanity.
3. Made a decision to turn our will and our lives over to the care of God *as we understood Him.*
4. Made a searching and fearless moral inventory of ourselves.
5. Admitted to God, to ourselves, and to another human being the exact nature of our wrongs.
6. Were entirely ready to have God remove all these defects of character.
7. Humbly asked Him to remove our shortcomings.
8. Made a list of all persons we had harmed, and became willing to make amends to them all.
9. Made direct amends to such people wherever possible, except when to do so would injure them or others.
10. Continued to take personal inventory and when we were wrong promptly admitted it.
11. Sought through prayer and meditation to improve our conscious contact with God *as we understand Him* praying only for knowledge of His Will for us and the power to carry that out.
12. Having had a spiritual awakening as a result of these steps, we tried to carry this message to alcoholics, and to practice these principles in all our affairs.

ANGER

A person who is angry on the right grounds, against the right person, in the right manner, at the right moment, and for the right length of time deserves great praise. This comment was seen on the cover of a book, since lost. What is the "right" of anger? Most of us who have been the target of hostility find it anything but right. It feels all wrong. In recovery, we are cautioned to avoid "hunger, anger, loneliness, and tiredness" as disruptions of our recovery walk. We can manage to avoid being hungry, lonely, or tired, but how can we avoid anger? Should we? Someone once said, "Anger is a divinely implanted emotion. Closely allied to our instinct for right, it is designed to be used for constructive spiritual purposes. The person who cannot feel anger at evil is a person who lacks enthusiasm for good." I have observed and experienced the benefits of healthy anger, providing energy to protest injustice and to right wrongs. Perhaps such a dynamic is not anger at all, but determination, courage, and resolution to put things right. In my experience if we embrace what we call anger before it becomes rage and hatred, we can harness this power for good and constructive purposes. So I find that anger has a valuable gift in its protest—energy against evil, sickness, and sin. I recall that Jesus was angry frequently, and I am sure it was for all the right reasons.

There is something about righteous indignation that provides strength to combat the unacceptable and unjust things and people of this world. Surely, anger never arises out of trivial matters, but always about something vitally important. I guess if we did not have good, God-given anger, we would be passive, timid, and unable to get steamed up about anything worthwhile.

Therefore, if any one is in Christ, he is a new creation; the old has passed away, behold, the new has come.

2 CORINTHIANS 5:17

What lies ahead of us this new year in our recovery? One thing is certain—we are never finished. There is always another step to take or a fresh opportunity to work the steps again. An unknown writer has captured this reality well:

> We only see a little of the ocean,
> A few miles' distance from the rocky shore;
> But oh! out there beyond—beyond the wave's horizon
> There's more—there's more.

The "more" that is ahead is God. Like the prow of a ship cutting through the uncharted waves, God in Christ is in front; he is our future. He is in all our tomorrows, in all our new beginnings. Although we may fear what lies ahead, we need not be full of dread. God is there already, and everything the future can bring us will have to meet him first before it reaches us. Whatever is in store for us, our Higher Power, Jesus Christ, will be our constant companion and ever-present friend and savior. He is our "more," and he is never finished with us. May we begin and finish each day of the year with him. Today is set aside by the church as the feast of the "Holy Name of Jesus." May *every* day be his this year.

Holy Jesus, in your name and with your help, each day there is always more of your holy love and life. Amen.

For through the Spirit, by faith, we wait for the hope of righteousness.

GALATIANS 5:5

Although we cannot control the future of our recovery, our attitude toward tomorrow affects our life today. When we "look forward" to what lies ahead, we are alive. This attitude is often called hope, or trusting God's providence. Being reassured and calm about tomorrow saves us from fear and anxiety today. The "priceless gift of serenity" is built upon our confident and forward-looking gaze into the future. "It'll be all right" is our motto. Filled with hopeful expectation, John Burroughs wrote these words:

> The stars come nightly to the sky;
> The tidal wave unto the sea:
> Nor time, nor space, nor deep, nor nigh,
> Can keep my own away from me.

What "my own" is, is what God has in mind. God's way is ours. He won't be rushed; all in good time. The future is in God's hands. Our own special days will come. One thing is certain: with trust in God's love, all future days will be good. Saint Paul said that the present time is not worth comparing with the future glory God shall give us. "We know that in everything God works for good with those who love him" (Rom. 8:28).

Jesus, teach me to wait in hope and look forward to each tomorrow with love for you. Amen.

Jesus looked at them and said, "With men it is impossible, but not with God; for all things are possible with God."

MARK 10:27

A very wise doctor once said, "It doesn't matter so much what disease a patient has, but it is extremely important to know which patient has the disease."

Two men had tuberculosis, both contracting the disease at the same time. They both went to the same sanatorium together. One was home in eighteen months, fully recovered and healthy. The other man was dead in six months. Why? There were no physical or biological differences, but the survivor faced his disease with courage, acceptance, and faith in God; the dead man faced his disease with complaints, anxiety, and despair—never once leaning on God. What a difference faith makes!

What kind of patients are we toward our disease, our particular condition? Has our sickness or stress made us aware of how weak and fragile we are? That's okay. We *are* helpless to control our compulsion, addiction, or obsession—on our terms. Yet we have unlimited help on God's terms. Will we accept this inescapable fact and "Let go, and let God"?

Holy Jesus, open my eyes to my helplessness. Open my heart to your love. Open my will to your care and control. Amen.

"Behold, I stand at the door and knock; if any one hears my voice and opens the door, I will come in to him and eat with him, and he with me."

REVELATION 3:20

The Lord has all the help we need. The question is, Do we want his help? Jesus asked a blind man, "What do you *want* me to do for you?" (Luke 18:41). The man had been blind all his life, a beggar. That's all he knew. Jesus knew that such a man may not want unfamiliar sight. He also knew that the unknown challenges of the life of recovery could be fearful. It was a good question. With great courage the blind man chose the path of sight.

Ask yourself: What do I want? Do I really want recovery, to risk getting healthy? Do I honestly want to take on such a responsibility? Do I want to take that First Step of the Twelve and admit my powerlessness over my anesthetic, and that my life has become unmanageable? Do I want to take the Second Step and believe that God can restore my sanity and sight? Do I want to take the crucial Third Step and turn my life and will over to God as I can and will know him in Jesus Christ?

Jesus doesn't work against our will. He calls us, but he will not force himself on us. Yet he is always with us, maybe right behind us, just like our shadow. Until we turn and risk a look, he will not be present to us.

Blessed Redeemer, increase my desire to answer your call and respond to your loving invitation. Amen.

"Come to me, all who labor and are heavy laden, and I will give you rest."

MATTHEW 11:28

Why do some people do so well in their Twelve-Step recovery and others do not? What can we learn from prisoners who survive concentration camps? The survivors managed to keep an attitude of faithful and hopeful optimism. They stuck to their plan. They hung on to their Higher Power. In many cases that plan and power was from Jesus.

When sickness and suffering are permitted to stir up and stimulate dependence on God, then victims begin to taste victory. When we lay our little crosses at the foot of the cross of Jesus, we enter into the Christ-life and share in his resurrection. We become free.

We become free from our selves. Ask yourself: Wouldn't it be wonderful not to have to carry the whole load? Can I turn loose of my sickness? Can I fire my old manager (me) and take on a new one (Christ)? Can I switch from self-control to Christ-control? I know it's up to me. Will I let Jesus take over?

Dear Lord, please take over. I'm tired of my management. Free me by receiving me as your servant. Amen.

"Fear not, little flock, for it is your Father's good pleasure to give you the kingdom."

LUKE 12:32

A wealthy woman once felt that God was calling her to the religious life. She thought that she would be able to give up everything in order to follow Christ, with one exception. She had a garden that was very important to her. It was a place for her to be alone, to be at peace with herself, and to find refreshment. She was unwilling and unable to give up the key to her secret garden. Her privacy was too precious to share even with God.

What a powerful symbol that is for us! Each of us has a secret garden, and we are often unwilling to give up the key to Jesus and let him in. We want him to keep his distance at times. We find it so hard to learn that if we let him into every space and place in our lives, he will give it all back to us, and then some!

Mother Teresa of Calcutta once said that "God has only our hands with which to bless the world." She spoke of our need to reach out to the poor and destitute around us. But we ourselves are also in need of blessing, a blessing we can find only by taking down our hands that hide our faces from Christ. When we turn loose and give up our need for privacy, we break the fear of Adam and Eve, who hid their shame and nakedness from God in their Garden of Eden. We too are ashamed, full of fear of being found out. Yet when we reach out to take Christ's hands, we will find our own blessing. All we need do is to come out from hiding.

O Christ, it's so hard to be honest and open with you. I am so afraid that you will find out all my secrets. Help me to know that only by being naked before you can I be clothed with your blessings and enter your kingdom. Amen.

"Whoever lives and believes in me shall never die."
JOHN 11:26

If we do give up and give in to Christ, what then? We are in for a treat! If we let down our guard and surrender, we find such release and relief we'll wonder why we took so long. Whenever our Lord comes into our life anew, we are truly "born again"– and again and again. Whether we greet him as an old friend or for the first time, all things are made new! This is truly "good news"!

With Christ we can live the Twelve Steps of our recovery program with the best and brightest of all "spiritualities"! Christ will turn our despair into a gentle, calm expectancy. He will turn the turmoil and anxiety within us into confident, joyous hope and serenity. Above all, he will surprise us with his grace and graciousness and make our recovery his triumph. He will give each of us his very special brand of peace.

Ask yourself: Am I ready to receive what Christ gives me? In spite of my pain, am I willing to accept his gifts as blessings I *need* and not just what I want? In spite of my pride, am I willing to let his spirit help control me? Am I prepared to allow Christ to take charge and help me become more open, honest, loving, caring, kind, and forgiving to *myself* and others? Each day can be my day of resurrection; am I ready? Will I believe and live?

O gracious Savior, give me new life. Grant me the power of your resurrection. Amen.

"Whoever exalts himself will be humbled, and whoever humbles himself will be exalted."

MATTHEW 23:12

It's unfortunate that the word *shame* has almost disappeared from our vocabulary. There is no question that feeling humiliated or "put down" is not healthy, but being humble and possessing a proper sense of shame is right! It is no disgrace to blush. Jesus commends the one "who humbles himself."

Unlike guilt, which is a judgment of our actions, shame is a feeling. It is the emotional reaction to our guilt. Like an itch that needs to be scratched, shame urges us to relieve our guilt. Healthy shame acknowledges the guilty act, shows sensitivity and responsibility, and moves toward forgiveness, confessing, "I have done those things which I ought not to have done." The church calls this healthy reaction to guilt "contrition," a true and accurate sense of sorrow for our sins. It is the pathway back to reconciliation. It is the urge to "make amends." Healthy shame is confessed, cleansed, eliminated, and forgotten.

Unhealthy shame is "scrupulosity," which is more than the temporary feeling of shame for real misdeeds. A scrupulous person has a constant attitude of self-hatred, self-reproach. and self-loathing and clings to feelings of unworthiness no matter how much forgiveness is offered. Such a person feels ashamed just being alive.

In either case, no matter how we suffer, whether from healthy shame or unhealthy scrupulosity, Christ invites us to give it all to him for his disposal. The Eighth and Ninth Steps are ideal occasions to answer his invitation. He wants us to love ourselves and be free, not live in the bondage of any kind of shame.

O loving Lord, bring me to the foot of your cross to accept your outstretched arms. Embrace me and release me. Amen.

"Nor will they say, 'Lo, here it is!' or 'There!' for behold, the kingdom of God is in the midst of you."

LUKE 17:21

What is the most immediate thing about you? Is it either yesterday or tomorrow? Is it not now—*only* now? The most vital reality we experience is what now lies within. Whatever we feel, think, will, or sense is now inside. To know ourselves is to gaze within, to look into the inner recesses of our being. It is there we find the in-dwelling Christ. And we don't have to wait.

Yet how fearsome a prospect it is to confront our own insides! It is even more awesome to think that is where the kingdom of God is! We are used to hearing from certain schools of psychology that our inner thoughts, drives, and urges are a witches' brew of evil and brutal energies, that our unconscious is dangerous and sinister.

But this is not so with Carl Jung, the great friend and mentor of Alcoholics Anonymous. He has said that at least 90 percent of the unconscious is golden. Imagine that! We need not fear the evil within us; we can mine gold in the royal kingdom within. We can look with reverent awe for the riches there.

If anything stimulates and reinforces our own self-esteem, it is the belief that God rules within us. When we accept that, everything changes. How can we lose?

How joyous, Lord, that you planted your own life and kingdom within me! Help me to keep my own little kingdom from rebelling against yours. Amen.

"But when you pray, go into your room and shut the door."
MATTHEW 6:6a

What is the "room" that Jesus spoke of? Houses in his day did not have rooms as we know them today. Most homes in Palestine had only one room. The word *room* meant "inner room of the soul." It did not refer to any objective, outward, physical place, but to something subjective, inward, spiritual. We all have such a place within. It was written of Catherine of Siena that "she had built in her soul a chapel which she resolved never to leave, whatever her occupation. No one could take that interior chapel from her and she never left it." Brother Lawrence once said: "It is not necessary for being with God to be always at church; we may make a chapel of our meekness, humility, and love." Jesus meant for us to make within us a temple for the Holy Spirit, where we may be still, where we may speak and listen to God—and hear no other voices. This is where the Eleventh Step directs us daily—to prayer and meditation, to conscious contact with God. The Eleventh Step is our daily chapel time in the privacy of our spiritual being.

If we must have a room within set aside for God, we can have a house. Why not have several rooms within? We can reserve one room for praise, one for petition, one for confession, one for adoration, one for relaxation, one for intercession, one for meditation. We can construct a special room for every special prayer need and furnish them all as we choose, with what we value most. We furnish our homes with meaningful, memorable, and pleasurable things. Why not furnish our "prayer house" in the same way? Why not make it as lovely, comfortable, and inviting to God as we can? Then ask him to move in and stay forever.

Thank you, Jesus, for reminding me of my own inner chapel. Help me construct many rooms in my soul for you. Amen.

So the Jews said, "See how he loved him!"

JOHN 11:36

One grandfather always had the gift of saying just the right thing. On a particular Thanksgiving Day he explained to his little grandson the custom of breaking the turkey wishbone. Eager to have his wish come true, the little boy was crushed when he wound up with the small end of the bone. "That's all right, my boy," said his grandfather with a smile. "My wish was that you would get your wish."

To want what is best for others is the key to full recovery. The Twelfth Step is an example of caring for others' welfare and recovery. When we begin to become healthy, we want to share our health with others. Recovery is too precious to horde; it must be given away. To genuinely desire the healing of others carries a power of healing in itself. The sincere tear shed for our brothers or sisters in their presence is an actual prescription for healing. Our love for one another is God's own medicine.

Jesus gives us new hearts—hearts to beat strongly within us with new power and health for ourselves. But our hearts get even stronger as they touch others' hearts with loving care and encouragement. The Twelve Steps and the gospel both thrive on active caring and support of each other.

Dear Lord, I know you are healing my heart. I also know you want me to help other hearts beat stronger too. Amen.

> *"What man of you, having a hundred sheep, if he has lost one of them, does not leave the ninety-nine in the wilderness, and go after the one which is lost, until he finds it?"*
>
> LUKE 15:4

There was once a mother who served stewed prunes on occasion. She had a young son who thoroughly hated them. When he refused to eat the prunes, she would say, "God won't like that. God doesn't like little boys who don't finish their prunes. God will be very angry." One night at dinner, looking at the last two prunes in the bowl, the boy finally had had enough. He did not care how angry God became. He was sent to bed. A few minutes later, a terrible thunderstorm broke loose—lightning flashed, thunder clapped, and wind and rain pounded his bedroom window. The mother thought her son would be terrified. When she arrived in his room, he was standing with his face against the window saying, "My, my. Such a fuss to make over two prunes."

This boy's understanding of God is very close to that of Jesus, who saw God as loving, understanding, and forgiving. The mother's view is close to that of those who fear God and use that fear to control others; it hardly represents "good news." Yet how many of us live with guilt and fear over some act or some thought? Compulsive persons, whose addictive diseases have often led to out-of-control behavior, feel overwhelming fear and shame. We are sure God is angry.

But Jesus says he is not! God is gracious. He loves us. His love is never withheld because of our weakness or rebellion. There is nothing that can separate us from him. He will come to our aid no matter how lost we are. Nothing we have done or will ever do "will be able to separate us from the love of God in Christ Jesus our Lord" (Rom. 8:39).

O Good Shepherd, when I stray, calm my fear and erase my shame so I can receive your care and love with joy. Amen.

*Then he said to Thomas, "Put your finger here, and see my
hands; and put out your hand, and place it in my side; do
not be faithless, but believing." Thomas answered him,
"My Lord and my God!"*

JOHN 20:27–28

Albert Einstein once said, "The most beautiful experience we can have is the mysterious. . . . Whoever can no
longer wonder, no longer marvel, is as good as dead." If
we begin to take a look at the mystery of the universe, we
see that as our knowledge increases, so does the wonder.
Ptolemy could only count 1,022 stars; Galileo, only 5,000
through his telescope; in 1916, astronomers' best guess
was 300 billion. That figure soon doubled, then trebled.
Now we talk of galaxies and metagalaxies, until the mind
turns to jelly. Our own galaxy is 100,000 times 6 trillion
miles wide, yet we know that it is but a tiny part of the larger,
unknown star system.

Yet what about the mystery of faith? How do I respond
to the enormity of Jesus the Christ in my life and in my
recovery?

Our positive responses to the world and to our Savior
are responses of faith: faith in the tangible and in the intan-
gible. In our scripture passage, Thomas accepted only the
tangible. He demanded hands-on proof. Some of us also
demand such concrete evidence. Yet we have faith in
astronomers' telescopes and findings as trustworthy without seeing or understanding for ourselves.

"Let go and let God" is such a slogan worthy of trust.
It has worked for millions. Why not trust what has worked
for others? Such trust is hard, almost unnatural—yet recovery dwells more in the supernatural. Just think where
"doing what comes naturally" led us.

*O Christ, the incarnate Word, my mysterious Lord, give me what
I need so much: Faith and trust in your healing, life-giving presence.
Amen.*

Being asked by the Pharisees when the kingdom of God was coming, he answered them, "The kingdom of God is not coming with signs to be observed."

LUKE 17:20–21

Part of "letting go and letting God" is not only surrendering to his will but also being open to his unexpected action. God has a way all his own that frequently surprises us. Just when we become comfortable with his regular ways, he does something quite irregular.

Joan of Arc, in George Bernard Shaw's play, is asked by her interrogator about her conversations with God: "How do you mean, voices?" She responds, "I hear voices telling me what to do. They come from God." Her questioner insists, "The voices come from your imagination." To this Saint Joan replies, "Of course, that is how the message of God comes to me." How many of us are ready for that? Does God speak to us through our imagination? Can we look for the kingdom of God within us?

Cardinal Cushing often told the story of the little girl who sat on her grandmother's lap to listen to the story of creation from the Book of Genesis. As this magnificent story unfolded, the grandmother noticed how quiet the child became and asked her, "Well, what do think of it, dear?" The little girl answered, "Oh, I love it, you never know what God is going to do next!"

Both Saint Joan and the little girl knew what Jesus teaches: we had better get used to expecting the unexpected from God. Who could have imagined that people like us, addicts of all shapes and sizes, once enslaved by our compulsions, could find God in our Twelve-Step fellowships? God can and will be present and active wherever he chooses, and "you never know what God is going to do next!"–except that it will be good.

O God of the imagination and the unexpected, help me to be open to new images and ways through which you may speak and act. Amen.

*And a great storm of wind arose, and the waves beat into
the boat, so that the boat was already filling. But he was
in the stern, asleep on the cushion; and they woke him
and said to him, "Teacher, do you not care if we perish?"
And he awoke and rebuked the wind, and said to the sea,
"Peace! Be still!" And the wind ceased, and there was a
great calm.*

MARK 4:37–39

Rembrandt fashioned one of his masterpieces from the
story of the storm on the Sea of Galilee. It shows the little
boat, filled with Jesus and his followers, colliding with a
great wave. You can feel the quaking of the thunderous
water as it hits the boat. The storm surrounds them. The
rigging is loose and flapping in the wind; the disciples
clearly show their fear. In the midst of all the storm and
panic, Jesus had to be awakened! He had such great trust
in God, his Father, that he could sink deep into the very
being of God without any concern.

Looking at this painting, we can say, "If only we could
learn to trust that way, to be like Christ asleep in the midst
of life's storms." With that picture in our mind, we can feel
that "everything is all right" no matter what kind of tem-
pest rages about us. Whether the storms are from fear,
worry, cravings, sadness, jealousy, or whatever else assaults
our program of sobriety and serenity, we are safe within
Christ's boat.

The example of Jesus asleep in the boat is our answer:
We are meant to be those who "let go and let God," just
as Jesus did all the way to the cross. We are not in control;
God is at the helm. That knowledge alone will calm our
stormy life.

*Jesus, give me your faith and trust in the Father. Help me to always
realize that I am God's child, so I may have peace and be still.
Amen.*

> *"Ask, and it will be given you; seek, and you will find; knock, and it will be opened to you."*
>
> MATTHEW 7:7

It's quite common to hear people seeking recovery say that their condition is based on circumstances. "I didn't get the breaks," "Luck was against me," "My boss (wife, husband) was against me," or "It's not my fault."

It's true that we became the way we are through no fault of our own. Fault has nothing to do with it. Blame is futile and fruitless. Why blame anyone? We simply have a disease, a compulsion, a condition that we surely did not plan or cause. Blaming anyone, including ourselves, will only prolong our agony. We have a no-fault condition.

We did not choose our distress. But we *can* choose life! Ask yourself: How long do I have to blame? How long will I resort to excuses? When will I learn that the only thing that matters is the desire to get well? When will I decide to surrender my life and will over to Christ for his healing? What have I got to lose except my own chains?"

Lord Christ, take my chains of shame and blame away. Help me choose your healing. Amen.

*"Take my yoke upon you, and learn from me; for I am
gentle and lowly in heart, and you will find rest for your
souls. For my yoke is easy, and my burden is light."*

MATTHEW 11:29–30

"But it's so hard!" Yes, it is. Nothing is more difficult than
surrender. Of course, it is fearful. Yet, why are we afraid
or ashamed to ask Jesus to come into our unmanageable
lives? Do we see him as a threat to our controlling ways?
We know that he is not some kind of fiend or thief who will
destroy us. We know he is the loving Good Shepherd, the
King of love. Yet we persist in our pride.

Like Adam and Eve, we would be "like God" (Gen. 3:5),
in control. To let God be God would mean that we couldn't
be in charge anymore. It is inescapable. At the very heart
of our humanity is our sin, our pride, our self-centered
stubbornness.

We should ask ourselves this: Isn't my own pride or self-
pity standing in Christ's way? My sickness is not my doing,
but my sinful pride is all my own, isn't it? My illness isn't
the problem; I am! Shall I continue to be stubborn in my
refusal to be helped? Don't I try to make myself greater
than Christ by rejecting his invitation, for whatever excuse
I offer?

*O divine Companion, drive away my stubborn pride. Break down
my wall of refusal. Conquer my self-centered will. Amen.*

*And the peace of God, which passes all understanding,
will keep your hearts and your minds in Christ Jesus.*

PHILIPPIANS 4:7

Most of us have witnessed a three year old in the midst of a temper tantrum. Soothing and soft words fall on deaf ears. Shouting and screaming back at the child fail. Sometimes nothing seems to work. Oftentimes such tantrums are cries for help, for someone else to take over. The fury comes out of frustration with a situation that is too immense and overwhelming to cope with.

We also can behave like frightened and frustrated children. Life often gets to be too much to handle! We cry out in exasperation and fury, "Please, please, for God's sake, somebody come and take this decision out of my hands; it's too big for me!" Then in the middle of our ranting and raving, we are picked up (still struggling and hollering) and put in our place. For a child that place is usually a crib, a song, or comforting and strong arms. For us it may be our meeting, our sponsor, a treatment center, or the arms of Christ. Like a screaming child, we may be begging for someone or something to take away the frustration by taking over for us.

That's where the structure and strong arms of our program and our Christian faith come in—both safe places to be. When we "let go" of our need to be in charge and "let God" take over, we can find the "peace of God, which passes all understanding" (Phil. 4:7). When we acknowledge God as "Father" and pray to him "*Thy* will be done" and not "*My* will be done," then we can finally feel safe, secure, and at peace.

Help me, O Christ, in the midst of my frustrations to know that I am not supposed to figure it all out or control everything. Pick me up and put me in my place, where I can be still and let your strong arms take over. Amen.

"You hypocrites! You know how to interpret the appearance of earth and sky; but why do you not know how to interpret the present time? And why do you not judge for yourselves what is right?"

LUKE 12:56–57

A young woman in college wrote the following letter to her parents. It was the first letter home in four months:

Dear Mom and Dad,

I'm sorry it has been so long since my last letter, but I didn't want you to worry about the fire in the dorm and my concussion, which happened when I fell out of the window trying to escape. I've been eager to tell you about the nice attendant from the service station around the corner who comforted me so before the ambulance came. I'm out of the hospital now, and feel great now that I am living with the nice service station attendant in his room over the garage. I know you will be happy to know that I really love him and that you will soon become grandparents.

In closing, let me tell you to stop worrying. There was no fire, I didn't fall out of the window, I didn't have a concussion, I am not living with anyone, and you are not going to be grandparents. I told you all those things because I got a "D" in biology and an "F" in history and I wanted you to put that into perspective.

How wise to consider several points of view! Perspective is so important, and what we think leads to what we do. Thought almost always precedes action, yet thinking can be inaccurate and miss the mark. In our program, we often fail to see our progress because of a faulty perspective. When we "let go, and let God" we can see our victories as well as pain and our problems. Like the college student, we need to see that things could always be worse. When we take our inventories, we need to see our strengths as well as our weaknesses and let God correct our point of view.

Dear Lord, keep my perspective clear and realistic. Help me see all sides and all angles before I act or react too hastily. Amen.

January 20

And he said to all, "If any man would come after me, let him deny himself and take up his cross daily and follow me. For whoever would save his life will lose it; and whoever loses his life for my sake, he will save it."

LUKE 9:23–24

How can you and I bear our pain if we give up our anesthetic? We probably can't. We've become dependent, addicted to a substance, a person, or an activity. We're hooked. But we can get unhooked. We must remember this about our distress: *We didn't cause it; we can't control it; and we can't cure it!* But God can create a miracle in us, anyway!

The Twelve Steps will help us bear our pain. The first three steps unhook us (these are the "give up" steps); the next three cleanse and reconcile us with ourselves (the "clean up" steps); the next three steps restore and reconcile us with others (the "make up" steps); and the last three steps maintain our freedom and health (the "keep up" steps). Even though our compulsion won't be cured, it will be "arrested" into a state of remission; we can soon become "well," even "weller than well."

Do we expect our recovery to be without any strain and pain, or will we risk the pains of recovery, taking courage from the pain Jesus endured for us?

O Christ of the cross, you endured pain and suffering for me. Help me bear my pain. Give me your courage. Amen.

*But Jesus on hearing this answered him, "Do not fear;
only believe, and she shall be well."*

LUKE 8:50

One of our greatest spiritual dangers, especially as we
walk the steps of our recovery, is "stinking thinking." Delusion comes in many forms. One false thought is the conviction that God cannot or will not help us. When we think
that way, we tend to allow ourselves to be dominated by
fear—fear of relapse, fear of the past, fear of guilt, fear of
embarrassment, fear of loneliness, fear of personal relationships, fear of being hurt again, fear of accidents. Whatever terror haunts us can lead to "stinking consequences."

When we think that God cannot or will not help us, we
leave ourselves wide open to these fearsome results. However, when we are convinced that God's power is greater
than any evil that could befall us, we can live with confidence and hope. We can also distinguish between fear
and sober precaution. Fear paralyzes and drives us. Precaution "leads us not into temptation and delivers us from
evil"; with it we avoid foolish mistakes and keep on the safe
steps of our program. A cautious person thinks clearly, sees
real danger, and can take reasonable risks.

When we are sure that "the whole world is in God's
hands," we can stand fast with Saint Paul when he said,
"We know that in everything God works for good with those
who love him, who are called according to his purpose"
(Rom. 8:28). What is God's purpose? Is it not that we
should love him and trust him? Love and trust make no
room for fear. So, listen to Jesus, when he tells us, "Do not
be afraid; . . . I am with you always" (Matt. 28:10, 20).

*Lord, keep my thinking clear of fear and full of proper caution.
Help me look to you in love and trust and not give way to worry
and anxiety. Amen.*

But deliver us from evil.

MATTHEW 6:13

Angels used to live in New Hampshire. In the White Mountains there once was an organization called the Blue Angels. Its members' cars had blue flashing lights on top. The Angels carried first-aid supplies, food, hot coffee, chains, tow ropes, gasoline, and other emergency supplies. These volunteers patrolled the winding, snowdrifted roads looking for stranded motorists. Anyone in distress was served and aided with no questions asked or lectures given. The help was given unconditionally, without charge.

We still have such angels. They are recovering people who follow the Twelve Steps and believe in Jesus the Christ. They aren't God's only angels, of course, but they offer what all angels give—love and service as an act of grace and goodness, with no strings attached except the hands of love.

We experience such generosity and kindness at every Twelve-Step meeting. We may not always see it, but the blue lights are flashing. The help for recovery is always there. Some of us have been discovered stuck and helpless, almost frozen in our snowdrift; we were rescued and personally carried or escorted to a meeting or church. Others found the flashing light of help on our own and came for recovery on our own. Yet one thing is clear—recovery and rescue are there always like an angel of God.

O Rescuer of my frozen life, send your angels to help me. Then help me be one of your angels in return. Amen.

> *"Whatever house you enter, first say, 'Peace be to this*
> *house!' And if a son of peace is there, your peace shall rest*
> *upon him; but if not, it shall return to you."*
>
> LUKE 10:5–6

The opposite of control is peace. We often say, "All I want is peace of mind," yet we keep on trying to force solutions and resort to white knuckle exertions in order to keep everything and everybody under control. Maintaining control is not peaceful. Jesus gives us his way—the way of "letting be" or "acceptance."

Our Lord calls us first to accept ourselves. He encourages each of us to be who we are. He also reminds us that we are to accept the lives of others as well. "Live and let live" is a message from the Lord as well as a slogan of all Twelve-Step programs. All recovery is a process of being delivered from the clutches of *control*. Self-control and other-control lie at the heart of our illness.

Jesus tells us that if we offer our peace, we cannot lose! Either our peace will "rest upon a son of peace" or it will return to us. When we freely give, what we volunteer will either "rest or return," without our efforts to control or manipulate the results.

Lord Jesus, help me to be willing to "let it be" and to turn loose of my urge to control others. Let your spirit of acceptance be upon me. Keep me from manipulating and planning my results. Amen.

"Peace I leave with you; my peace I give to you; not as the world gives do I give to you. Let not your hearts be troubled, neither let them be afraid."

JOHN 14:27

What if we don't have peace? How can we give what we do not have? We get it from Jesus. He gives it. We receive it. The Prince of Peace gives us a peace beyond understanding.

How do we go about receiving such peace? By asking for it. By letting go of our discontent and our troubled hearts. We have so little confidence in our own self-worth that we are never content with the way we and others are.

Yet our discontent can work *for* us too. Our sense of uneasiness can be so great that we become exhausted and just quit! That's a wonderful place to start! Rather than remaining restless we can rest in Christ. We can place our concerns in his lap. This will take the focus off ourselves and others and place it on our Lord.

Christ has what we desire. He can calm our troubled and fearful hearts. He has soothing words for each of us. He yearns for us to take what he has for us—his peace.

O, Prince of Peace, give me the peace you have just for me. Help me receive it as the gift it is. Amen.

John answered, "Master, we saw a man casting out demons in your name, and we forbade him, because he does not follow with us."

LUKE 9:49

It is amazing how little control Jesus exerted over others. His power was the power of attraction, not force or manipulation. He held out an invitation, not a weapon. When his followers saw someone doing good works and healing without using Jesus' name, he told his disciples to "let them be." If they are doing good, that is to everyone's benefit, even if they don't seem to have the right credentials.

How different we often are! We try to get people to do it our way or to follow our rules. Forcing others into our mold just does not work. Applauding and accepting others' good results and appreciating the distinct differences in people is much more productive.

It is so easy to give advice and try to shape others into our own idea of recovery. Is your friend abstinent and sober? Are the other members of your group more open, secure, and loving? Are they growing in confidence and enthusiasm for the Twelve Steps? Well, that's all that matters! They are with us, not against us.

Lord Christ, help me to be at ease with others and with their ways of recovery. Keep me from my own harsh judgments of others in recovery. Amen.

> *Then Peter came up and said to him, "Lord, how often shall my brother sin against me, and I forgive him? As many as seven times?"*
>
> MATTHEW 18:21

When our brother sinned against us, when our father rejected or abused us, when our mother shamed or condemned us, when our sister ridiculed or hurt us, or when anyone caused us pain, it was so easy to keep score, to remember, and to resent. We can find so many times when we can blame someone else for our past disappointments and our present situation. Past resentments can become a way of life, as we nurse and harbor old hurts and grudges. Forgive them? How can we? We have every reason to be bitter. They are to blame! We are their victims! Our resentment is justified.

Of course it is. So is our anger, rage, and hatred. But will our resentment and blame serve justice? Will revenge settle the score? Will our hate or self-pity solve anything? Our Twelve-Step program doesn't think so. Jesus didn't think so.

In fact, what our recovery program offers and what the Twelve Steps offer is the way out—the way of peace and serenity, the way of forgiveness. Healing comes from self-forgiveness and other-forgiveness, from "Live and let live."

Lord Christ, cleanse me from the devastation of my resentments. Let my past pain be buried. Give me your peace. Give your way of forgiveness. Amen.

> *"Judge not, and you will not be judged; condemn not, and you will not be condemned; forgive, and you will be forgiven."*
>
> LUKE 6:37

Jesus wants us to be free. The Twelve Steps want us to be free as well. Both want us to "live and let live." We can "live" if we forgive ourselves, and we can "let live" if we forgive others. One hand washes the other.

Our Lord yearns for our freedom and release from the prisons of our own minds and hearts. He offers "the priceless gift of serenity." But we cannot receive this gift while the corroding acid of bitterness and the malignant cancer of resentment eat away at our souls, doing more damage to us than any past offender could.

Jesus calls us to release the bitter past, to let go of the resentment, and to let justice be served by God. Though we may have every reason to be bitter, he would rather have us be better.

To be better is to be cleansed and healed from the pain of our hurtful past. To "live and let live" is to allow the injustices of the past to be purged on the funeral pyre of Christ's redeeming love. This love is Christ's own presence, his gift of himself. It will come only through the prayer of surrender to him.

O, healer of souls, give me freedom and release. Burn away all my bitterness, so that I can live in the fresh sweetness of your love. Amen.

> *And as they continued to ask him, he stood up and said to them, "Let him who is without sin among you be the first to throw a stone at her." And once more he bent down and wrote with his finger on the ground. But when they heard it, they went away, one by one, beginning with the eldest, and Jesus was left alone with the woman standing before him. Jesus looked up and said to her, "Woman, where are they? Has no one condemned you?" She said, "No one, Lord." And Jesus said, "Neither do I condemn you; go, and do not sin again."*
>
> JOHN 8:7-11

When Jesus told some scribes and Pharisees who had caught a woman in the sin of adultery, "Let him who is without sin among you be the first to cast a stone at her," no one could meet that test, so no stone was thrown.

Under the Law of Moses, she deserved her punishment, but Jesus brought a new law into the world, a law measured by *mercy*, not justice. If we receive what we deserve, and if justice is served, no one is safe. We are all doomed.

There is a story about a recovering person who had completed twenty years of the program successfully, had been active in church and community affairs, and was an outstanding citizen. When this person died and appeared before Saint Peter, the entrance requirements were laid out: "You need two thousand points to get in." After rehearsing all the achievements of his entire life, the applicant was told, "Good, that's worth three points!" "In that case," he said, "only the grace of God will get me in!" "That's right," answered Saint Peter, "that's worth 1,997 points. Come right in!"

O, Christ, my savior, help me to seek and serve mercy before justice, to forgive before I condemn. Let me be an instrument of your love in myself and for others, and live more by grace than law. Amen.

But he said to him, "A man once gave a great banquet, and invited many; and at the time for the banquet he sent his servant to say to those who had been invited, 'Come; for all is now ready.'"

LUKE 14:16–17

We are those whom Jesus has invited to come to his banquet. The feast he beckons us to is now. All is prepared. The table is set; the food is served. "Come to the table, get it while it's hot!" we are urged. To wait or hold back may spoil the meal.

The call of Christ is to come to a festive and joyous feast. What is it that keeps us from such a celebration? Perhaps somewhere we didn't hear or receive the invitation. Perhaps we did not really believe that the party would be fun. For whatever reason, we have no excuse now. Surely we feel our hunger and thirst. Surely we know we need to be fed, and most surely we could use some joy and celebration.

Thank God, he is patient with us and keeps on sending his invitation. His call is always in the present. It never stops. He is ready to feed us at any time, as long as that time is *now*. His feast never grows cold; he is never unprepared. We can hold back out of fear or shame or indifference, and we may miss out.

But we need not keep on missing out. Jesus is ready at any time to receive us. All we need do is stop making excuses and come sit down at his table.

Gracious Lord, rouse me to accept your invitation. Remove my laziness, dissolve my excuses, calm my fears. Get me to your table now. Amen.

The night is far gone, the day is at hand. Let us then cast off the works of darkness and put on the armor of light.
ROMANS 13:12

Why is it so hard to hear the invitation of Christ? It is as if we are deaf and dead to his voice. His words bounce off us as if we were a stone wall. Yet he can penetrate our deafness, and even in our deadness we can hear the voice of the Son of God, calling us to be with him. Even if we have become dull or dead to Christ, he can break through. Saint Paul reminds us that we have no time to procrastinate. He says, "Besides this you know what hour it is, how it is full time now for you to wake from sleep. For salvation is nearer to us now than when we first believed; the night is far gone, the day is at hand" (Rom. 13:11–12).

Don't we really know? Aren't we aware? We know we need to be alive and awake. We know we have been asleep much too long. Christ is ready to undo any death we are experiencing. He has no wish for us to be sleepwalkers; but desires only our freedom and new life. Yet this life is our choice. As hard as he shakes us, we must hear and wake up on our own.

Heighten and increase my awareness, O Christ, so that I may hear, wake up, and live in you. Amen.

And he said, "Truly, I say to you, no prophet is acceptable in his own country."

LUKE 4:24

A man once wrote the Department of Agriculture about the dandelions in his lawn. "Dear Sirs," he wrote. "My lawn is infested with dandelions. I have pulled them and sprayed them. I have used every device known to humanity. But still the dandelions keep multiplying. I am at my wits' end. Can you help me?" The department wrote back, "Dear Sir, since you cannot get rid of your dandelions, we suggest that you learn to love them. You might even eat them."

There are dandelions in everyone's life that simply must be accepted, even if it is not easy to do so.

At the head of our dandelion list are our compulsions and addictions. We did not choose them any more than we chose the color of our hair. But acceptance is the key to serenity, so is change. We can find help by admitting and accepting our condition and then turning to the Twelve Steps and to Christ for our healing and recovery. Desperate weed control or complaining will never help. Our program and our Lord will.

Dear Lord, please help me to accept myself and seek the serenity of your grace so I may live and triumph over my condition, and not wear myself out by straining or complaining. Amen.

ARGUMENTS

I have noticed that when someone says he agrees with you in principle, he's invariably getting ready to argue with you. Arguments are not usually productive; however, discussions usually are. Arguments are basically battles between two people insisting that they are right. It is a win-lose proposition. No one seeks to lose an argument. Winning is the goal. Unfortunately we become blinded to the other side and can only see our truth. This is so common in religious arguments. Spurgeon said, "It seems odd that certain who talk so much of what the Holy Spirit reveals to themselves, should think so little of what he has revealed to others." Someone jokingly said, "Any argument has two sides, and they're usually married to each other." Unfortunately, we often forget that there are two sides.

An argument can be transformed into a discussion by remembering that there are two sides and that both sides should win, not just one. A win-win encounter will provide learning on both sides and each will benefit by the conversation. *Listening and learning* is as important as *showing and telling*. Asking questions and being curious about the other's ideas and opinions will enrich and bless the matter under review. Understanding should be the goal, not winning points.

I have found I can avoid arguments by prefacing opinions as mine alone, and that I could be wrong! Being right is not so important if you are the only one who thinks so. Before I impute some thought or feeling to another, I try to remember to say, "I could be wrong, but it seems to me that you are not feeling well today. Is that right or am I imagining things?" This way, I clear the way to be agreed with or corrected without any attack or presumption on my part. It seems to work.

And he said, "Take heed that you are not led astray; for many will come in my name, saying, 'I am he!' and, 'The time is at hand!' Do not go after them."

LUKE 21:8

Over a thousand years ago, a Spanish kingdom was under attack by foreign invaders. For many years, one small fort withstood all assaults, thanks to a remarkable leader called El Cid. When their great leader died, his followers had an idea. They dressed his body in his armor, tied a sword in his hand, and placed his corpse on his horse. With El Cid's body in the lead, the Spanish forces charged. But they were quickly defeated, for this act fooled no one. A desperate trick that collapsed led to despair instead of victory.

We are often tempted to trick our way through a step or a meeting. We continue to deceive ourselves and cover up the truth. Trying to prop up old bodies or dress up dead ideas is a constant temptation. We yearn for our old ways, our old fun times, our fond memories of happy experiences. Yet we know they are dead and can never return.

Recovery includes mourning and grief, and grieving is a necessary step to health and recovery. The first objective of grief work is acceptance of reality. This is Step One of recovery: "We admitted we were powerless and our lives were unmanageable." This is the truth. It cannot be changed or dressed up or propped up to life. Thank God, our Lord is not a lifeless body or a stage prop. Christ is alive, powerful, and actively winning our new life of recovery with us.

Heavenly Lord, keep my eyes clear and my search honest. Show me truth and help me accept it, as I lean on your strength and life. Amen.

*I appeal to you therefore, brethren, by the mercies of God,
to present your bodies as a living sacrifice, holy and
acceptable to God, which is your spiritual worship.*
ROMANS 12:1

H. G. Wells once said, "Until we have found God we begin
at no beginning, we work to no end." This could be our
motto for our recovery and release from addiction. Until
we find God, our recovery can't begin or get anywhere. Our
discovery and devotion to God is not a special and unique
cure for addictive diseases. God is every person's need. God
is as necessary to life as air, water, and food.

Human beings instinctively worship. We bow down and
devote our energy and loyalty to something. This is not an
option. We *must* believe in some important cause, group,
activity, or person. Our tragedy is that we choose such false
and unreliable gods. The first commandment in the law
is: "Thou shalt have no other gods but me." Only the God
of Abraham, Isaac, and Jacob, only the God and Father
of our Lord Jesus Christ is worthy of worship. Only the creator, redeemer, and sanctifier—the only God—is worthy of
our devotion. Only he can heal us. Wealth, fame, pleasure,
power, or knowledge cannot substitute for God in Christ.
These things may come our way, but not by worshiping any
of them. Jesus said: "Seek first his kingdom and his righteousness, and all these things shall be yours as well"
(Matt. 6:33).

Don't let me put anything before you, O God. Amen.

And, having been set free from sin, have become slaves of righteousness.

ROMANS 6:18

The First Step of our Twelve-Step recovery is often called the "desperation step." In desperation we admit that our lives are unmanageable and that we are powerless over our addiction. The Second Step prepares us to acknowledge that only a Higher Power can restore us to sanity and clarity. Then we take the crucial Third Step, the "surrender step." It is the step of greatest importance and greatest difficulty. It is the "Fish or cut bait" of our program, where we must truly submit our lives and wills to God. These words may inspire us:

> Surrender isn't giving up
> something you don't want . . .
> It's giving up what you do want.

For years we tried to hang on to what we wanted. Recovery is giving up our need to hang on and placing ourselves into God's hands. We give ourselves to him. When we "drop ourselves into God's lap" we can stop running and fighting. We are safe and sound from now on—as God wills, not us.

Thank you, Lord, for being there to accept my surrender. I'm tired of running my life. Take over, please. Amen.

*"If you then, who are evil, know how to give good gifts to
your children, how much more will your Father who is in
heaven give good things to those who ask him!"*

MATTHEW 7:11

Honesty is an important key to our program of recovery.
Self-awareness is being able to look ourselves in the mirror and not just see the blemishes! We are so prone to count
our vices and overlook our virtues. Of course it is not easy
to admit our defects, but it seems even harder to see our
strengths. We seem to have a strange double standard. We
count as a vice or "character defect" anything we have *ever*
done . . . only once! Yet we count as a virtue or asset only
those qualities we display *all the time.*

When we struggle through our first Fourth Step, we often
list many more faults than virtues. Yet an accurate and balanced inventory is necessary to continued recovery. Maybe
one Fourth Step isn't enough; we may need to repeat the
process several times. The inventory will get less difficult
as we realize that a true balance sheet lists both assets and
liabilities.

Why this difficulty with accurate inventory and honest
self-awareness? Could it be that we don't think that we are
loved by God? Most of us accept and love our children no
matter how many faults or how many virtues they possess.
We just love them. If we believe that God is our Father,
surely he loves his children that much more. Jesus reminds
us that if we know how to give good gifts to our children,
surely God our heavenly father is even more generous!

*Lord Christ, you called us to be honest and straight. Help me to
see what is true and live with the truth and nothing but the truth.
Amen.*

"I came not to call the righteous, but sinners."

MARK 2:17

The central character in Tennessee Williams's great play *A Streetcar Named Desire* is Blanche, a refined Southern lady who has her share of compulsions and weaknesses. Her life is falling apart, and she expresses her panic by talking too much. The more she is afraid the more she talks and the worse her plight becomes. Love and acceptance continually elude her, and she winds up lonely and alone. Her "talk-aholism" repels those who might love her. Then Blanche meets Mitch, the last person she would be likely to seek out. He is overweight, sweats profusely, and is coarse and dull; it is not surprising that he feels lonely and unloved too. In a beautiful moment in the play, Blanche pours out her grief over a past tragedy. Mitch hugs her and says, "You need somebody and I need somebody, too. Could it be you and me, Blanche?" At first, she is shocked and insulted. Then, suddenly, with a soft cry, she accepts Mitch's arms around her. Through her sobs, she says, "Sometimes there's God, so quickly."

Many of us have felt God's sudden embrace. As we have tried to walk the pathway of recovery upon the Twelve Steps, when we needed love the most, when we were even desperate and despairing, "there's God, so quickly." Just when we had given up and lost hope, strangely and without logic or reason, God lays his healing hands upon our sick souls and we find new health. Isn't it awesome the way this happens when we are at our lowest point, when we know we are completely powerless and out of control?

O great Physician, put your arms around me. Lay your hands upon me. For I am sick and in need of your healing. Amen.

God was in Christ reconciling the world to himself, not counting their trespasses against them, and entrusting to us the message of reconciliation.

2 CORINTHIANS 5:19

The great Leonardo da Vinci had a violent argument with a fellow artist just before beginning his work on *The Last Supper.* Leonardo was so bitter and full of rage toward his enemy that he painted his fellow artist's face into the face of Judas Iscariot on his painting. But when da Vinci tried to paint the face of Jesus, he could not find the features he wished. As hard as he tried, Jesus' face escaped him. He finally concluded that his frustration was Jesus' own doing, because he had painted his enemy's face on Judas. He painted out the face of Judas and began again on the face of Jesus, this time with success. Leonardo learned that you cannot, at one and the same time, paint the features of Christ into your own life and also paint any other face with the features of hatred and bitterness.

We cannot see Christ if we do not forgive and "paint out" hatred and resentment toward anyone. Pardon and peace go hand in hand; no recovery, no serenity is possible without the sweetness of forgiveness.

Jesus, teach me to forgive and forget all hurt and bitterness, so that I may see your face. Amen.

Pray constantly, give thanks in all circumstances; for this is the will of God in Christ Jesus for you.

1 THESSALONIANS 5:17–18

God has a special way of answering our prayers. He sends us what we need, rather than what we request. A poem by an unknown author says it well:

> I prayed for strength that I might achieve;
> I was made weak that I might obey.
> I prayed for health that I might do great things;
> I was given infirmity that I might do better things.
> I prayed for riches that I might be happy;
> I was given poverty that I might be wise.
> I prayed for power that I might have the praise of men;
> I was given weakness that I might feel the need of God.
> I prayed for all things that I might enjoy life;
> I was given life that I might enjoy all things.
> I received nothing that I asked for—all that I hoped for;
> My prayers were answered—I am most blessed.

Prayer is our conversation with our Higher Power. For recovering Christians, prayer is our dialogue with Christ. He is our prayer partner. When our thoughts turn toward our Lord, we are praying. When we look at the facts of life through the eyes of Christ, we are praying. Prayer is our consultation with our Lord.

One of the best prayers for our hearts was given to us by Saint Thomas Aquinas:

Give us, O Lord, steadfast hearts, which no unworthy thoughts can drag down; unconquered hearts, which no tribulation can wear out, upright hearts, which no unworthy purpose may tempt aside. Amen.

Dear Lord, give me a heart that beats for you in prayer. Amen.

This I command you, to love one another.

JOHN 15:17

The king of Denmark once went out alone on horseback. A visitor to the country was surprised to see the king unattended and asked one of the citizens if the king didn't have a bodyguard. The citizen replied with pride, "We are *all* his bodyguard."

One of the best things about our Twelve-Step program is the care and concern we all have for one another. In a real sense "we are all each other's bodyguard." We have a stake in the recovery of each person. We value each other. We protect each other. We strengthen and inspire each other. Our fellowship becomes our family, our fortress, and our energizer.

There is a wedding prayer that says, "Now our joys are doubled, because the happiness of one is also the happiness of the other. Now our burdens are cut in half, since when we share them we divide the load." In our fellowship of recovery, we double our joys and cut our burdens in half. Meetings are not the whole program, but the program wouldn't work without them. We are a recovering society, a family, a flock—not isolated individuals. We need each other. There are no isolated Christians; there are no isolated people in recovery.

Remember the old hymn?

Blest be the tie that binds our hearts in Jesus' love;
The fellowship of Christian minds is like to that above.
Before the Father's throne we pour united prayers;
Our fears, our hopes, our aims are one; our comforts and our cares.
We share our mutual woes, our mutual burdens bear;
And often for each other flows the sympathizing tear.

Thank you, Lord Jesus, for my Christian family and my Twelve-Step family, both one in your healing love. Thank you for giving me companions and friends who enrich my life. Amen.

*For the Son of man also came not to be served but to serve,
and to give his life as a ransom for many.*

MARK 10:45

Over eighty years ago, the Salvation Army was given responsibility for a leper colony in India. A Salvation Army officer named Shaw, who was a medical missionary, took charge. During his rounds he came upon three lepers chained together, their shackles cutting into their diseased bodies. Shaw ordered them released at once. The guard protested that it wasn't safe; the men were dangerous criminals as well as lepers. But Shaw insisted, and the three were unchained. Two weeks later Captain Shaw had his first misgivings about freeing the criminals. He had to leave the colony overnight and feared leaving his wife and child alone. But, full of Christ's courage, his wife encouraged him to go—and said she was not afraid. The next morning when she went to the front door she found the three criminals lying on the steps. One of them said, "We know doctor go. We stay here so no harm come to you."

Love and compassion are risky, yet only by love is love born. The risks of love in Christ are countless. They don't always appear to have been worthwhile. Yet without such risks, no gains would be made at all. To walk the Twelve Steps is to take a risk each step of the way. Each time we work a step, go to a meeting, talk with our sponsor, open ourselves to prayer and meditation, we make ourselves vulnerable. Yet our risk is our triumph. No matter how yesterday went, success is for today, and to love is to succeed.

O Christ, when I am in danger, when I am at risk . . . keep me keeping on, so that I can live through my failures and use them to learn to love and win on your terms. Amen.

"Therefore you also must be ready; for the Son of man is coming at an hour you do not expect."

MATTHEW 24:44

Two men met in a graveyard. One was crying over the grave of his wife. So was the other. They looked at each other with tear-flooded eyes. One was more upset than the other. He sobbed, "I loved her so much. She was everything to me. I am lost without her. She was so wonderful and kind and loving." His crying grew louder.

The other man said, "I know, so was my dear wife."

"But you don't understand! She was my whole life."

"So was mine, my friend," said the other.

But the first man, with anguish in his eyes, screamed, "You don't understand! I never told her!"

As recovering Christians we all have someone to tell before it's too late. Is there someone we love and cherish who has not heard our words of love and appreciation? Someone we take for granted? Even if there is no special person, tell God, tell your group, speak your love before it's too late.

Lord, why do I hold back my words of love? Loosen my tongue and make me speak my love. Amen.

"When you pray, say: 'Father, hallowed be thy name. Thy kingdom come.'"

LUKE 11:2

People have called God the Unmoved Mover, Eternal Energy, the Unknown Absolute, the First Principle, the Life Force, Supreme Intelligence, Life Essence, The Force, and the favorite of Twelve-Step groups: Higher Power. The list of names could go on almost endlessly.

If you want to know God best, Jesus said, then follow my example and simply call him Father. Whatever Father means to us is less important than what it meant to Jesus, who gives us a clear answer through the words and actions of his own life. We are God's children. He is a parent who loves us. He empowers us. He saves us. He accepts us. In our recovery, he gives us life now and life eternal. With Samuel Wesley we can praise our God in these words:

> "Thou our Father, Christ our Brother,
> All who live in love are thine;
> Teach us how to love each other,
> Lift us to the joy divine.
>
> Mortals join the mighty chorus,
> Which the morning stars began;
> Father-love is reigning o'er us.
> Brother-love binds man to man."

Dear Lord and Father of us all, keep me in close and loving relationship to you. Through Christ, our Lord. Amen.

But he said to me, "My grace is sufficient for you, for my power is made perfect in weakness." I will all the more gladly boast of my weaknesses, that the power of Christ may rest upon me.

2 CORINTHIANS 12:9

Abraham Lincoln once said, "I have been driven many times to my knees by the overwhelming conviction that I had nowhere else to go." Most of us who now find recovery in Christ from our old addictions know the truth of Lincoln's words. We were "driven to our knees." The miracle of our lives is that when we were the lowest, we met a solid foundation that kept us from sinking lower. Our elevators had reached the basement. What is so wonderful about our Lord is that when we do sink to our knees, we then have something to stand on. When we finally run out of our own power, we can rely on God's power; we can pray with John Baillie:

O holy spirit of God, abide with me;
   inspire all my thoughts;
   pervade my imagination;
   suggest all my decisions;
   order all my doings.
Be with me in my silence and in my speech,
   in my haste and in my leisure,
   in company and in solitude,
   in the freshness of the morning and in the weariness of the evening;
   and give me grace at all times humbly to rejoice in Thy mysterious companionships. Amen.

We know that the best thing that could ever happen to us is to have to reach out in our lowest point—and then find God. We find him most powerfully when we are most weak.

Most loving Lord, thank you for being there at the lowest spot in my life. Take my hand and pull me up. Amen.

For he says, "At the acceptable time I have listened to you, and helped you on the day of salvation." Behold, now is the acceptable time; behold, now is the day of salvation.

2 CORINTHIANS 6:2

"God grant me the Serenity to accept the things I cannot change; Courage to change the things I can; and the Wisdom to know the difference."

Every Twelve-Step program uses this familiar Serenity Prayer at some point of the meeting, and many people use it every day. But the complete prayer, which is attributed to the theologian Reinhold Niebuhr, goes on:

"*Living one day at a time;* accepting hardship as a pathway to peace; taking, as Jesus did, this sinful world as it is, not as I would have it: Trusting that you will make all things right if I surrender to your will; that I may be reasonably happy in this life and supremely happy with you forever in the next. Amen."

Living in and for the present is vital to recovery and health. Yesterday is gone; tomorrow is out of reach. "Behold, now is the acceptable time; now is the day of salvation" (2 Cor. 6:2).

Thank you, Lord, for this day, for new life and a new start. Open me up to your presence now, so that I do not put you off. Amen.

[He] said to the man, "Stretch out your hand." He stretched it out; and his hand was restored.

MARK 3:5

One of the most powerful customs in the chuch takes place during the wedding ceremony. As the couple begins to exchange their vows, first the man takes the woman's hand. After declaring his promises, they must *turn loose* and release each other before the woman in turn takes the man's hand in hers. The power in this symbolic action is profound. It signifies the freedom of choice in the joining of two lives. There is no coercion or force. One freely chooses, releases, and then allows the other to freely choose.

This action is of greater importance than joining the convenant of marriage—it is the shape of all life: embracing and loosing. We grasp, and we let go; we take, and we relinquish; we close, and we open. The symbol of the hand closing its fingers around another hand is familiar to us who yearn and churn to get and keep. But the other motion is harder and less familiar—to turn loose, release, let go, and allow the other to stay or depart. The unclasped hand is open, vulnerable, and makes an invitation, not a fist or a wrestler's hold.

Christ has open hands—open arms, eager and willing to enfold and comfort and hold us close—as long as we wish, but he will not clasp or grasp us without our willingness to be embraced. Our lives are made up of countless openings and closings, of receivings and takings. Our recovery program works the same way. It's ours for the taking—never there to "take" us.

O Christ, you open your hands to me and you embrace me when I ask. Keep me opening and embracing in the best way possible. Amen.

"Is not this the carpenter, the son of Mary and brother of James and Joses and Judas and Simon, and are not his sisters here with us?" And they took offense at him. And Jesus said to them, "A prophet is not without honor, except in his own country, and among his own kin, and in his own house."

MARK 6:3–4

A World War II navy man tells the story of what happened aboard his destroyer when news of the war's end came, and the sailors were ordered to destroy all the big shells on board. "When they started their work," he said, "the men treated those shells with great respect. They cradled them in their arms very carefully and carried them to the side, where they eased them overboard. But there were hundreds of shells to be destroyed, and as the day wore on, the men became more and more careless. Toward afternoon's end, I actually saw them tossing the shells to each other and even contemptuously kicking them overboard."

When the love, power, and peace of the Twelve-Step program first comes into our lives and we feel the energy of it, we treat it with great reverence. As time goes by, we may begin to take it for granted. As Jesus' neighbors did, we find that "familiarity breeds contempt." We can get lazy, tired, and careless, and we can lose respect for recovery's own special kind of power. When that happens, our program doesn't explode, it just collapses.

Lord Christ, you mean more to me than I can ever say. You have given me healing and hope in my program of recovery. Please keep me full of care and truly careful about what I care about so much. Amen.

"Rise, take up your pallet and walk."

MARK 2:9

In C. S. Lewis's *Screwtape Letters*, the goal of the devil is to keep Christians in a "Christianity *and . . .*" state of mind and away from the knowledge that they are in a state of grace. The devil tells his demons to keep Christians talking *about* Christianity *and* psychology, Christianity *and* politics, Christianity *and* marriage. "Keep the emphasis away from "Christianity *is*."

When we concentrate on what our life in Christ *is*, we are alive and well. Trying to figure out the Twelve Steps, the slogans, our sponsor's wisdom, the supportive honesty of our group leads to a kind of confusion called "analysis paralysis." Accepting and living the Twelve-Step life as God's gift is living in grace. Jesus simply says, "Rise! Get up, stop thinking about it and start walking."

The saying "If it works, don't fix it" applies to our walk with Christ and our program. We are pilgrims traveling our road with Christ, not spectators on the sidelines, thinking *about* grace. We are *in* a state of grace, and grace is our heartbeat, giving us the power we need to get up and walk at all. It is futile to worry about the relationship between Alcoholics Anonymous and the church, Overeaters Anonymous and religion, or Emotions Anonymous and faith or to compare and contrast the Twelve Steps and Christianity. They all belong to God, and they work!

O, Christ, help me to relax and enjoy your presence, in my religion and in my program, to stop trying to remove the wonder and awe from my recovery and simply accept the wonderful reality of your healing power. Amen.

> *"The Son of man has come eating and drinking; and you say, 'Behold, a glutton and a drunkard, a friend of tax collectors and sinners!'"*

LUKE 7:34

In *Zorba the Greek*, we encounter a person who lives life to the hilt. The most attractive thing about Zorba is that when he runs out of words to express what he feels, he dances. When Zorba dances, his whole being moves. The counterpoint to Zorba is "the boss," who is uptight, inhibited, grim about work, leisure, and life itself—a real "workaholic."

The author portrays the dynamics between these two opposite numbers, the free one and the frozen one. Eventually Zorba's zest for life gets through to the boss, who finally "thaws out" and turns to his friend and says, "Zorba, teach me to dance." Someone has called this request "one of the greatest moments in contemporary literature."

We can have great moments like this. When we turn to Christ he will become our dancing master and "teach us to dance." Our icy, tense existence will thaw and turn to joyous warmth. Jesus has been called The Lord of the Dance, and he invites us to dance and live with him. He calls us to "life abundant," and more than that: he shows us how! Each beat and note of the Twelve Steps has its own gracefulness and rhythm. Each element that enriches our recovery sounds its own special chord. Together, our life in Christ and our Twelve-Step program blend into a "harmony of health" that never ceases.

O, Lord of life, may my heavy feet become light with your dance of love and joy. Take away my grim heaviness and "lighten me up" with the sounds of your symphony. Amen.

"Pray to your Father who is in secret; and your Father who sees in secret will reward you."

MATTHEW 6:6b

Toward the end of his life, the great jazz musician W. C. Handy, feeble and totally blind, was invited to play his trumpet at the first inauguration of President Dwight Eisenhower. When the Father of the Blues played his magnificent "St. Louis Blues," the audience was thrilled by every clear, mellow note. The radiant joy on W. C. Handy's face was even more thrilling. No one had the courage to tell him that Eisenhower had left the ballroom an hour before Handy's performance. He had played his best for an absent president.

We often feel the same. We play our best and think God is absent, or not listening. This is *never* so! God is always listening, attentive and open to our concerns. In fact, he hears any tune we can manage to play. He sees and finds our needs before we do and matches our necessities with his grace. He never stops working with and through us and others to help lead us to find him. Our Lord is never outside, but always present, doing more for us than we can ever dream.

In our blindness we do our best. In our feebleness we try and strive. Jesus knows. He cares. Our "Father who is in secret" will reward us. We may never know or understand, but every expression, every thought, every feeling directed and given to God in Christ will contain its own reward, its own grace.

Lord, sometimes you seem so secret that you seem to be missing. Help me to accept your mysterious and awesome ways as beyond my knowing, but above all keep me in your love and care, no matter how lonely I feel. Amen.

"Do you not yet perceive or understand? Are your hearts hardened? Having eyes do you not see, and having ears do you not hear?"

MARK 8:17–18

The great scientist George Washington Carver was responsible for an agricultural revolution in the South. But the most special thing about him was that he talked to God, and he would hear God talk to him. God always said, "Behold, George Washington Carver, what do you have?" And Dr. Carver would answer: "A sweet potato, Lord." And God said, "What can you do with it?" "I can bake it, fry it, boil, or even mash it, Lord." "But what else, George Washington Carver, Behold!" From persistent gazing, probing, watching, and experimenting, Dr. Carver developed more than 300 products from the peanut, 118 from the sweet potato, and 75 from the pecan.

When we live in open expectation, "Behold!" we too can discover and develop new products in our lives. The wonder of recovery is that there is so much to see if we only look and are willing to look longer and deeper. There are messages to hear, if we will pay attention and listen. Our slogans may appear trite, yet each has a power and a depth that is inexhaustible.

Dear Lord, grant me sharper sight. Help me to see and hear farther, deeper, and clearer. Help me not to turn away from the obvious. Amen.

*"'Yet because this widow bothers me, I will vindicate her,
or she will wear me out by her continual coming.'" And
the Lord said, ". . . Will not God vindicate his elect, who
cry to him day and night . . . speedily[?]"*

LUKE 18:5–8

A mother with many children was telling a friend about
her day: her husband was on a business trip, the washer
broke down, it was pouring down rain, the roof was leak-
ing, and the children were wild and out of control. Everything possible was becoming impossible. She summed up
her plight by saying, "I even got a busy signal when I called
Dial-a-Prayer."

There are days like that. Those of us who suffer from
addictive compulsions can have weeks, even years, that go
wrong. What if God really is too busy for us? Of course,
we know in our heads that this could never be, but our
hearts often mislead us. Reality frequently disappears when
our emotions claim us. The facts are otherwise. The good
news of the gospel of Christ is the same joyous message,
loud and clear: God loves us! This is *the* indisputable fact
of all life!

No matter how or why things fall apart we are still loved,
and God is on the line every second. Maybe we fail to call,
or misdial, or give up too soon, or maybe we don't hear
or don't like God's answer. He *always* replies: sometimes
yes, sometimes no, sometimes not yet, and more often, "I
have my own suggestion and plan, my child." God's grace
works in ways beyond our understanding and quite often
against our puny plans. But he always has better plans. Perhaps we can learn to accept whatever comes as the occasion for a blessing even in the midst of chaos and pain.

*Blessed Lord, help us to be persistent and patient. Keep us persist-
ent in our prayers and patient with our expectations. Amen.*

"Lo, I am with you always, to the close of the age."
MATTHEW 28:20

When we are down and out, lost, and scared, we are often more sensitive to God's presence and power. It is a mystery that when we appreciate our own limitations, we are better able to open ourselves to God's limitless strength. As often as tragedies do occur, they are never God's will. He only wills life. The intention of God's rule is always to be found within our response to his love and salvation, not in our fear and despair over accidents.

By an accident of birth, we have become addicted persons. Who knows why? We are not responsible for our illness. We are responsible for our response to it, however. Many of us in the "recovering community" have wondered if we *had* to become addicted in order to find God. Sometimes it seems that way. But God's control is beyond our comprehension. We simply don't have the answers. Nevertheless, we do know that our best clues to God's mysterious will is found in Jesus—in his teaching, ministry, suffering, death, and resurrection. Our response to the concrete, down-to-earth demonstration of the entire "Christ event" is our answer and our salvation.

In every act and action of Jesus our Lord, he is love and life. That fact we can trust and rely on—no matter what. Even in the midst of disasters worse than we have ever seen, even if our nightmares of nuclear holocaust come true—we are still in the loving hands of our Lord. He's still in control. He has the last word: "I love you."

Lord, thank you for my weakness, my ignorance, and my folly. In my frail and limited life, I find you and your healing strength. Amen.

"If I then, your Lord and Teacher, have washed your feet,
you also ought to wash one another's feet."

JOHN 13:14

If anything can keep us away from God, it is our pride—
the towers of Babel we build to our own egos. Each of us
has his or her own Babylon, our prized possession or
accomplishment. We compulsively hearken to our "own
thing," our self-fulfillment. At these times, we say, "I am
the Lord my God; and I shall have no other gods before
me." We know this is wrong. We know this does not work.
Because the harder we strive for "self-actualization," the
more the actual Self of God seems to elude us.

Human autonomy and independence are appealing ideas.
But they are idols. Yet they have great power over us, and
they become the actual gods of too many. The temptation
to worship the "sanctity" of our person is the tempter's call
to move us away from the sanctity of his person—the Body
of Christ.

The word *worship* comes from two words: *worth* and *ship*,
what we give worth and value to. To worship is to bow down
to what we find worthy and valuable, to "turn our will and
our lives over to the care" of that "god." Jesus taught us the
way out of such idolatry. He demonstrated in his own life
that true freedom from all our little self-made gods comes
in serving the one and only God. The way we serve and
worship the true God is by serving others. Servanthood is
freedom.

O gracious and good Lord, help me shut my ears to the tempter's
call to put myself first. Keep my priorities straight. Teach me your
life of service. Amen.

> *"But while he was yet at a distance, his father saw him and had compassion, and ran and embraced him and kissed him."*

LUKE 15:20

Imagine how you might feel if you were the captain of a slave ship. Picture the burden of guilt and shame you would carry if you had to transport chained human beings in squalor to a life of degrading slavery. Such a person was John Newton, who was overwhelmed by his part in this despicable traffic. His sin was more than he could bear. He knew he was "a wretch" in a wretched business. His repentance was total. He turned to God for forgiveness. What he received was beyond his expectations. Like the prodigal son in Jesus' parable, he found a waiting, loving Father, who welcomed him home with a celebration! Some time later he wrote these familiar words:

> Amazing Grace, how sweet the sound
> That saved a wretch like me
> I once was lost, but now am found
> Was blind, but now I see!

John Newton became a clergyman and wrote other hymns, preached stirring sermons, ministered to other "wretches," and completed his life as a tribute to God and a gift to humanity.

How like the recovering addict! The person who once was wretched, lost, and blind and who once caused seemingly endless pain can be saved! Yes, saved. Not only can we find such saving health; we learn, like John Newton, that the grace that saved us is truly amazing, and the grace that we can share with others is more amazing still.

O Savior and Lord, save me from my sin and wretchedness. Lead me safely to you. Lift the blindness from my sight. Keep me coming home to you, to receive your welcome. Amen.

> *"But the tax collector . . . beat his breast, saying, 'God, be merciful to me a sinner!' I tell you, this man went down to his house justified rather than the other; for every one who exalts himself will be humbled, but he who humbles himself will be exalted."*
>
> LUKE 18:13–14

Christ does not ask those of us who are trying to recover from our compulsions to wallow in remorse. But how can we reach out for help if we feel no need for forgiveness? "To have no shame" can mean we have become numb to the twinges of conscience within us. Jesus does not *blame and condemn* our shortcomings; however, he does want us to *see and admit* our character defects. Why? So they can be removed, of course. Our Lord wants us to feel our shame only long enough to get rid of it. We need to feel the burden before we can lay it down. That's how the tax collector Jesus used as an example of humility got rid of his burden. His pleas for mercy were heard; "he went down to his house justified." He confessed, he was forgiven.

Some of us, however, imagine guilt where there is none. Becoming addicted or bald, having asthma or diabetes, not being pretty or rich are not occasion for guilt. The way we were created is not our fault. We are responsible for our actions, what we actually did. Lying, cheating, stealing, hurting others—that's where guilt belongs. Shame makes a proper fit. Then we can "humbly admit" what we have done and take the humble and cleansing steps that remove the guilt and erase the shame.

The Talmud says, "A sense of shame is a lovely thing in a man. Whoever has a sense of shame will not sin so quickly; but whoever shows no sense of shame in his face, his father surely never stood on Mount Sinai."

Soften my heart, Lord. Deliver me from callous pride. Lead me to love you enough to admit my guilt, feel my shame . . . and then find your forgiveness. Amen.

> *Therefore, as it is written, "Let him who boasts, boast of the Lord."*

1 CORINTHIANS 1:31

Our imaginations seem capable of creating an endless array of religious organizations. Yet there are only two religions. One is followed by those who expect salvation by doing. The other is made up of those who have been saved by something done. The first thanks human beings; the second thanks God. The first is false; the second is true.

Before we entered the recovery program of the Twelve Steps, we belonged to the first group. We tried over and over again to accomplish our recovery by our own efforts. When we gave up and surrendered our valiant efforts at self-salvation, we found it had already been taken care of by Jesus Christ. We cannot save ourselves. No one can be his or her own savior. Our choice is clear—we can keep on in futility, trying to accomplish the impossible, or we can give up, "let go and let God," and accept the salvation accomplished on Calvary. As Saint Paul exclaims, "For by grace you have been saved through faith; and this is not your own doing, it is the gift of God—not because of works, lest any man should boast. For we are his workmanship, created in Christ Jesus for good works" (Eph. 2:8–10).

Savior, you are my religion. Your mercy and love I look to and cling to. Keep me from trying to do your work. Amen.

Such is the confidence that we have through Christ toward God. Not that we are sufficient of ourselves to claim anything as coming from us; our sufficiency is from God.
2 CORINTHIANS 3:4–5

When the power of addiction claims us, we forget the awesome power of God. We have tried so many times and in so many ways to control our addiction or our addict. We are actually embarrassed when we are asked, "Have you tried God? Really tried him?" We think we have. Yet something made our attempts halfhearted and our faith weak. Maybe there is something about God we forgot. Perhaps we overlooked his love and friendship. Benjamin Franklin, worried about a nation turning away from God, asked:

Have we now forgotten that powerful Friend? Or do we imagine we no longer need His assistance? I have lived a long time; and the longer I live, the more convincing proofs I see of this truth: that God governs in the affairs of men. And if a sparrow cannot fall to the ground without His notice, is it probable that an empire can rise without His aid?

As we struggle to create a new empire of health to replace our old kingdom of addiction, have we "forgotten that powerful Friend," Jesus Christ? An officer of George Washington said in a difficult time, "General, we are lost; everything is lost." Washington replied, "Sir, you do not know the resources and genius of liberty." These words can be our motto in recovery. We must never forget or overlook "the resources and the genius of liberty" found in the Twelve Steps of recovery that Jesus gives to all who fight with him.

Dearest Friend, help me trust your resources and genius in my recovery. Amen.

He said to them, "Why are you afraid? Have you no faith?"

MARK 4:40

A story from the Jewish tradition tells of a man lost in a jungle. He tried frantically to find his way, but remained hopelessly lost. Suddenly, he was filled with terror. He saw in the distance what seemed to be a wild beast coming toward him. He could not run. He was frozen with fear. As the beast came closer, the man was filled with relief. It looked like a domesticated animal. As the beast came closer, he could see it was a man on a horse. Stirring up all his courage, he moved forward to meet the man. When he reached up to shake the man's hand, he looked into the eyes of his own brother!

Although this life contains many beasts of prey, most of them of the human kind, we can meet our own brothers and sisters if we live through our fear. Many friends appear to be enemies, even ferocious animals, at a great distance, yet as distance is removed, as we grow closer and extend our hand of friendship, we may find our own family.

We experience such closeness in our Twelve-Step families. Yet even within such recovering groups there will be fear, mistrust, and distance. When we look outside our groups to the church, the temple, the civic club, the neighborhood, we often find the same elements. When we begin to realize that we are all human, with the same fears, hopes, and dreams, perhaps we will move through our suspicion and fear and reach out to others in love.

It is in love that we find fear's antidote, because "there is no fear in love, but perfect love casts out fear" (1 John 4:18). Jesus is perfect love.

Dear Christ, help me to be fearless, and to be full of love. Create more trust in me, and let me see my brother and sister in more places as I move closer to everyone. Amen.

*I am the door: if any one enters by me, he will be saved,
and will go in and out and find pasture.*

JOHN 10:9

Studies of schoolchildren have shown that they are happier and feel freer to play when they are in playgrounds that are fenced in. Fences and walls do not always make prisons; they can also provide security.

The boundaries created by a fence, a wall, or even a curb help create distinctions between here and there, known and unknown, safe and dangerous. Those who enter foreign lands often become confused, disoriented, and even sick. At such times, we run to the safety of the familiar. We latch on to people who speak our language. We may flee to our hotel room, where at least we recognize our own clothes and luggage! We are relieved to see a McDonald's! In such cases, familiarity breeds security, not contempt.

Our Twelve-Step boundaries and fences are wonderful security blankets, especially when we are confused. Order, direction, simple principles, and straightforward slogans provide the security we need to clear up our confusion. Above all, the same faces, the same accepting smiles, the same understanding eyes give us our bearings back and set us back on the right path.

We are comfortable with our fellow addicts. Our own relatives, old friends, those at our church and at our job often seem unfamiliar and unable to speak our language. The word *family* comes from the word *familiar.* Home is where we are comfortable and at ease instead of confused and in dis-ease.

*O Christ, you are my true home and have always been with me,
but I know I can be with you better in my recovery than in my
addiction. Help me become more familiar and at home with health
than sickness. Amen.*

> *"The eye is the lamp of the body. So, if your eye is sound, your whole body will be full of light."*
>
> MATTHEW 6:22

A man once built a cabin with shelves around the walls. One evening he was visited by a friend. As the evening progressed, the visitor became extremely restless. When his host asked about his agitation, his friend replied, "If you will forgive me, it's those shelves. Every one of them slopes down to the right." "Do they?" said the surprised owner of the cabin, "I never noticed." The visitor was a carpenter by trade. He was disturbed because he saw those shelves against a true vertical, which ran like a plumb line through his mind. The owner of the cabin, on the other hand, was at ease with crookedness, and even unaware of it.

Among the first steps to recovery is awareness. Without truth and the ability to see a "true vertical," we remain off center. We may even be comfortable that way. How will we see rightly unless one with the true eyes of a carpenter shows us? Jesus was a carpenter. He still is. With his eyes and with his true perspective, we can measure life and see reality.

The yardstick that Jesus used most often was "straight love," caring that showed itself in straightforward compassion. True love bears true fruit. So much of our recovery program exists to provide us a chance to follow the yardstick of Christ-like love in action: in twelve active, loving steps that set us on a course from our false and flat horizontal to a true and lofty vertical.

O Carpenter of Nazareth, give me your yardstick and plumb line of love, that I may keep myself straight upon your measured Twelve Steps of life. Amen.

During World War II there were times when the Allied advance on Germany was halted. Towns, terrain, tanks, bad weather, gun emplacements, and many other obstacles could all stop an army. Sometimes a river would call a time out while facing a bombed out river bridge, calling for a pontoon bridge to be pieced together across the water.

A century earlier during the Civil War, General Stonewall Jackson's army had to stop as it looked over to the other side or a river. The general ordered his engineers to plan and build a bridge. He also issued another order to his veteran wagon master and simply told him to get this army over that river NOW! Looking around, the wagon master immediately organized his men in scavenging all the logs they could find, trees they could cut down and anything else that could be jerry-rigged into a bridge. Before the next sunrise old Stonewall was told by his wagon master that all the guns, caissons and wagons were all on the other side. General Jackson asked about the engineers. He was told that they were still busy in their tent drawing up detailed plans for a bridge.

This story reminds me of the times in recovery when we have to get it all right in our heads before we act. We wait until we learn more to take that fourth step, or delay making amends until we are ready. So much of our recovery happens by osmosis, trial, and error and just "doing it." Every meeting declares, "keep on coming back," and going to more meetings, listening and learning, doing the steps, living the slogans, and taking action—all these activities provide most of our recovery. We are active Twelve-Steppers not passive thinkers. Most of the steps are action steps: Turning over, making an inventory, making a list, humbly asking, making amends, Continuing to take inventory, seeking conscious contact with God, and carrying the message . . . are all actions, not just words or ideas or insights. A passive or inactive recovery is no recovery at all. Recovering Christians are especially busy. They are busy going to church, studying, serving, praying, loving, and doing the work of ministry.

"And when you fast, do not look dismal, like the hypocrites, for they disfigure their faces that their fasting may be seen by men. Truly, I say to you, they have their reward."

MATTHEW 6:16

You've probably heard this story before. A woman returned to her car in a crowded mall parking lot and found a note under the windshield wiper. It said, "I have just smashed into the rear of your car. The people who saw the accident are watching me. They think I am writing down my name and address. They are wrong."

Isn't this a common type of deception? When others are watching, we cover up so that we "may be seen" to be good or responsible. We are also clever at denial and rationalization. Unfortunately, our cover-ups merely delay the inevitable. Saint Paul reminds us: "Do not be deceived; God is not mocked, for whatever a man sows, that he will also reap" (Gal. 6:7). We know that, don't we?

We may, but it's easier to evade and avoid than to face the music. It's even harder to face the truth when we are burdened with a compulsive addiction that is more powerful than our basic honesty and decency. That's the bind we're in! We don't like lying, excusing, and covering up—we just can't seem to help it. It's true that we can't control our addiction, but we most certainly can control our heart. That is, we may be powerless over drinking, food binges, gambling, or other compulsive activities, but we still have the power of our basic honesty and decency, and we can *admit* our powerlessness. That's the first step to freedom, and it's one we can take!

O God of truth, release my honesty and help me withhold deceit. Give me courage to admit my powerlessness. Amen.

"For where your treasure is, there will your heart be also."
MATTHEW 6:21

A great third-century Christian said, "Idolatry is the principle crime of the human race, the highest guilt charged upon the world, the whole cause of judgment." Martin Luther, centuries later, paraphrased Jesus when he said, "Where you hang your heart, there is your god."

Anything can become an idol, the object of our heart: food, status, success, sex, power, money, fame, gambling, a person, cars, alcohol, drugs, boats, computers, houses, furniture, gardens—the list is endless. Idols never present problems to us when it is obvious that they *are* idols. The moment we realize that they are only poor substitutes for the real thing, they cease to be worshiped and to claim our hearts. When we begin to "be restored to sanity," our moment of truth arrives. It finally dawns upon us: we not only worship idols; we have surrendered our life and will over to the care of lesser gods that enslave us and tear us down. When we decide to bow down only to God the Father, Son, and Holy Spirit, we are freed from our addictive idols and lifted up.

Twelve-Step programs and Christian faith testify to the "Higher Power" of God, who in reality is the "Highest Power." By submission and surrender to him, "lower powers" that now control us can be controlled by God Almighty, not by us.

Sovereign and Lord of all life, save me from the clutches of lesser gods. Help me worship only you and keep all lesser attractions in their proper place below you. Amen.

*But if we have died with Christ, we believe we shall also
live with him.*

ROMANS 6:8

An old Indian legend tells the story of a tribe near Niagara Falls that had a ritual of sacrificing one of their most beautiful daughters each year to the "great god of the waters." One year the chief's own beloved daughter was chosen by lot to be the sacrifice. There were no exemptions, even for chiefs. When the fateful day arrived, the chief could not be found to preside over the ceremony. The ritual went on without him. The Indian maiden was tied into a canoe to be swept over the falls. As her canoe was pushed into the rapid current, another canoe came out of hiding to join her. It was the chief, her father, who had come to his daughter's side to join her in death.

To the Christian this tale is familiar. It is the central fact of the cross. More than a noble sacrifice and certainly more than a pathetic tale of wasted love—the cross of Christ is the power and presence of God himself. Saint Paul sees in the cross of Jesus the very essence of our own: "But if we have died with Christ, we believe that we shall also live with him" (Rom. 6:8). It is the "with him" part that is so full of good news. We don't go over the falls alone.

Of course, as Christians we know that new life lies at the bottom of the falls. We also know of the surrender of the Third Step, when we allow the current of the program to sweep us over the waterfall of "ego death" and "self-control." To "let go and let God" is as fearsome as this. To turn loose of the control of our old compulsions is to be swept away in terror "out of control" and "powerless." Yet it is in this surrender that we find our salvation.

*O risen Lord, help me to trust you and surrender to you. As I submit
to the death of my old sick life, I know you will give me a new
life of health. Amen.*

And Jesus said to Simon, "Do not be afraid."

LUKE 5:10

Samuel Johnson said, "Unless a man has courage, he has no security for preserving any other virtue." Courage is the basic virtue. Of what use is wisdom if you don't have the courage to act wisely? Of what value is love if you don't have the courage to love? Of what importance is truth if you don't have the courage to speak it? Of what consequence is faith without the courage to embrace it? Courage activates all other goodness.

It also requires honesty. It takes courage to confront the truth of our unmanageable loves and then admit it. It takes courage to surrender our lives and wills to God as we understand God to be. It takes courage to make our Fourth and Fifth Steps. To face our moral life and honestly take our inventory and then admit our findings to another human being, make our best efforts "to make amends," continue our inventory, maintain our conscious contact with God, and share our program with others—all our Steps take courage.

The Twelve Steps are for the brave. We walk the way of recovery facing fearful truths—with every person who walks along with us. We can be courageous because we do not walk alone. We are with one another and God. It is knowing that we have the support and friendship of our companions that supplies the courage we often lack. Saint Paul experienced this as a prisoner awaiting trial and possible death: "And so we came to Rome. And the brethren there, when they heard of us, came as far as the Forum of Appius and Three Taverns to meet us. On seeing them Paul thanked God and took courage" (Acts 28:14–15).

Increase my courage, O Christ. Strengthen my will to walk with you bravely. May I take courage from my friends. Amen.

Then Jesus, crying with a loud voice, said, "Father, into thy hands I commit my spirit!"

LUKE 23:46

A television humorist once complained about his psychotherapy sessions. "I go to this doctor and pay him seventy-five dollars an hour, and all he does is ask me the same question my father used to ask me all the time: 'Who do you think you are, anyway?'" A good question. Perhaps it is *the* question for us all to ask.

Jesus knew who he was. He was his Father's Son. His relationship with God was intimate, close, and personal. Who are we? First of all, we are creatures. We have been created by a loving God in his own image. Why were we created? In order to become his adopted children, brothers and sisters of Jesus. When we realize that what God has in mind for us is similar to the intimacy he has with Jesus, we can rejoice, as if we were orphans taken in off the street.

Every day we are being shaped and molded into the Father's family. Part of that shaping comes from following the Twelve Steps. Through the gospel and the steps we are being offered the closeness of a child's relationship to a parent. To know this is to join Saint Paul as he says: "You have received the spirit of sonship. When we cry, 'Abba! Father!' it is the Spirit himself bearing witness with our spirit that we are children of God, and if children, then heirs, heirs of God and fellow heirs with Christ" (Rom. 8:15–17).

O Father of our Lord Jesus Christ, shape me and mold me into your image and likeness of love and adopt me as your own loving child. Amen.

Anyone whom you forgive, I also forgive. What I have forgiven, if I have forgiven anything, has been for your sake in the presence of Christ.

2 CORINTHIANS 2:10

Bishop Phillips Brooks once said: "If there is any good that I can do or any kindness that I can show, let me do it quickly, for I shall not pass this way again." Recovery is a process of healing old hurts, memories, and resentments. Steps Eight and Nine should not be delayed too long, since they exist to drive out the old poisons of the past. A woman in recovery said, "In this life, if you have anything to pardon, pardon quickly. Slow forgiveness is little better than no forgiveness."

Real, cleansing forgiveness is a forgetting—a real canceling out of the past. When a hurt is forgiven, it is as if it never happened: it is gone—forgotten as a dream—never to return.

What is the way to such forgiving and forgetting? The method best used is the apology. Its usefulness is immense. As someone once said, "An apology is a friendship preserver, costs nothing but one's pride, always saves more than it costs, is a device needed in every home." Apologies form the core of Steps Eight and Nine and are essential to lasting recovery.

O forgiving Lord, quickly drive out from my heart all resentments, so that I forget as I forgive and so that I apologize as I remember. Amen.

"For the gate is narrow and the way is hard, that leads to life, and those who find it are few."

MATTHEW 7:14

A woman once went on a journey to a distant city. She was unfamiliar with the route, became confused, and took the wrong road. She stopped her car and asked a passing stranger, "Can you help me? I am lost." "Where are you headed?" asked the stranger. "I'm going to Boston," the traveler answered. "Then you are not lost. You know where you are going. You just need directions."

We who walk the daily road of recovery know that we are never lost—just confused at times. We know where we intend to go: to the land of health and wholeness. We just need directions and we need them continually—the Twelve Steps and our Lord Jesus Christ. We need the Big Book, meetings, sponsors, and our total program. In the same way, we cannot walk with Christ and be truly rich in the Lord without Scripture, worship, study, fellowship, and service. We all need direction.

Although it is attractive to think we can find our way alone, the facts of life and of recovery make it plain to us that we often become disoriented and mixed up. Without the encouragement, wisdom, and stability of others we would really become lost and alone and sick all over again. Thank God, we cannot travel alone, we must have a company of friends along with us on our pilgrimage.

O Jesus, keep me oriented, with companions and on the right road. Help me ask for and receive directions in my program and in my faith. Amen.

For me to live is Christ, and to die is gain.

PHILIPPIANS 1:21

Alfred, Lord Tennyson once wrote these words:

> . . . More things are wrought by prayer
> Than this world dreams of. Wherefore, let thy voice
> Rise like a fountain for me night and day.
> For what are men better than sheep or goats
> That nourish a blind life within the brain,
> If, knowing God, they lift not hands of prayer
> Both for themselves and those who call them friend?
> For so the whole round earth is every way
> Bound by gold chains about the feet of God.

Without voicing our prayers we are indeed no better than sheep or goats. Without speaking out our hearts' desires, our feelings, our thoughts, to our friend, we are, without a doubt, blind and dumb. Prayer is our lifeline with God. That great man of prayer Saint Thomas Aquinas prays for us all in these words:

Bestow on us, O Lord our God, understanding to know Thee, diligence to seek Thee,
Wisdom to find Thee, and a faithfulness that may finally embrace Thee. Amen.

The goal of all prayer is the goal of our life: God. The purpose and final objective of every prayer is to be in the loving embrace of God. To be with him is our goal, our life, our all. Our prayers are the highways to heaven and him.

Lord Christ, be with me always. It is your presence alone that I seek. Amen.

"And the King will answer them, 'Truly, I say to you, as you did it to one of the least of these my brethren, you did it to me.'"

MATTHEW 25:40

There is a nineteenth-century painting that shows a long row of beggars waiting in a soup line on skid row. They are all ragged and dirty, but around the head of one, barely visible, is a halo. One of them is Christ! We may not see a halo around the head of our needy brothers and sisters in this world, but if we see with compassionate eyes we will see Christ. To serve and care for those who are down and out is to serve our Lord.

To care for such persons sometimes seems fruitless and wasted effort. Yet such love and care is indeed profitable. The payoff is the wonderful power of a fresh start.

We who are suffering from addictive diseases may not identify with skid-row bums. Yet how many times have we been ashamed to admit our condition? How often have we found acceptance only among our "own kind"? We may not be the same, but the scenario is similar. Without love and embrace, there is only despair. Without acceptance, without someone risking giving us another chance, the dream of a fresh start vanishes. Thank God for the wonderful fellowship of recovering addicts, who love us back to life.

O Christ of the downtrodden, give me fresh starts and new chances. Above all, give me people who believe in me and care. Amen.

He who does what is true comes to the light, that it may be clearly seen.

JOHN 3:21

There is a lovely church in a valley in Switzerland that has no electricity. At the end of each pew, next to the pulpit and lectern, and around the altar are candlesticks, with no candles. Whenever an evening service is held, every worshiper and each of the clergy bring lighted candles. As each enters the church the glow becomes brighter and brighter, until the nave is bathed in a gentle light. If even one family is absent, its pew goes unlighted, and the total effect is diminished. Each family knows its light is necessary to illuminate the church; everyone is needed.

We know that one of our greatest human needs is to be needed! Somehow we must believe that someone counts on us, that we are necessary somewhere! In this modern world of mass everything, we find it hard to believe in our own individual importance. But we must, or we shrivel up and die. Our light goes out. Recovery in Christ is God declaring, "Let there be light!" Our new life in Christ is like a plant on a windowsill that greets the dawn. Each tight little bud and leaf begins to open up as the entire plant turns to drink in the life-giving light of the Twelve Steps.

This kind of blossoming takes place over and over again in our recovery. Tight, inhibited, depressed, lonely, and frightened people relax, unfurl, and open wide to the new light of truth and love in Christ—as each person relies and depends on the other. What is most marvelous about the light of Christ is that we all need it, and it needs us! It's all needed! As we soak in light, we reflect and add to its fullness. A glow of health begins to shine.

Dear Lord, you are my light. You are the light of the world. Thank you for giving me the insight of your Twelve-Step program. Help me share the light I have with others. Amen.

Paul, an apostle of Christ Jesus by command of God our Savior and of Christ Jesus our hope.

1 TIMOTHY 1:1

An old folk proverb goes: "It ain't what you don't know that hurts you; it's what you know that ain't so." Before our walk in Twelve-Step programs, how many opinions did we have that we now know just "ain't so"? We thought the primary cause of our slavery was our weakness, or our sinfulness, or our insanity. Above all, we thought we were hopelessly lost, even cursed and damned. Many such thoughts flowed through us. But they "ain't so"!

The good news of recovery and of Christian life is that what we once thought is wrong! We are sick, and need to be healed. Our addiction is a disease that we did not choose. Yes, we are also weak, sinful, and crazy at times, but our primary condition is being sick. Of course, we need to be strengthened, cleansed, and enlightened, but first we need healing. First things first. We cannot even see what is really strong, good, or sane until we find healing.

The best part of what "ain't so" is that we are not lost, cursed, or damned, and that there is hope. That hope is where it has always been: in "Christ Jesus our hope" (1 Tim. 1:1). He is our physician, and his practice extends everywhere: in our Twelve-Step fellowship, in the church, and wherever the sick cry out from darkness and distress.

A famous minister was once told by a person he helped, "You are a good man." His reply was, "I'm not a good man. I am sinful, selfish, and sick; Jesus Christ has laid his hands on me, that's all." And that's everything.

O great Physician, lay your hands upon me. Bring me health, strength, goodness, and sanity. Help me receive your loving touch with hope and joy. Amen.

"Truly I perceive that God shows no partiality."

ACTS 10:34

There is a historic old church in Sweden that is significant for many reasons, but the most striking thing about it is the life-size Christ the King on the wall at the back. It lies directly in the path of the steps to the pulpit. The preacher can see—indeed, must see—it as he or she mounts the pulpit, but it cannot be seen by the people. When asked about this great figure of Christ, the church guide told this story:

One Sunday, King Charles XII made an unexpected visit to the church. When the preacher saw the king come in, he threw away his prepared sermon and spent the time extolling the king's virtues and talking about how much King Charles was doing for his people. A few days later, that magnificent carving of Christ the King arrived as a gift from the Swedish king. Along with the present came a letter in which the king ordered that this figure of Christ be placed on the wall behind the pulpit steps so that, thereafter, anyone who walked up those steps to preach would be forced to see the one who was supposed to be praised.

It is so easy to be impressed by position and power. We become awed by the success and status of actors, politicians, and royalty. Yet we know that we are all simply human, all equal and precious in the sight of God.

Thank God the original founders of Alcoholics Anonymous meant "anonymous" to signify the absence of status. In our Twelve-Step fellowship there are no officers; everyone's rank is equal. That equality is one of great honor, however, which comes from the King of Kings, who is always the one to be praised. By honoring Christ and his kingship, we all become kings and queens.

Praise to you, Lord Christ, by whose honor and glory I am glorified and honored. May I always be forced to see you first and foremost. Amen.

[Jesus said to the blind man], "Go, wash in the pool of Siloam" (which means Sent). So he went and washed and came back seeing.

JOHN 9:7

The Twelve-Step program is like the Pool of Siloam. The steps cleanse, refresh, and remove blindness. As we plunge into the clear pool of our program and allow ourselves to be washed and awakened, we can only respond as the healed blind man, "One thing I know, that though I was blind, now I see" (John 9:25). Our blindness disappears, and new sight and clear insight appears—yet we don't know how.

We go to the meetings, we live the steps, we accept the slogans, we rely on our sponsor, and we depend on the support of the group—trusting—without figuring it out or knowing how it works. At the same time, we know that Christ is doing better things for us through our program than we can ever dream of or deserve.

Even if some of us never see or acknowledge Christ within it all, we rely on what produces the results, sobriety and serenity. As we surrender and trust in the program, we effectively give our life to the loving Christ whether we speak his name or not. Jesus doesn't need the credit. He simply rejoices in the healing. And when healing happens, we experience the "Amazing Grace" of "I once was lost but now I'm found, was blind but now I see."

O healing and cleansing Christ, may I obey your command to wash in your pool and receive the grace you have in store for me. Amen.

But Jesus said to him, "Follow me, and leave the dead to bury their own dead."

MATTHEW 8:22

The Gospels never report that Jesus went to a funeral. He was not disrespectful or callous about grief and sorrow. Indeed, he did grieve. He was just too involved in life to have time to stop and grieve over the past for very long. His focus was not on death and loss; he came to give us a vital present and a promising future. Jesus is the Lord of life, not death. Our opportunity is in the life we live and will live, not the deaths and losses that have taken place.

Life is for living relationships, for life lived with others. The primary "other" with whom we are to relate is Jesus, who calls us to follow him. Since he is no longer here in the flesh to follow, he has given us each other. Our recovery group is an ideal opportunity to live in vital relationship with others who are our equals. No one's life is valued any less or more than anyone else's in the eyes of Christ. Nowhere is this more important than in our Twelve-Step relationships.

There is no rank or status in Alcoholics Anonymous. We are all equally important in God's ranking. Jesus wants us all to honor each other as brothers and sisters, and that's how we can follow him.

Lord Jesus, thank you for calling me to life as your gift of today and to life with others, who are my brothers and sisters. Amen.

Jesus said to him, "If you would be perfect, go, sell what you possess and give to the poor, and you will have treasure in heaven; and come, follow me." When the young man heard this he went away sorrowful; for he had great possessions.

MATTHEW 19:21–22

There once was a little boy who was eagerly looking forward to his birthday gift from his favorite uncle, who always had a knack for picking out just the right toy. This year, however, the uncle decided his nephew was old enough to start receiving clothing, and sent him a sweater. At his mother's prompting, the little boy obediently sat down and wrote his thank-you note: "Dear Uncle George: Thank you for the sweater. It is what I've always wanted—but not very much. Love, Jimmy."

Such an honest answer is refreshing, but even more revealing of our attempt to live the Twelve Steps. We want Christ to be our "Higher Power." We want to follow him and leave all our other attachments and compulsions behind—but not very much! At least, not enough to override our addiction. Unless we get as excited about God and the Twelve Steps as we are by our favorite substance or activity, we'll choose to stay in our state of disappointment and dis-ease.

God created us with the power of choice—not over our addiction (which is no one's fault)—but over our choice between "me" and "God." God also created a desire for him deep within us, which, although dormant in many, is still more powerful than any other attraction. If we choose to use God's help, through our recovery program, to uncork that desire, then we can rejoice and sing, "This is what I've always wanted—very, very much!"

Jesus, you invite me to join you, to follow you, but sometimes I hold back. Increase my yearning for your grace. Make it stronger than my possessions, especially my addiction. Amen.

"He who has seen me has seen the Father."

JOHN 14:9

This ancient Hindu story helps us get a perspective on God:

"What are you reading?" a passing stranger asked a holy man sitting by the roadside. "I am reading a Sacred Book," he answered. "What is it about?" the stranger asked. "It is about God," the man replied. "Who is God?" asked the stranger. "God," said the holy man, "is the Lord of the world." To which the stranger replied, "I only believe to exist what I can see with my eyes." The holy man rose, held the open book up to the stranger at a great distance and told him to read. "How can I read this when you hold the book at such a distance!" the stranger shouted. Then, the holy man held the book so close to the stranger that it touched his nose. "Can you read now?" "But how should I be able to read when the book is so near? Again I cannot make out anything." "Indeed, you cannot see," said the holy man. "You cannot focus your eyes on the print because you are blinded by your own faulty perspective."

A child once said from her perspective, "Jesus is the best picture God ever had took." Poor grammar, that's true, but glorious theology. Seeing God in the life, teaching, ministry, death, and resurrection of Jesus Christ is the very core of Christian belief and hope. It can't be any clearer and closer than that, unless we are standing too far away or miss what's right under our noses. Our Twelve Steps reveal the same reality even when we fail to see it. Are there not times when we are so close to the program that we lose our focus? Don't we also fail to see because we stand too far off? Maybe we need to always find the proper place to get the right picture—the picture that really fits our need. Using the eyes of Christ can always help provide the right view.

O Christ, you are always there. Help me to keep the right focus and not to try to see you at too great a distance, or take your closeness for granted. Clear up my stubborn blindness. Amen.

"Greater love has no man than this, that a man lay down his life for his friends. You are my friends."

JOHN 15:13–14

What can be more straightforward? Jesus shows us in the clearest way what and who he is. He is our friend. This demonstration was on a tree—the tree of Calvary, the cross of his crucifixion. As he hangs there he says, "I love you with the greatest love possible." Directly to us, he is saying, "I love you so much, I will go this far for you. I will go to this length to show you and make it real to you. I will go this far to move you."

It is the love of God in Christ that "saves" us. It is Christ's love that breaks our pride and fills us with gratitude and true worth. As recovering Christians, nothing can move us to love and appreciation for Christ and each other more than to consider his sacrifice of love upon the cross for all of us. The words to the old hymn express it well:

> When I survey the wondrous cross
> Where the young Prince of Glory died,
> My richest gain I count but loss,
> And pour contempt on all my pride.
>
> Were the whole realm of nature mine,
> That were an offering far too small;
> Love so amazing, so divine,
> Demands my soul, my life, my all.

When we stand at the foot of the cross and gaze upon our Lord's great love for us, the Third Step flows naturally from our grateful hearts. Such love drives us to our knees. Our pride vanishes. Yet in its place a new sense of belonging and value fills us. We are his beloved friends! What better knowledge on which to base our self-esteem?

O Christ, lead me often to Calvary, where I may see your great love and friendship for me. Amen.

"Truly, truly, I say to you, he who believes in me will also do the works that I do; and greater works than these will he do, because I go to the Father."

JOHN 14:12

An old story has been passed down about an angel who greeted Jesus on his arrival in heaven after the Ascension. "Lord, who have you left behind to carry on your work?" the angel asked. "A little band of people who love me," answered Jesus. "But Lord, what if they fail when their trials come? Will all you have done be defeated?" "Yes," Jesus replied, "if they fail, all I have done will be defeated." The angel persisted: "Is there nothing more?" "No," said Jesus. "What then, Lord?" asked the worried angel. "They will *not* fail," was Jesus' answer.

How can Jesus say that? Anyone can see that there is failure, not "great works," in Christianity. We have witnessed everything from executions and wars to persecution and terrorism, all in the name of Christianity! Many of us among the company of the addicted have been shunned, shamed, ridiculed, condemned, and abandoned by our Christian brothers and sisters. Isn't that failure?

It is, but it is not complete failure. Jesus told the angel in the story that he left a *little* band. Jesus told his disciples that "those *who believe in me* will do the works I do." Our Lord placed his trust in the hands of a few—just a handful. God has always trusted a tiny little crew to do his work. Thank God, he has scattered his "little band" throughout the world, in all sorts of places. Wherever his works of love exist—even in the midst of evil—there is Christ's own victory. There is "the little band of people who love me and who will not fail."

O Christ, please cleanse me and count me among your little band. I do love you and want to serve you. Help me stay on your path of winning love. Amen.

"And when he has found it, he lays it on his shoulders, rejoicing. . . saying to them, 'Rejoice with me, for I have found my sheep which was lost.'"

LUKE 15:5–6

One of the earliest paintings of Jesus portrayed him as a young shepherd carrying a lamb across his shoulders. Many of us have seen such portrayals. Some of us see ourselves in the lamb. The thought of being carried safely in the arms of our Lord is comforting and soothing.

However, to be picked up and carried is difficult for many of us to accept. Thoughts like "I'm too heavy" or "I'm too embarrassed" or "I'm too dignified" or "I'm not helpless" fill our minds until we have to admit: "I'm too tired; I'm too sick; I'm powerless." To surrender and submit to the strong arms of a Savior humiliates the proud but brings joy to the weary and sick.

What keeps us from being helped is our fierce self-sufficiency. Sheep are not self-sufficient: wayward, unruly, stubborn, or stupid, perhaps, but hardly autonomous and independent. If we do identify with animals, we like to think of ourselves as being clever as a fox, strong as a horse, wise as an owl, but it's humiliating to think we are sheep in need of a shepherd.

Good Shepherd, please help me to allow you to pick me up and carry me much sooner, before I become exhausted. Teach me to rely on you every day. Amen.

> *"Truly, truly, I say to you, the hour is coming, and now is, when the dead will hear the voice of the Son of God, and those who hear will live."*
>
> JOHN 5:25

Children often go right to the core questions. A story is told of a group of children whose kitten has died. "Why did Jesus let this happen?" they ask. Then they ask the deeper question, "Why does everyone die, and why does Jesus allow it?" They decide to ask the expert, the minister of their church. He gives a very profound, theological, and orthodox answer and sits back in satisfaction. One little boy turns to his elder brother and says, "He doesn't know either, does he?"

Unfortunately, no one seems to have the answer. Why are we addicted and afflicted? Why did we have to suffer and cause others to suffer? We just don't know. However, we do know how to get better and where to turn. The how is our Twelve-Step program of recovery. The where is to Jesus Christ our Lord and Savior. We don't know the solutions to the puzzles of life, sickness, and death, but we do have remedies!

Why life, sickness, and death? Jesus never tells us. He just lives, dies, and lives again for us.

Dear Lord, you suffered and died for me; why did you have to go through such pain? I know you didn't say. For whatever reason, thank you for loving me so much. Was that the reason all along? Amen.

"If you abide in me, and my words abide in you, ask whatever you will, and it shall be done for you."

JOHN 15:7

"One day at a time" means that our program is not for sprinters, it is for long-distance people. The sprinter does not have to worry about pace, since the race is short, over in one burst of explosive energy. The long-distance runner has to pace the race and even gain strength along the way. Too fast is too bad. The Chinese have a saying, "Consider the worm, his day is but two feet long." Such a small distance is appropriate for such a small creature, and it's a full day's work!

Too often in recovery "we want what we want when we want it." We dive impulsively into the program, jumping from the First to the Twelfth Step. Some of us even try to be sponsors in our first month of recovery! Such a fast pace is not progress. Our program is for steady, healthy, lifelong growth. We are growing oaks, not alfalfa sprouts. Solid success takes time to develop a strong trunk and limbs with roots planted firmly in the Lord's soil. If we go too fast, we'll be easily uprooted and wither away.

Jesus wants our recovery, but he sets his own condition on our growth. Jesus says you first have to "abide," make your home in me and in my words. He is emphatic. He means *unless* you abide in me, *only* if you abide in my words, will your desires be granted. It takes time to abide, to live in a home. It takes time to live in Christ and in our program. Are we striving to make a home or are we just visiting?

Lord, keep me living in you and in my program of recovery as a permanent resident, patiently growing into a firmly rooted tree. Amen.

> *"Father, if thou art willing, remove this cup from me; nevertheless not my will, but thine, be done."*
>
> LUKE 22:42

A great philosopher has declared that the agonizing struggle that Jesus went through in the Garden of Gethsemane is and shall forever be the highest moment in the history of religion. Naturally, that is one person's opinion. Obviously, Good Friday and Easter are more vivid and memorable events. Why call the Garden of Gethsemane the highest? Perhaps it was because Jesus' agony and struggle in the garden led to the decision that resulted in the crucifixion and resurrection. Without the struggle of will in the garden, there would have been no cross and empty tomb.

Haven't we had our gardens of torment when we cry out to God to "take this cup from me!"? Haven't we—don't we still—grapple with God as we try to assert our will, our desires, our needs? But if we follow Jesus and take the Third Step—to surrender our life and will over to God—Easter is ahead. It comes only through a cross of pain, but as the old hymn says, "If we can't bear the cross, then we can't wear the crown."

The Third-Step garden makes the cross and crown happen. From the complete and unconditional surrender of life and will to God flows the strength and resolve to rise again to new lives of serenity, love, and service! The wonderful fact of recovery is that our garden of the Third Step is always there. The marvel of recovery is that with each daily surrender comes new power to continue to recover.

Dear Christ, you gave me a pattern in the Garden of Gethsemane to always use as I take my Third Steps over and over again toward my new crosses and my new resurrections. Amen.

"My God, my God, why hast thou forsaken me?"
MATTHEW 27:46

A Chinese tale tells the story of an old farmer and his only son. One night the old man's horse escaped, and the neighbors came to comfort him in his loss. He said, "How do you know this is bad luck?" Several days later, his horse returned with a herd of wild horses. Now his friends congratulated the farmer for his good fortune, but the old man said, "How do you know this is a good thing?" His son broke his leg trying to tame one of the wild horses. Again the neighbors gathered, this time to bemoan this new misfortune. "How do you know this is ill fortune?" asked the old man. Soon a war lord came to recruit able-bodied youth for his army, and the farmer's son escaped conscription because of his broken leg. In true fashion, the farmer's friends expressed their pleasure over such good luck. Here the story ends, but it could go on forever.

What a true picture of recovery and of the church! It seemed a bad day when we discovered our addiction. It seemed a bad day when we gave up our anesthetic substances and our compulsive behaviors. It seemed a bad day when Christ cried out in pain and anguish on the cross. Yet in the mystery of recovery time and again what seemed bad becomes good and good luck is followed by bad. Yet God always has the last word. He brings Easter out of all Good Fridays, even as new Good Fridays follow our new resurrections. Easter is always the final word.

Almighty Christ, grant me the will and willingness to accept good and bad days as a part of your mystery toward the final good day in your kingdom. Amen.

We love, because he first loved us.

1 JOHN 4:19

A wise Christian saint was once asked the secret of becoming perfect. He said:

The sole secret is a hearty love of God, and the only way of attaining that love is by loving; . . . Begin as a mere apprentice and the very power of love will lead you on to become a master of the art.

Yet we are not loved for our loving natures. Christ, our supreme Lover, loves us despite our lack of love — not because we possess so much of it. What is wonderful about Christ's love is that he loves us anyway! Saint Paul was aware of Christ's great generosity: "But God shows his love for us in that while we were yet sinners Christ died for us" (Rom. 5:8).

If we cannot respond in grateful love to Christ's sacrifice, we are indeed dead. Who will reject his outstretched arms? Who will turn away from his love? It's our choice.

Christ, I fear most the loss of your love. Take me into your loving arms. Teach me how to love. Amen.

So we know and believe the love God has for us. God is love, and he who abides in love abides in God, and God abides in him.

1 JOHN 4:16

Nothing is more beautiful than love. It puts forests, flowers, and sunlight to shame. Yet as beautiful as it is, love is more practical than pretty. Real love gets down to the real world, where there's no "prettiness." Yet there is beauty. Recovery is not overpopulated with pretty people either, but all people struggling to recover are beautiful.

The sight of Jesus bowing under the weight of the cross—his stumbling, falling, bruising crash to the stones, his cries from the cross, his sweat, his blood, his dying breath—none is a pretty sight. Yet how beautiful! We have tried for centuries to capture the beauty in that ugliness. Some of the greatest works of art have tried to portray our crucified yet beautiful Savior. Here is God in our flesh, cruelly betrayed, tortured, and nailed to the cross—what could be uglier? Nothing. Unless something more beautiful than beauty was there on that hill. Unless the ugly horror was transcended and transformed—made holy.

And it was. Each time we kneel at the foot of the cross, as we gaze in wonder upon our suffering Savior, no beauty can compare. The glory is overwhelming:

In the cross of Christ we glory, towering o'er the wrecks of time;
All the light of sacred story gathers round his head sublime.

Bane and blessing, pain and pleasure, by the cross are sanctified;
Peace is there that knows no measure, joys that through all time abide.

See, from his head, his hands, his feet,
Sorrow and love flow mingled down!
Did e'er such love and sorrow meet,
Or thorns compose so rich a crown?

Jesus, may your beautiful cross of love be ever before my eyes and in my heart. Amen.

> *But in fact Christ has been raised from the dead, the first fruits of those who have fallen asleep. For as by a man came death, by a man has come also the resurrection of the dead. For as in Adam all die, so also in Christ shall all be made alive.*

1 CORINTHIANS 15:20–22

If God is good, why do we suffer? This question is universal and as ancient as humanity. It is still being asked. Buddhism began in order to provide an answer. When one eliminates all desire, Buddha said, all suffering vanishes. Yet suffering remains, and we still ask why a loving God would create a world full of suffering, injustice, and death. Some have said that God causes suffering as punishment. Others say that God simply has no control over or interest in his world and that accident rules. Unfortunately, we don't know. We simply must accept the suffering of addiction as a mystery.

Yet one thing is certain. No matter how much we suffer—God loves us. He takes no pleasure in our pain. In fact, there is every reason to believe that God in Christ takes the pain of our addiction upon himself. The cross is our answer. Even though he deserved no pain, he took all our sin and suffering as his own. He embraced our condition and loved us unto life and glory. As baffling and mysterious as suffering is, even more wondrous is our Savior's love for us upon the cross, drawing us all unto his loving, healing arms. As we sink into his cross, we fall into his death and then leap up with him on Easter. He is risen. So are we.

Lord, I fall into your loving arms upon the cross and trust your Easter in my life. Amen.

"For he makes his sun rise on the evil and on the good,
and sends rain on the just and on the unjust."

MATTHEW 5:45

Many people who have visited Reims cathedral in France hear the story of the glorious rose window that is the jewel of that church. During World War II, the rose window was shattered. Immediately after this disaster, the townspeople rushed from their homes and laboriously and lovingly gathered up every single bit and piece of lead and glass. When the war ended, the town called in skilled artisans to build a new rose window using the shattered fragments of the old—now made even more magnificent through their devotion.

In our God-given freedom, we are vulnerable; we can be shattered and crushed. What was beautiful and precious in our lives can become broken and shattered. But God picks up our pieces and saves them for the time when we can be "put back together again."

Christians are not insulated from hurt and harm; God doesn't prevent disasters in our lives. He sends sunshine and rain on everyone. After all, God's own Son suffered unspeakable pain. Disciples are called to follow their master, for better or worse.

Nevertheless, in every collapse and decay are the seeds of new life and new glory. God does not want anything to go to waste; he will help us gather up the bits and pieces of our lives and rebuild us into stronger and even more beautiful windows—for his love to shine through. He may not protect us from all harm, but he will always restore and renew us to a shining new Easter resurrection of our very own, in a life that begins today.

O, risen Lord, keep me close to your side. Keep me from despair. Keep my hope alive. Make me a new window to your glory. Amen.

Jesus said to her, "I am the resurrection and the life; he who believes in me, though he die, yet shall he live."

JOHN 11:25

In A. J. Cronin's *The Keys of the Kingdom*, Father Chisholm is a missionary priest who works most of his life against overwhelming odds and in spite of countless failures. One day he is talking to a farmer who is moaning over the loss of his garden to a recent flood. "My plantings are all lost; we shall have to begin all over again," he cries. Father Chisholm quietly replies, "But that's life, my friend: to begin again when everything is lost."

That is also the way of the cross and resurrection, the mystery of Good Friday and Easter. The life of a Christian is a continual round of dying and rising again. Life is made up of many deaths and rebirths. Our plantings are often washed away, yet we start over; it is inevitable. No one sees this pattern of grace any better than those of us who live in the recovering community. We are "born again" all the time. Each meeting, each prayer, each connection with our sponsor, each book we read all greet us with the fact of loss and life. Something dies, yet something also rises. That's recovery. Recovery is renewal, change; it is dying to the old and rising to new life.

No real recovery is ever static. A lively recovery is always in flux. The Twelve Steps are for "stepping" not "standing." Being "born again" into the Twelve-Step new life is a process of active kicking and screaming. It is the way of God.

Dear Lord of life as well as death, help me to accept your cycle of loss and gain and to surrender myself in trust to your presence in all my dyings and risings. Amen.

"Thy kingdom come. Thy will be done, on earth as it is in heaven."

MATTHEW 6:10

A great musical composer was asked: "If you had to spend the rest of your days on a desert island, which of your four hundred compositions would you take with you?" "I'd take some blank paper," he replied. "My favorite composition is always the one I will write tomorrow." Even in the worst of circumstances, one can hope, create, and find beauty and meaning—even on a desert island.

To the Christian believer, hope is not the same as a Pollyanna's wishful thinking. A sense of comforting strength rests in our hope in God's promise to make "his kingdom come" in our lives. Christian hope is "blessed assurance" in the midst of life's struggle, even in the middle of hell itself.

The victory that we find in our life struggles with our addiction rests upon the conviction that our striving is joined to Christ's own warfare against disease and eternal death. Although we are united with Christ in his suffering and death, as Christians we shall also be "united with him in a resurrection like his" (Rom. 6:5). Such is his will that will be done, his will for life.

Above all, we know that we have already won by the victory of Christ and are guaranteed the benefits of his suffering, death, and resurrection. Saint Paul said, "Thanks be to God, who gives us the victory through our Lord Jesus Christ" (1 Cor. 15:57).

O Divine Master, who taught us to pray, keep my hope alive in your kingdom and in your will, not mine. Amen.

"And behold, some are last who will be first, and some are first who will be last."

LUKE 13:30

The new minister of a church insisted on leaving written instructions and notes for his staff. A janitor who could not read or write was soon found out when he failed to respond to the written messages. He lost his job as a result. This man, however, was no ordinary person. He was brilliant, although unlettered. He began his own business and became very wealthy. One day, his banker was astounded when he discovered his customer's illiteracy and exclaimed, "Good heavens, man, just imagine where you would be if you could read and write!" His reply was, "Yup, I'd be a janitor in an Episcopal church."

The saying, "When you get lemons, make lemonade," illustrates the fact that something bad often leads to a greater blessing. If we don't fail or come in last sometimes, we would never move on to something better. Whatever happens in our life, nothing is outside of God's grace. "Recovering folk" often feel like leftovers. Yet God in his grace takes the cast-offs and the castaways and creates new and wonderful miracles of success, if we let him.

Carl Sagan has often said that nothing in creation is ever wasted. In fact, he states that the very stuff of the original universe, from billions of years ago, exists in the cells and elements that make up our present bodies. We are all billions of years old! God continues to use, rearrange, and reuse what was into what is and what is into what will be. When we offer ourselves to God in the Third Step, we are making his recycling work that much easier.

O Christ, friend of the last and least, I give my leftover self and all its cast-off pieces to you to rebuild and renew. Amen.

> *"No one puts new wine into old wineskins; if he does, the wine will burst the skins, and the wine is lost, and so are the skins; but new wine is for fresh skins."*

MARK 2:22

Now and new go together. Without now, anything new is meaningless. Without the nowness of Christ's presence, we wither and decay. The new wine of recovery must be poured into new wineskins. The fresh new insights of the Twelve-Step program must fill fresh, soft skins that will allow the new wine to expand and mellow.

Holding on to destructive old ideas and attitudes will cause the old skin to rupture; it will not give or yield. When the freshness of Christ and our program is poured into old, rigid skins, they won't hold or hold up. The old package can't contain the new.

However, the new can contain worthwhile contents from the old. Think of that! We don't have to completely throw away what was valuable in our past. On the contrary, what was creative in the past can become fresh elements of the present. Good and mellow old wine can be easily welcomed and merged with the new. Only the old bottles and packages have to go!

If our program is not working for us, perhaps we are trying to fit the new program into our old package. But with an open and new wineskin of our own, we can contain the healing of the new wine of Christ and our program. Furthermore, we can pour the contents of our seasoned wine into the new embrace of the wineskin of recovery.

O Christ of the now and the new, help me be a fresh, yielding, and supple wineskin so I may receive your new wine. Help me discard my old, rigid, and dried-up wineskin, and pour whatever good, old wine I have into your fresh new container. Amen.

Rollo May said, "It is an old ironic habit of human beings to run faster when we have lost our way." There have been times when I have confused mere action for achievement. Aimless action may feel better than being stuck, but it can cause destructive accidents. Sometimes we rush our recovery. Action is essential, but action that is full speed ahead rarely takes root. One of our best slogans is, "Easy does it." This hardly means that recovery is easy, but that we shouldn't rush things. Frenetic activity without reflection or understanding frequently leads to discouragement and burnout.

Each step contains a wisdom component that invites a trusting acceptance before the action. We accepted our powerlessness, came to believe, made a decision, were entirely ready, and had a spiritual awakening. Our action is guided action. Guided by the steps and slogans and traditions and promises.

In every recovery group there are those enthusiastic ones who go from the first to the twelfth step, skipping the rest in between. Soon they learn. Soon we learn that "haste makes waste" and that recovery is a lifetime endeavor. We have plenty of time. Thank God. Jesus walked this earth. He did not dash from place to place. He had time. He took time. He takes time for us. He never resented interruptions. When the woman reached out to touch his robe, he took time for her. When the lame, blind, dumb, and afflicted called out to him, he took time for them. When the children came to him, he took time for them. He takes time for you and me. Recovery takes time for you, too. Why not take time for recovery? Good things take time. We cannot force our program. Let it take root in you and blossom on God's good schedule.

"There is a lad here who has five barley loaves and two fish; but what are they among so many?"

JOHN 6:9

A three-year-old boy was playing with his father's leather tools and accidently blinded himself with an awl. The year was 1812. Seventeen years later, as a youth of twenty, he invented a system that allows the blind to read. His name was Louis Braille. His tragedy was turned into a blessing for many thousands. Helen Keller said of her handicaps: "I thank God for my handicaps, for through them I have found myself, my work, and my God."

Such inspiring examples of triumph in the midst of tragedy are more frequent than we suspect. The Hallelujah chorus was written by Handel when he was fifty-six years old and paralyzed on his right side. Mozart wrote some of his best music while living in poverty, Beethoven, when he was deaf.

Our compulsive disorders are handicaps. The addictive disease we suffer from is painful and even tragic. Yet the consequences of it are not automatically tragic. The outcome can be victorious and inspiring. We may not have the distinction of being great musicians, writers, or statesmen. We can be great, however; pain and suffering can fashion us into loving human beings. Suffering can be our pathway toward humility and kindness, through the Christ who suffered and died for us all.

To embrace our weakness and our pain, to endure the stress and strain of our handicapped lives is the pathway of the cross, the avenue toward new life and love. To face into our need and helplessness is to come face to face with the truth of God's great love for us.

Look upon me, O Christ, from your cross, and heal me of my lack of faith and hope. Take my pain as an offering to yours, and give me your Easter victory now. Take my meager loaves and fishes and multiply them through your grace. Amen.

"Blessed are those who hunger and thirst for righteousness, for they shall be satisfied."

MATTHEW 5:6

Once there was a man who searched for God without ceasing. He was determined to find him. He went from church to church and meeting to meeting without success. Finally, at a riverbank, he encountered a wise old sponsor. "Show me how to discover God!" the man pleaded. "I will introduce you to two friends of mine who will help," the sponsor said, "but you must do exactly as they say." The sponsor's two friends led the man into the river until the water was over his head. They held him down, keeping his head under water. Because he trusted the sponsor, he went along at first, but soon he began to panic and struggled violently. The men persisted and kept him under, until his lungs were about to burst. Then they let him up, sputtering and gasping for air.

When the man regained his composure, the wise old sponsor asked, "Tell me what you thought about when you felt you were drowning?" The man replied, "I thought about air, how I had to breathe, how I wanted air." The old sponsor said, "This is what you have yet to learn: when you want to walk the Second and Third Steps, when you want God the way a drowning man wants air, then you will find him."

When Rudyard Kipling was on his deathbed, his last words, uttered with his last breath, were "I want God." That is what Jesus tells us. Our blessedness lies in wanting God the same way, with our whole being, with a consuming hunger and thirst for his righteousness—and we shall be filled.

O, righteous Lord, never let me rest and be satisfied with anything less than you and your righteousness. Give me an aching hunger and a burning thirst for you. Amen.

*Put on then, as God's chosen ones, holy and beloved,
compassion, kindness, lowliness, meekness, and patience.*
COLOSSIANS 3:12

When the news of the Battle of Waterloo was first received in England, it was brought to the south coast by ship and then sent on by semaphore signals upon high places. The message came through: "Wellington defeated," and then fog rolled in and concealed the signal flags. This news of defeat spread gloom throughout the land, but when the fog lifted the signals were completed: "Wellington defeated the enemy." The nation's joyful response was that much more intense because of the darkness that preceded it.

So much of our life in recovery contains signals yet to be finished or messages temporarily hidden by fog. We are blessed in recovery by our Christian faith. This faith is based on God's victory in Christ, who turned the defeat of the cross into the triumph of Easter. The cross is the incomplete message. The empty tomb is the final answer. Christ is risen. He is alive. He is with us, and we live with him. His risen life is with our recovery and in the Twelve Steps, alive, powerful, and effective. Nothing can ever defeat our Lord. Therefore, we cannot be defeated.

Risen Lord, you are always victorious. Help me never forget your victory is mine too. Amen.

"I have said this to you, that in me you may have peace."
JOHN 16:33

> When in danger, when in doubt,
> Run in circles, scream and shout!

This old rhyme is not advice; it's a description of what we generally do when we are fearful and confused. We know it's futile, but we do it anyway!

This tendency is addressed in the British navy by a custom known as "the still." In cases of sudden disaster aboard ship, the call for "the still" is blown. This is a whistle for the crew to come to complete silence. When "the still" is blown every man aboard knows what it means: "Prepare to do the right thing." This moment of calm has helped avoid many a catastrophe that "running in circles, screaming and shouting" could cause.

The personal life of Beverly Sills has been full of tragedy, including a child born deaf, never to hear her mother's magnificent voice. She was asked how she copes. She spoke of a "stillness" and said:

When "the stillness" comes, you simply realize that it is not important for everybody to love you. It's more important for you to love them. It turns your whole life around. And the very act of living becomes the act of giving.

Twelve-Step recovery speaks of such a "stillness." It is a deep, calming presence of peace within the center of our life. We call it "serenity." We call it "priceless." It comes from God as we surrender our fear and doubts to him. The Third Step sounds the first notes of "the still" for us.

Lord, may I seek my serenity in you and be at peace and then listen as you guide me to do the right thing. Amen.

"Depart from me, for I am a sinful man, O Lord."

LUKE 5:8

In 1839 Dr. Thomas Burgess, a member of the British Royal College of Surgeons, wrote these words:

We can make an individual laugh against his will, by tickling the soles of his feet. We can make him cry by corporal punishment. We can make him tremble with fear by the same means. We can rouse his anger by striking him. But we can only make him blush by appealing to his conscience. No physical means can produce blushing; it must be solely a moral stimulus that will excite a true blush.

We sometimes hear that we need to get rid of our hang-ups, our guilt; we hear that guilt and shame are wrong and destructive. That is not entirely true. Only false guilt arising from mistaken and misplaced judgment is wrong. Only imposed shame and coercive put-downs that are unjust and unfair are destructive. True guilt and honest shame are essential to our moral fiber. Guilt is a measurement of wrongdoing and failure. Shame is what we feel when we *know* we are judged guilty correctly. Guilt tells us we were wrong; shame is what makes us blush by appealing to our conscience. Without an accurate evaluation of our guilty deeds and without an appropriate sense of shame, we cannot take the Fourth Step.

O Loving Lord, may I realize my guilt and feel my shame—so that I may amend my life through your healing forgiveness. Amen.

"Rejoice with me, for I have found the coin which I had lost."

LUKE 15:9

A little three year old wandered away from the family campsite at a national park. The family searched, then more families joined in. Soon the entire park population was involved. After one day of looking everywhere, and just before losing hope, the child was found by the father. After being tucked into bed, the rescued child said, "Gee, aren't you all glad you found me?"

If anything is made clear by Jesus about our heavenly Father, it is how much he rejoices over our rescue. Jesus illustrates this by the stories of a lost coin found by a housewife, a lost sheep found by a shepherd, and a lost son found by his father. God is like that, Jesus says; there is much rejoicing among the angels in heaven over just one rescue!

If any place brings such rejoicing by God and heaven, it is a Twelve-Step meeting or a church gathering. When the lost are found, God is around. And his joy surrounds us. Naturally, we are prone to thank some other source for our rescue: luck, or our resourcefulness, determination, or good sense. Yet it is God who discovers us, uncovers us, cleanses and cleans us up. When we find clarity in the midst of confusion, doubt, and fear, we have found God and he has found us.

Dear God, to know you rejoice when I am found is such joy to me. Help me to never stop looking for and finding you, and myself. Amen.

> *From that time Jesus began to preach, saying, "Repent, for the kingdom of heaven is at hand."*
>
> MATTHEW 4:17

Two brothers were once convicted of stealing sheep and were branded on the forehead with the letters S T, which stood for "sheep thief." Unable to bear the shame, one brother fled to a foreign land, where he still had to explain his brand. He wandered from land to land, hoping he could escape his guilt, but finally died in bitterness, buried in a forgotten grave. The other brother repented of his crime. He did not go away but bore his shame, acknowledged his guilt, and resolved "to make amends." He stayed with his people, determined to win back their respect. As the years passed, he gained a reputation for great honesty and kindness. One day a stranger came to town and saw the old man with S T branded on his forehead. He asked someone what the letters meant. A villager said, "It happened long ago and I have forgotten the details, but I think the letters are an abbreviation for 'saint.'"

Such is the choice for us. We can run and hide. We can deny and dispute. But we cannot escape. The only way of healing is to surrender and face the facts. When we repent and make amends, we turn toward the light of truth and health. The process of giving ourselves over to the healing, purging, cleansing love of God has the power of the holy within it. There is no power stronger on earth than the courage to face our past. Almost every saint worthy of sainthood had to become free of his or her yesterdays. We are not called to spectacular sainthood, but we are called to repentance, to truth, to forgiveness, and to new life in all our todays. Our Lord Christ bears in his own wounds our past shame and guilt—all we need to do is embrace his present love to remove our stain.

Dear Christ, I lay open at your feet in my shame. Forgive me and hear me. Amen.

"What did you go out into the wilderness to behold?"
LUKE 7:24

A man with a terrible toothache met a friend, who noticed his face full of pain. "What's wrong, John?" he asked. "I have a horrible toothache, and this is my dentist's day off, and aspirin doesn't help," said John. His friend replied, "When I have pain, I go to my wife for relief. She hugs me, kisses me, caresses me, and comforts me so much, I forget about my pain." John said, "That's wonderful! Is she at home now? I'd like to go see her!"

When we share our solutions to life, it doesn't mean we can use somebody else's program. One man's relief may be none of our business! We can't take what is not ours. Each of us has our own recovery, and we can use only what belongs to us and fits us.

We aren't to blame for our pain, but we are responsible for finding our own dentist, making our own appointment, sitting in our chair, and claiming our own health with the Twelve Steps. Our toothache may not be our doing, but our search for relief certainly is.

Jesus seldom healed anyone until that person showed a willingness to sincerely and honestly seek out healing. Expecting relief and being open to even better health than we can imagine, we receive more from Christ than we could ever ask or expect! The Twelve Steps work the same way if we are willing, honest, and open to receive the blessings of recovery. It all starts with us.

O Christ, as I seek relief from pain, please increase my will for health. Amen.

"I am the light of the world."

JOHN 8:12

The spirit of the Eleventh Step is captured by Brother Lawrence, who wrote:

Pray remember what I have recommended to you, which is, to think often on God, by day, by night, in your business, and even in your diversions. He is always near you and with you; leave Him not alone. You would think it rude to leave a friend alone who came to visit you; why, then, must God be neglected? Do not then forget Him, but think on Him often, adore Him continually, live and die with Him; this is the glorious employment of a Christian; in a word, this is our profession; if we do not know it we must learn it.

An ancient writer wrote, on a similar note:

Whoso draw nigh to God one step through doubtings dim,
God will advance a mile in blazing light to him.

Our recovery is not just "one step through doubtings dim" but Twelve Steps that we repeat over and over again! Every step, no matter how halfhearted or weak, is a major step. God will blaze his light into our darkness. The more we practice the presence of God through "prayer and meditation," the greater and clearer our light will be. God's light is pure and bright. It is shining in the Scripture and plainly written in the Twelve Steps. The more we read, contemplate, and study our Bibles, our Big Book, and our Twelve-Step literature, the greater the light will be in our hearts and minds. God in Christ wants our enlightenment. He is the light of our world. Without him there is no light. With him is no darkness at all.

O light of my world, shine on me and drive the darkness away. Amen.

> *Let us then with confidence draw near to the throne of grace, that we may receive mercy and find grace to help in time of need.*

HEBREWS 4:16

A great Christian teacher once said, "Have thy tools ready. God will find thee work." How can we serve others in recovery? What can we do to fulfill Step Twelve? Unfortunately, here there are no guidelines or rules. The Twelfth Step is a "sharing of self" step. The power of telling our story is one of being available and ready. God will provide the jobs—if we don't wait for spectacular projects. Albert Schweitzer once said:

Always keep your eyes open for the little task, because it is the little task that is important to Jesus Christ. The future of the kingdom of God does not depend on the enthusiasm of this or that powerful person; those great ones are necessary too, but it is equally necessary to have a great number of little people who will do a little thing in the service of Christ.

God does his work of recovery and salvation with many hands. Every act of kindness or assistance to others ranks the same with God. There is no better or best. Every time someone lightens the burden of another, God is powerfully present.

O Christ, you noticed the small details. Help me be ready to help and serve in small ways, every day. Amen.

"For nothing is covered that will not be revealed, or hidden that will not be known."

MATTHEW 10:26

In Florence an artist named Donatello refused to accept a block of marble from the quarry because it was not perfect. Michelangelo took this rejected stone and carved his famous statue of David from it. The same Michelangelo once gazed upon another rock, covered with filth and garbage, and said, "There is an angel inside that rock, and I will get it out."

Imperfections often hide beauty. Soiled material can be cleansed and transformed under the right hands, through the right eyes. How often we fail to look under the surface or seek the worth in what seems worthless. John Ruskin one day took some common mud that he found and put it under his microscope. He discovered that it held four things: sand, clay, carbon, and water. He looked deeper and saw in the sand the potential sapphire; in the clay, the opal; in the carbon, the diamond; in the water, the snowflake.

With the loving and caring eyes and hands of Christ we can be made beautiful. We are always precious in his sight. He sees our goodness even when no one else can. And in our programs of recovery we encounter similar appreciation.

We often say, "Expect a miracle," yet miracles are not magic conjured up through the bizarre or the strange. Miracles are made from the commonplace: common people, bread, some fish, a manger, a cross. Our full saying is, "Expect a miracle. I am one." You and I are the stuff of miracle and personal transformation. Our commonplace lives can be changed by the higher power of Christ.

Dear Christ, behold me and hold me in your hands. Fashion me into a miracle of new love and life. Amen.

"Blessed are the meek, for they shall inherit the earth."
MATTHEW 5:5

The spirit of our human "declaration of independence" from God is summed up in William Henley's "Invictus": "I am the master of my fate: I am the captain of my soul." Ironically this proud poet was later shaken by personal disaster and found himself humble and broken. To his surprise and gratitude, out of his weakness and dejection, he found love and healing as he desperately turned to God. He discovered the true captain and master of his soul — he discovered his "Higher Power." William Henley deeply regretted writing "Invictus," with its prideful words that have enchanted and deceived so many.

How familiar this story is to us who are beginning to recover from our controlling ways, from our dependency and our codependency. Those of us who are addicted to drugs used to be so sure we were in charge — until our substance took charge and we realized how helpless we really are to shape our own lives. Those of us who are addicted to people or behaviors were just as determined to be captains and masters of the situation. We all ended up defeated and helpless.

To be helpless, however, is the opposite of being hopeless. To realize our helplessness simply acknowledges that we need help! We all do. The Twelve Steps of recovery are the help we need, along with the healing love of Christ Jesus, who is our soul's true captain and master. To know where our help comes from is our hope. This hope is our only health, our only chance of victory.

Dear Christ, my master and captain, I thank you for my helplessness. I praise you for my hope: you and the Twelve Steps. Amen.

*"Holy Father, keep them in thy name, which thou hast
given me, that they may be one, even as we are one."*

JOHN 17:11

The simple, staggering, and unvarnished faith of Christians has always been that God is like Jesus, so much so, that we worship Jesus as the Son of God.

One way to look at this is in light of the simple principle of universals and particulars. The grace we see in Jesus is the specific example of the universal attitude of God's habitual and eternal grace. Music, we say, is a universal, and the works of Mozart, Brahms, or Beethoven are particular, specific, supreme examples of music. Beauty is a universal, and the Parthenon, the Taj Mahal, or Michelangelo's *David* are particular, specific, and supreme examples of beauty. Drama is a universal, and the works of Sophocles, Shakespeare, and Miller are particular, specific, and supreme examples of dramatic art.

No one has ever heard universal music or seen universal beauty or drama; we know them only through concrete, specific examples. This is the Christian belief and understanding of our Lord Jesus. He is the particular, specific, and supreme example of the universal we call God. Because of this belief, Christianity has been called the "scandal of particularity."

Jesus is not merely the "Higher Power" whom I choose to call God; he is the prime and fullest expression of God yet to grace this earth. Through him, all our other healing programs of grace, like our Twelve-Step programs, draw their power and pattern.

Lord Jesus, I thank you that you are so real, close, and human. I give you my love and devotion as the most concrete and specific revelation of God. Amen.

*"Woe to you lawyers also! for you load men with burdens
hard to bear, and you yourselves do not touch the burdens
with one of your fingers."*

LUKE 11:46

A salesman came to the front door and met a little boy
who answered the doorbell. As he looked down at the child,
the salesman asked, "What is your name, son?" "My name
is Jimmy Don't," the boy replied. Little Jimmy had been
told "don't" so many times he thought it was his last name!

We have many such words like *don't* that stick in our
hearts and minds. There are words like *should, ought,
always, never, nothing, nobody,* and *everyone.* It's fun sometimes to count the times you hear such words at a meeting
or in church. If we hear too many, we just might become
like Jimmy. The words of recovery sound more like these:
*can, do, may, decide, choose, listen, learn, love, think, trust,
talk,* and *feel.* They have a positive, fluid ring to them.

Jesus encountered a religion made up of the burden of
law. Endless regulations and rules controlled all of life and
stifled the spirit. The Pharisees tried so hard that they had
over a thousand "don'ts." Imagine learning a thousand
"Thou shall nots," much less obeying them! Thank God the
Big Book and the New Testament are both testimonies to
freedom and hope. They lift, not restrict. Thank God our
Twelve Steps are stepping stones to possibility. Thank God
the gospel is the good news of promise. Thank God we can
do more than we cannot.

*Please help me, Lord, to hear and speak the words of hope, to live
with optimism and be open to the possible. Amen.*

"Why do you seek the living among the dead?"

LUKE 24:5–6

When a recovering Christian begins to live again and to experience freedom from the power of an addiction—that beginning is "Easter." The discovery of God's liberation and new life is our resurrection experience. It is for us a rising again and a coming alive—a bursting forth from the death-like tomb of our diseased compulsions. When God's liberating life breaks through and rolls away our tombstone, we can sing with this unknown Christian:

> Sing, soul of mine, this day of days,
>   The Lord is risen.
> Toward the sun-rising set thy face,
>   The Lord is risen
> Behold He giveth strength and grace;
> For darkness, light; for mourning, praise;
> For sin, holiness; for conflict, peace.
>
> Arise, O soul, this Easter Day!
> Forget the tomb of yesterday,
> For thou from bondage art set free;
> Thou sharest in His victory
> And life eternal is for thee,
> Because the Lord is risen.

Haven't we found light, praise, holiness, and peace? Are we not set free from bondage? Isn't this victory? Isn't this Easter? Doesn't Easter dawn whenever he breaks the chains of addiction? Most Christians in recovery think so. We thank Christ for our deliverance. We thank him every day.

Jesus, you are my Easter Day. You roll away my tombstone. Your risen life has raised me up. I thank you more than I can ever say or sing or pray. Amen.

"Have you never read, 'Out of the mouth of babes and sucklings thou hast brought perfect praise'?"

MATTHEW 21:16

When children are asked questions, watch out for the answers! Recently a group of elementary and high school students were asked: Where do you look for God? Where do you see God? Some of their responses are revealing.

One eleventh-grader answered poetically: "I find him in the morning mist/beyond the shining sun/among the wild flowers/in the city lights." Another reflected deep cynicism. "God is a nonexistent security blanket," he said. In the same vein, another thought that "God is a ventriloquist, and we are his dummies." A twelfth-grader found God not only "in solitude, in friends, in nature, in beauty, in other people, babies, those over sixty-five, in my family, but even in New York City!"

Perhaps the best of all answers came from a high school student who asked, simply, "Why? Did you lose him?"

Someone once said something like this: "When I lost God, I moved." God is in our recovery program of Twelve Steps. He is not lost. We may go astray, stop going to meetings, fail to work the steps, quit reading the literature, neglect our sponsor's help, and forget our prayer and meditation. When we then lose the feeling of God's presence, it is we who moved, not him. He's not hiding.

O Jesus, I know that I can see you and find you if I just follow your command to seek, knock, and ask for you. Amen.

"You received without pay, give without pay."
MATTHEW 10:8

Two friends were talking about honesty after a meeting. The program that night was about being straight and straightforward with each other. All at once one of the them said, "Mary, there are times when you seem distant and cold, and you make it hard for me to get close to you because you don't respond, and you make others feel uncomfortable too!" Mary glanced at her friend and shouted, "Why can't you let somebody be who she is!?"

Mary's friend was working very hard on "honesty and straight talk." Unfortunately, she wasn't working equally hard on "acceptance." The conversation between Mary and her friend illlustrates perfectly what's involved in the Serenity Prayer: change and acceptance. Mary wanted acceptance; her friend obviously wanted change, especially in Mary.

The Serenity Prayer links change with courage. It took courage to confront Mary honestly and to risk the anger of her response. It took courage for Mary to respond. But the prayer also links acceptance with serenity. Neither Mary nor her friend seemed very serene. Both were too involved in "change"–either achieving it or resisting it. Perhaps if we were all to work harder on accepting ourselves and others we would reduce the pain that comes from trying so hard to change others. Isn't there wisdom in that?

O blessed Lord, help me to keep change and acceptance in balance, and keep me from trying to change others. Amen.

"Truly, I say to you, he shall not lose his reward."
MATTHEW 10:42

Joyce Kilmer wrote these words about a friend who died:

> Rich joy and love he got and gave;
>   His heart was merry as his dress;
> Pile laurel wreaths upon his grave
>   Who did not gain, but was, success!

As recovering Christians we are surrounded by such friends, people who have gained none of the externals of success—who may not even be "gainfully" employed—but who are winners. Why? Because they deal in getting and giving the internals of success: joy, love, and merry hearts.

There is a football team that claims never to have lost a game. The scoreboard, for them, is merely an external measure of points. The members of this team measure themselves by an internal instrument—their own self-esteem. A winner never loses, regardless of the score. Jesus appeared to lose on Good Friday. His friends and enemies alike saw an apparent defeat. But he was only temporarily out-scored—the game was not over. Easter broke through as he burst forth from the tomb and gave us all an endless victory. We are all winners in Christ—no matter what may happen to us on the outside. Saint Paul puts it well: "In all these things were are more than conquerors through him who loved us" (Rom. 8:37); "Thanks be to God, who gives us the victory" (1 Cor. 15:57).

Our Twelve-Step team is also God's victory. Hundreds of recovery groups are providing hope and health to apparent losers everywhere. What is even better—we can actually see thousands of personal Easters taking place right here and now.

O Christ of the least, the last, and the lost, help me to realize that when I walk with you and the Twelve Steps, I'm already winning. Amen.

"And why are you anxious about clothing? Consider the lilies of the field, how they grow; they neither toil nor spin; yet I tell you, even Solomon in all his glory was not arrayed like one of these."

MATTHEW 6:28–29

A story is told about the father of the great poet Emily Dickinson. On evening at dinnertime, the fire bell started ringing madly. All the people in the little town came running out, clutching their napkins and silverware, looking for the fire. There stood Emily's father. He had just seen a gorgeous sunset and didn't want anyone to miss it, so he rang the fire bell to get everyone's attention before the beauty faded!

No doubt many thought he was crazy; getting that excited by a sunset is unusual for most of us. We look at God's beauty and get a bit inspired for a spell and then go on about our business. Sadly, many of us lose our excitement, our compulsion to shout to all, "Come, look and see!" Not so with Jesus. Throughout his teaching ministry, and especially in the Sermon on the Mount, he draws our attention to similar wonders: birds, lilies, salt, light, and so much more. He calls us to accept and appreciate the marvelous works of our creator. Furthermore, he calls our attention to our own inner world of beauty.

To "Let go and let God" is to relax, rest, and be at home with all the beauty around us and within us in the world of nature and in the human world. Jesus calls us even further: "to consider"–to really pay attention. Our program also beckons us to "come, look and see," to accept an invitation "to consider" recovery.

O Lord of all beauty, inspire me to consider your world, others, and myself. Amen.

"And I, when I am lifted up from the earth, will draw all men to myself."

JOHN 12:32

When Michelangelo was a young man, he was given a remnant of an ancient Greek statue. It was only part of a human form, yet Michelangelo was attracted to it. He was so drawn to this piece of marble that he never let it leave his mind. It was the first thing he looked at in the morning and the last thing he saw at night. During the day he would feel its texture and drink in its beauty. He was drawn constantly to this lovely thing. After months and years of adoration, the beauty of this classic form literally became a part of the great sculptor's own life. The artist absorbed an ancient beauty that came out in his own fresh creations.

What a marvelous symbol of our program of recovery and of our Christian faith! Whatever piece we look at, appreciate, and devote our attention to, however small, actually imprints and molds us with its beauty and goodness. As we lovingly engage ourselves with our program and our Lord, we become transformed little by little by such grace. Our model of the Twelve Steps and our model in Christ conforms us to the very essence of health, wholeness, and love. What a grand thought to keep in mind. We can, like Saint Paul, look forward to saying, "It is no longer I who live, but Christ who lives in me" (Gal. 2:20).

Beautiful Savior, you are my model and most treasured work of art. Not that I could ever hold or possess you, but you allow me to love you and become part of your life of beauty. Amen.

Jesus answered him, "If a man loves me, he will keep my word, and my Father will love him, and we will come to him and make our home with him."

JOHN 14:23

Over a hundred years ago, a man and a woman met and married and were soon thought to have "perfect companionship." Robert Browning and Elizabeth Barrett were poets. Robert lovingly teased Elizabeth about her dark complexion, calling her his "little Portuguese." Some time later Elizabeth presented her husband a collection of poems, *Sonnets from the Portuguese.* The first poem Browning read included these lines:

> The face of all the world has changed
> Since I first heard the footsteps of your Soul.

These words are the perfect reflection of a tender human love; but they also mirror the image of Christ and his church, of recovery and the afflicted. The face of our world changes when we hear the Twelve Steps and the gospel. We can actually see change when we hear spiritual footsteps, when we detect the sounds of souls.

What does a soul sound like? If a soul is the life or spiritual vitality of a person or group, then in the life-soul of recovery in Christ many of us will hear love, acceptance, hope, peace, faith, courage, and joy. These footsteps have changed the face of our world.

O blessed Lover of my soul, change the face of my world with the sounds of your spirit. Amen.

"You shall call his name Jesus, for he will save his people from their sins."

MATTHEW 1:21

Dun Scotus was a wise English philosopher of the Middle Ages, but he became mixed up in an early version of an IRS audit. His tax mistakes were so stupid that our word *dunce* memorializes his stupidity. General Burnside is remembered today, not for his Civil War heroics, but for his bushy whiskers or "sideburns." Our most popular lunch, the sandwich, is all we recall today about the Earl of Sandwich, who did a lot more than put meat between two hunks of bread. But, praise God, we remember Jesus the way he was and is.

The name of Jesus, which could also be translated Joshua or Jeshua, literally means: "God who saves." He did, he is, and he will. In Japanese, Jesus sounds like yes. How wonderful! Yes, Jesus saves. We see that in neon signs, on small roadside churches, on roofs right next to "Coca-Cola" and "visit Rock City," but the message is true and completely accurate: Jesus does indeed save. His name is true.

When we pray in the name of Jesus, or call upon his holy name, we invoke his salvation, his healing power of love. For to know his name is not merely to speak it, but to know him. To know him is to receive him and to connect with health and redemption. When we say yes to life and to recovery, we are meeting the "God who saves"—wherever we may be.

Wonderful and mysterious love, I give my life to you. I say yes to you, Lord Jesus, my Savior. Amen.

"The cup I shall drink, you shall indeed drink."

MATTHEW 20:23

Charles Schulz, the creator of "Peanuts," gathered some of his cartoons into a book called *Security Is a Thumb and a Blanket*. The last page shows a small boy kneeling beside his bed at night, and the caption reads: "Security is knowing you're not alone."

Life can be lonely and impersonal, yet it need not be. When we walk into a Twelve-Step meeting, our isolation can cease—if we so choose. Our loneliness can be immersed in the rich experience of personal sharing as we recover together. The cups we drank were indeed also drunk by our recovering friends. We share our illness; we also share our recovery.

Christ offers his companionship to us as well. He was born in a stable; he never owned his own home. In fact, he said he had no place to lay his head. Yet he was not homeless or alone. He was supremely "at home" and has helped humanity also be at home—with him. G. K. Chesterton reflected on Christ's homeless birth at Bethlehem with these words:

> To an open house in the evening
> Home shall man come
> To an older place than Eden,
> And a taller town than Rome.
> To the end of the way of the wandering star,
> To the things that cannot be and that are,
> To the place where God was homeless,
> And all men are at home.

Lord, with you I am never alone, nor am I homeless with my recovering friends—help me be at home with myself. Amen.

"Bear fruits that befit repentance."

LUKE 3:8

Imagine reading your own obituary in the paper. It can happen. It did happen some years ago. A man woke up and read his death notice in the paper. Another man had died, but the obituary was about the reader. The story called him "a merchant of death," since he was the inventor of dynamite and had made a huge fortune from explosives and weapons of war. Shaken by this story, he changed his life completely. A "power greater than himself" came into his life that morning. Facing the truth about himself, this munitions king became a great man of peace. From that moment on, he gave his "life and will over to" humanitarian causes. He is known today as the founder of the Nobel Prize—Alfred Nobel.

The first few examples of personal change in A.A.'s Big Book are like Alfred Nobel's—sudden, dramatic transformations. Few of us can expect such instant insight; most stories of recovery are not like that. Recovery and faith more often come by following the Twelve Steps and Holy Scripture step by step, day by day.

O Word of truth, dear Lord Christ, help me to see and hear who I am. Break through my blindness so I may wake up and change into the person you want me to be. Amen.

And he said, "He who has ears to hear, let him hear."

MARK 4:9

A recent widower gave these instructions to the stonemason who was preparing the tombstone for his late wife: "I want 'Rest in Peace' on both sides. Then, if there's enough room: 'We shall meet in heaven.'" After the memorial stone had been erected, he read the following:

> Rest in peace on both sides
> And if there is enough room,
> We shall meet in heaven.

Who was really to blame for this mistake? The widower spoke well enough. The mason listened well enough. But there was no feedback. There was no "checking it out." The speaker failed to get confirmation; the listener failed to repeat and clarify the instructions.

In the same way, jumping to conclusions, hasty judgments, and on-the-spot evaluations can sabotage our program of recovery. In our denial, without realizing it, we frequently hear only what we want to hear. We often think to ourselves, "Why listen to this speaker? We have nothing in common. I'm not like that. I'm not that bad." Prejudice works that way—we pre-judge before we even hear. Perhaps the real truth is that in ways we have yet to discover, there in that person we might have seen ourselves but for the grace of God.

Dear Christ, you were often misjudged and misunderstood. Help me to really listen to your words and not just hear what I want to hear. Amen.

"For the Holy Spirit will teach you in that very hour what you ought to say."

LUKE 12:12

A school superintendent and a principal were observing a seventh-grade class in session. As they entered the room, they heard the teacher say to a tall boy, "Carl, will you please open the window?" After Carl had obliged, the teacher said to the whole class, "I just don't know what I would do without Carl! He's the only one who can reach and open the window for me." After they had left the class, the principal said to the superintendent, "Did you notice what a loving thing that teacher did for Carl? He is large for his age and awkward. The children call him Clumsy Carl. He is a slow learner, has low self-esteem, and badly needs encouragement. That window really didn't need opening, but Carl needed to open it. He desperately needed recognition, and the teacher, bless her, was responding to that need."

Like Carl, we often need the encouragement and recognition we receive in our program. Every chip, every birthday, every hug and pat on the back—every time we are asked "to open the window," we grow in self-esteem and get better.

We also need to be like that teacher. We grow when we look for opportunities to recognize and ask others to help—even when it doesn't need doing! People need to be needed, loved, and recognized. Saint Paul says it well: "Therefore encourage one another and build one another up. . . . Be patient with them all" (1 Thess. 5:11, 14).

O Christ, my encouragement, help me to give my recovering friends and fellow Christians many "encouraging words." Keep me open also to receive the support I need. Amen.

"Love your enemies, do good to those who hate you, bless those who curse you, pray for those who abuse you."
LUKE 6:27–28

Hattie worked in an office. She was an "old hand" and had worked her way up to a managerial position. Yet she was stern, uncompromising, and unforgiving. She was efficient but cold as ice. Her subordinates called her Hateful Hattie. Whenever new workers arrived, they were warned about her. But Hattie never changed. One day a new employee named Helen arrived. She ignored the warnings and made a determined effort to love Hattie. It was not easy, but Helen persevered and never let her love be turned aside. Then, without warning, Heavenly Helen, as she was beginning to be called, died. When Hattie heard the news, she sobbed: "Helen was the only Christ I ever knew."

We have met many Christs in our Twelve-Step groups. Even though we have plenty of Hatties, including ourselves, some Helen keeps on loving us in spite of our spitefulness. It's easy to push people away, but it's hard to stand up and move through barriers of fear, mistrust, and hatefulness. Love is a hard act, not an easy feeling. Christ showed us how—he loved us to the end, even as we drove the nails into his body. He lives now to make Hatties into Helens.

The miracle of love is a mystery of "tough *acts* for others." The difficult path of caring for others, sharing with others, and daring toward others creates our own healing. Love is never turned aside but keeps on and brings lover and beloved both to life!

Loving Savior, direct me to love the unlovable, to reach out to the unattractive and hateful. Be with me, so that I don't turn aside and turn them off. Amen.

"Blessed are you when men hate you, and when they exclude you. . . . Rejoice in that day, and leap for joy, for behold, your reward is great in heaven."

LUKE 6:22–23

One evening a terrible storm struck an army post. At the Officers' Club, the rain was driving against the windows, the wind was howling, and hail was falling. Through a window, a woman saw a soldier outside in the midst of the storm, faithfully standing guard duty. "O dear," she said, "look at that poor boy out there in the storm." A woman standing nearby said, "My dear, it's perfectly all right. He's only a private."

Can we ever imagine Christ saying that? Yet how often have his followers said, "He's only an alcoholic," or, "She's only a drug addict." We have a bagful of "onlys." The people who live in the slums, the maids, street cleaners, garbage men, the foreigners in our world—all can be looked upon as being "only" or "just" or "merely." How unlike our Lord: how unlike recovery.

To recover from our disease, we must eliminate the tendency to see any human being as "only" anything. If we must label or tag anyone, let it be as a brother or sister, friend or fellow. Twelve-Step groups do not recognize rank. Neither does the gospel. We are each so precious and valuable that there can be *no* belittling permitted. We are all equally important to God and to each other—whether we like it or not.

O merciful and most loving Christ, keep me from ever looking down on any human being. Keep me from looking down on myself. Amen.

"Salt is good; but if the salt has lost its saltness, how will you season it? Have salt in yourselves, and be at peace with one another."

MARK 9:50

The tragic conflict of Christians in Northern Ireland is a heavy burden for both Roman Catholics and Protestants to bear. The damage done to Christ's own body by this uncivil war is beyond calculation. A young Irish boy was asked what he thought could be done to end the violence and death. He said, "I think we'll have to bring in someone who doesn't believe in God."

What's crucial, however, is not belief *in* God but belief *about* God. Anyone who believes that God can be served by violence is deluded. God is a God of peace, brotherhood, and love. To call upon God at the same time that we shed blood is to demonstrate that we don't know what God is about. To act in destructive ways in the name of religion is to worship the god of war and bloodshed, not the Prince of Peace.

Actions of love are acts of true worship. Recovery, the Twelve-Step way, and the gospel of love are messages of peace. These can save the world.

O Prince of Peace, do not let my actions reflect false belief about you. Keep my belief in you in harmony with your acts of love and peace. Amen.

"Let what you say be simply 'Yes' or 'No'; anything more than this comes from evil."

MATTHEW 5:37

There was once a plumber who wrote a letter to the government agency in charge of plumbing regulations. In it he said he had discovered that hydrochloric acid was great for cleaning out clogged drains. A bureaucrat wrote back, "The efficiency of hydrochloric acid is indisputable, but the corrosive residue is incompatible with metal permanence."

The plumber was delighted. He wrote back and said he was glad the government agreed with him. The same bureaucrat sent a second letter, "We wish to emphasize that we must refrain from assuming any responsibility for the production of toxic and noxious residue with hydrochloric acid and, consequently, must most emphatically recommend some alternative procedure."

Again the plumber misunderstood, and again he wrote back saying he was glad the government agreed with him. Finally, in desperation, the bureaucrat wrote, "Don't use hydrochloric acid. It eats hell out of the pipes!"

Thank God, the core of our program of recovery in Christ is simple. The straightforward messages and procedures of the Twelve Steps and the gospel are crystal clear. The slogans and the Scriptures ring with pure tones of faith, hope, and love. The hard part is not the understanding. What's hard is the acceptance and the performance.

Lord, you are so straightforward. Help me to be the same. Amen.

Once a golf pro, who was known for his huge ego, was challenged to play golf at $100 a hole by a man in dark glasses, using a white cane to guide his way. "How could I take you on, man? You can't even see," the conceited pro blustered. "That's true, I can't see a thing. I am totally blind," the challenger replied. "But I was once a champion before I lost my sight. I think I can whip you." The golf pro pondered the situation. He was down on his luck and needed some cash. So, he thought, "Why not?" If this jerk was insane enough to take him on, it was his own fault if he lost his money. "Was that $100 a hole you said?" The blind man confirmed the bet. "I sure don't know what's causing your recklessness. Are you sure you're not joking? When will the contest begin?" "Any old night will do," answered the blind man, "especially one with no moon out."

Sometimes there are advantages to being blind. I remember a movie in which the heroine was blind and had the advantage over her attacker in the dark. So many of us in recovery grieve over our condition and our past misery. We actually think we are handicapped. I have heard many people in recovery declare their "attitude of gratitude" in having to be in recovery and how the program has blessed them in their affliction. Maybe in some ways we are blind, but we are blind to things we no longer want to see any more. Who wants to see life as an unrecovered addict? Who wants to keep living at the expense of everyone else? Who wants to keep on apologizing, making vain promises, lying and deceiving our loved ones? Who wants to live without God? Perhaps we are luckier than anyone else on earth. Who or what can match the wonder, joy, and peace of walking the Twelve Steps with Jesus Christ?

Through him then let us continually offer up a sacrifice of praise to God, that is, the fruit of lips that acknowledge his name.

HEBREWS 13:15

Our most serious sin is our independence that ignores God. If one thing is clear in any person's life, it is that God does not accept our rejection. He will not allow us to ignore him. Catherine Marshall pictures this well:

If your every human plan and calculation has miscarried, if, one by one, human props have been knocked out, and doors shut in your face, take heart. God is trying to get a message through to you, and the message is: "Stop depending on inadequate human resources. Let me handle the matter."

Our entire life of recovery could revolve around those five words "Let God handle the matter." Our prideful independence is our major problem and the root of our disease. Our acceptance of God's direction and control is the heart of new health and deliverance. When we admit our powerlessness in the First Step, we place the matter in the hands of one who really matters. Emerson describes this surrender to God's care as "prayer," and he calls prayer "the contemplation of the facts of life from the highest point of view." Such trust in God's care is the foundation of recovery.

O Christ, keep my prayers constant and even toward your power and love for me. Never let me stay away too long. Amen.

"My friends, do not fear those who kill the body, and after that have no more that they can do. Therefore I tell you, do not be anxious about your life."

LUKE 12:4, 22

Some of the saddest and most dangerous of human beings are the selfish "survivalists" who arm themselves and their little group against the threat of the rest of humanity. Even a popular love song echoes that urge: "Only you and me *against* the world." When threats are seen everywhere and "being on guard" is a daily obsession, there can be no true living, only existence. Yet what is existence that is drenched in fear? Where is the happiness in that?

A great man once said, "The root of all happiness lies in the capacity to live in a world that makes you unselfish because you are not overanxious about your personal place." Yet where does this capacity come from? A lot comes through the grace of our Lord Jesus Christ, as well as from our Twelve-Step programs. What better way to eliminate fear and replace it with fellowship and peace? Our true safety is surrender. We can find a triumphant trust by letting Christ teach us his way. He shunned survival and chose the freedom of sacrifice instead of the slavery of security. We can choose the same freedom. He and his program of peace will drive out our fears if we let him.

My safety and security are only to be found in you, Lord. Keep me aware of where my salvation is—in you alone. Amen.

Do not be conformed to this world but be transformed by the renewal of your mind, that you may prove what is the will of God.

ROMANS 12:2

There is a school of acting known as "method acting." Using this technique, the actor absorbs and totally identifies with the character portrayed. The identification becomes so intense that the feelings, attitudes, and thoughts of the fictional character take over, almost possessing the actor. The actor is "transformed" into the character in the play.

In the same way, as recovering Christians we can act our way into a new way of thinking, instead of trying so hard to think our way into a new way of acting. Saint Paul calls this the "renewal of our mind." We have a motto that says, "Fake it till you make it."

Saint Paul tells us it helps to imagine what God wants. Sometimes we need to pretend. The word *imagine* comes from the word *image*, which means "likeness" or "mirror." Imagination and imagery can guide us to new ways of renewing our minds. One recovering Christian, for example, was tormented by anxiety attacks; she had tried everything, she thought. Finally a wise sponsor suggested she change her direction of thought and make a complete commitment to God's will, and to imagine that this might mean God wanted her to accept her anxieties and give all her torment and weakness to him. She didn't just think about it. She did it. It worked. She was transformed by accepting this new form of surrender.

When we submit to God's viewpoint we begin to act according to his will and way. The Twelve Steps and the gospel then become the means to "prove what is the will of God" and then to follow it.

Lord, teach me to ask what you want first, to use my imagination, and then to surrender and do your will. Amen.

*That according to the riches of his glory he may grant you
to be strengthened with might through his Spirit in the
inner man.*

EPHESIANS 3:16

A philosopher said, "The quest for tranquillity must of
necessity begin with self-examination." Indeed, we do seek
tranquillity, which we call the "priceless gift of serenity."
But does serenity begin with examining ourselves? Most
of us would find it impossible to start our recovery with "a
searching and fearless moral inventory." Thank God, this
is saved for Step Four! As Christians in recovery we know
that we could not stand the sight of our inner self until
"strengthened with might through his Spirit."

Our recovery in Christ does involve cleansing. Taking our
own inventory, sharing what we have searched out and
found, and being willing to have God remove our moral
defects – all act like fresh, clear rinse water in recovery. Yet
isn't it wonderful that God accepts and embraces us long
before we are scrubbed clean? If we thought we had to get
shiny and dressed up in our "Sunday-go-to-meeting"
clothes, we would never walk into a meeting!

First we "give up" our act, then we "clean it up." This is
a familiar road to recovering Christians. The road to our
Lord is the way of repentance. First, we repent. "Repent"
means to surrender and turn to the Lord, right where we
are in our sin and shame, in our soiled and shameful condition. After we turn to our Lord, we express our sorrow,
make our confession, and begin our rehabilitation. But we
don't have to be rehabilitated to turn to God! If we never
begin our Fourth Step, we are still loved and welcomed into
our Savior's arms.

*Thank you, Jesus, for accepting my surrender. Thank you for giving
me courage to examine myself so that you may also cleanse me.
Amen.*

*Then the King will say to those at his right hand, "Come,
O blessed of my Father, inherit the kingdom prepared for
you from the foundation of the world."*

MATTHEW 25:34

There is a legend about the last day on earth—the Judgment Day that Scripture tells us about. In heaven on this
final day, everyone is joyfully celebrating, singing, dancing, and embracing their loved ones. Everyone is jubilant
except Jesus, who is standing sadly at the gates to heaven,
looking down and beyond. He is asked why he is not joining in the festivities and joy all around him. Jesus answers,
"I am waiting for Judas."

The power of this story should touch the heart of every
person in recovery. God in Christ is such pure, forgiving
love that he yearns to embrace his betrayer. All his followers
let him down and were restored to fellowship with Christ.
The same reunion awaits Judas. Each of us has sold out
Christ many times in many ways. Only the self-righteous
and proud among us could deny our guilt. We all have some
Judas in us. Yet we are always welcome, even at the last day.

What is good news to us is that Jesus waits for us and
will embrace us when we return. What is bad news is we
have to choose; we have to move toward him. Of course,
he will help us return, but he refuses to pull us into heaven.
We make that journey by our own choice. We don't have
to walk alone, or even trudge along without assistance. But
we do have to decide that's the way we'll head. Once that's
decided, we'll get there. That's how the Twelve Steps work.
They are a sure and steady stairway to heaven as well. But
we have to walk them, and we travel hand in hand with many
other pilgrims.

*My blessed Lord, receive me and draw me up to you. I choose to
be with you forever. Amen.*

"Leave your gift there before the altar and go; first be reconciled to your brother, and then come and offer your gift."
MATTHEW 5:24

In the very early days of the church, those who wished to make amends for their wrongs were given something called penance to do. Soon it became the custom to perform acts of penance in a special place called a "penitentiary." This was a room set aside for penitents to say their prayers, do their acts of penitence, or spend time in silence. The whole idea was to "pay for" the sin by demonstrating honest and sincere repentance.

In the Eighth and Ninth Steps we enter our recovery "penitentiary"—our time for making amends. To make amends is to mend ourselves by acts of honest sorrow for the hurt and harm we have caused. The end result is healing, not punishment. The goal of our amending is wholeness, not shame. What we seek is cleansing forgiveness and a new life.

Every attempt should be made to make these steps of reconciliation. Our recovery depends on eliminating all the old guilt and shame as well as healing whatever old hurts still remain. Whether the healing takes place or not, the attempt to make amends is essential. Our healing rests on our willingness to show our sorrow and demonstrate our desire for healing. The rest is up to God. We must try. We can never know if forgiving love awaits unless we ask.

O Christ, increase my desire for forgiveness. Give me the courage to ask for it, even if I am refused. Amen.

"And whatever you ask in prayer, you will receive, if you have faith."

MATTHEW 21:22

Most people, whether they are religious or not, yearn for the security of a spiritual home. Most of us want inner resources to provide us with hope, courage, and peace of soul. We all need a philosophy or faith to see us through this life. Marcus Aurelius once said, "Man must be arched and buttressed from within, else the temple wavers to the dust." Jesus calls this inner structure and framework faith. In all that he taught and did, he demonstrated that without faith we can do nothing, but with it, all things are possible.

The spirituality of recovery is faith. When we receive such faith we are never alone, never forsaken. Through such faith we receive guidance, comfort, peace, love, and joy. William James said, "Every sort of energy and endurance, of courage and capacity for handling life's evils, is set free in those who have faith." The Twelve-Step program of recovery and the Christian life are deep wells of faith for us. When we dip into both we will be refreshed and renewed each day. As James Allen once urged:

Light up the lamp of faith in your heart. It will lead you safely through the mists of doubt and the black darkness of despair; along the narrow, thorny ways of sickness and sorrow, and over the treacherous places of temptation and uncertainty.

It will also guarantee our recovery.

Increase my faith, Lord. Grant me a steady supply from your own deep well. Amen.

"A new commandment I give to you, that you love one another; even as I have loved you, that you also love one another."

JOHN 13:34

A young, innocent girl from the country went to seek work in a large city. She was given one of those enormous job applications to fill out: name, address, family history, job experience, references, and so on. When she came to the question, In case of emergency, whom should we notify? she called the personnel manager over and said, "I don't understand this question." The manager said, "Well, you know, if some accident happened to you on the job, or some emergency arose, who should we call?" She said, "Why the nearest human being, of course."

Whom do we consider "the nearest human being" in our lives? Often the nearest and dearest person is not the one next to us or even someone in the same house. For Christians that "nearest human" is Jesus. His great love and power come through his humanity, his identification in our earthly life. Of course, he is God divine, but we meet him in his humanity. He is not beyond us, but our "nearest human being." Above all, he is in *every* human being—we can count on his presence at every Twelve-Step meeting.

The reality of Jesus as a man is wonderful and a wonder. We can relate to a close friend who is like us. We cannot connect with a God beyond and unlike us. Thank God we can turn and embrace Christ as brother and friend as well as worship him as King and Lord.

Thank you, Jesus, for being so near and alike and not far away and different. Amen.

"Glory to God in the highest, and on earth peace among men with whom he is pleased!"

LUKE 2:14

It is our custom to greet one another with "Hello" or "Hi," and to bid each other farewell with "Good-bye" or "So long." We can think of many other greetings and farewells. During the days of Jesus one word said it all: "Peace." In Hebrew the word is *shalom*. It is still heard as commonly in Israel as it was in Jesus' time.

Shalom cannot be fully translated into English; it means so much: "to be whole, sound, complete, and healthy." Such peace is more than the absence of conflict; it is also the presence of a living, dynamic vitality of wellness. To be in "shalom" is to experience healthy personhood, healthy relationships, and healthy institutions. It covers the earth. The angels sang "Shalom on earth, good will to men." Jesus said, "My peace I give to you; not as the world gives do I give to you" (John 14:27).

Isn't this the goal of recovery? To gain the "peace of the program" is to experience more than just the absence or remission of our illness. It is to gain a healthy "shalom" with Christ and our program. Shalom is to live well, to have a good life, and to be filled with the lively goodness of God. Beer commercials promise such a "good life"; one says, "It doesn't get any better than this!" Oh yes it does!

Jesus, give me your "Shalom" each day, and in every encounter with others may my hello and good-bye convey your "peace." Amen.

*"'And the things you have prepared, whose will they be?'
So is he who lays up treasure for himself, and is not rich
toward God."*

LUKE 12:20–21

In San Francisco there is a storefront funeral parlor with
a sign that reads: Why walk around half dead when we can
bury you for $99? It's refreshing to see a mortician with
a sense of humor, as well as one that's so cheap! Sadly
enough, however, there are too many sad, sick souls eager
to accept such an offer.

In our Twelve-Step world we make the opposite offer:
Why walk around half dead when we can offer you a new
life for no charge at all? Of course, we know this offer is
not really without cost. True, we don't charge dues, send
bills, or sell our programs for money. The priceless prize
we offer *does* cost, however. Our payment is the surrender
of our addiction, our life, and our will to God.

We invest our life in God, and we reap the benefits and
dividends of the Twelve-Step recovery. We can't buy recovery. We can only receive it or achieve it by declaring
bankruptcy. Then we become rich out of our own poverty,
so rich, in fact, that no mere financial fortune can compare with our wealth.

The early Christians felt filled with such a fortune—the
richness of God's grace in Christ. Saint Paul shouts with
his good fortune: "O the depth of the riches and wisdom
and knowledge of God!" (Rom. 11:33). Recovery is to
vibrate with the same joyous wealth in our Higher Power,
Christ.

*Jesus, you have made me rich beyond my wildest dreams. Thank
you for enriching me in my poverty and weakness. Amen.*

"And as for that in the good soil, they are those who, hearing the word, hold it fast in an honest and good heart, and bring forth fruit with patience."

LUKE 8:15

Most everyone has been caught in a traffic jam. We are helpless. All we can do is wait. Some superhuman people who live each day with turtlelike traffic have learned to accept such circumstances and make the most of it. They sing, play games, listen to tapes, read, talk, study, or meditate in the midst of the mess. A few tolerant souls just remain unruffled and patient.

Yet the majority of us seethe, shout, curse, or blow our horns in frustration. We become like children who cannot tolerate obstacles — certain our frustration is permanent — and throw a temper tantrum. Of course, this seldom helps; frustration will always return. It's guaranteed.

Once a man bought a suit at a used clothing store and found a fifteen-year-old ticket for a shoe repair job. The store was still in business, so out of curiosity the man took the ticket to the store to redeem the shoes. When he presented the ticket, the repairman looked at it, went in the back, then came back and said calmly, "They'll be ready next Tuesday."

Recovery is often like that for us. We get stuck, or we find that we still have to wait! The quality we need most is patience. Frustration breeds anger and impatience, yet no one can be called patient without encountering and dealing with frustration. Unfortunately, learning to be accepting and patient is on-the-job training. Serenity is born in the midst of struggle, and the greater the struggle, the greater we need patience.

Jesus, you are so patient with me. I want immediate relief, even immediate patience and serenity. Slow me down and calm me, please. Amen.

"So you have sorrow now, but I will see you again and your hearts will rejoice, and no one will take your joy from you."

JOHN 16:22

Have you ever greeted someone with "Good morning" and heard the reply, "What's good about it?" It's easy to find a happy mood quickly dampened by someone else's gloom. Gloom and doom are contagious; our joy is easily taken from us. There is an old story about a man about to jump from a high bridge to certain death. A brave and cheery policeman approaches the man with a proposition: "Let's take ten minutes now. I'll take five minutes to tell you why life is worth living and then you take five minutes to tell me why it's not." When each had finished, they joined hands and jumped off the bridge together.

Negative and pessimistic thoughts are powerful. To spread depression is a grave and dangerous practice. Others just might join our misery. To feel our own pain and sadness is natural. To express our sorrow is healthy. But we should not pull others down and put out their light as well. We all have a responsibility not to overburden others as we unburden ourselves. The Twelve Steps go up, not down. We are walking toward a star-studded roof garden of recovery, not down into a dark cellar of gloom.

The word *gloom* is never mentioned in the New Testament. *Glory* and *joy* appear hundreds of times. The Christian in recovery is able to stand with Saint Paul when he says: "We rejoice in our sufferings, knowing that suffering produces endurance, and endurance produces character, and character produces hope, and hope does not disappoint us, because God's love has been poured into our hearts through the Holy Spirit which has been given to us" (Rom. 5:3–5).

Dear Christ, lift my spirit so that I may lift others up and not pull them down. Amen.

> *"Now when these things begin to take place, look up and raise your heads, because your redemption is drawing near."*

LUKE 21:28

Those of us who suffer from addictive diseases know how important forgiveness is. We have done so much that needs to be forgiven. And while we have been forgiven many times before by our loved ones, co-workers, and friends, we've gone on to repeat our out-of-control behavior. Others have forgiven us, but we could find no forgiveness deep inside ourselves. How can we forgive ourselves when we are hopeless?

As crucial as forgiveness and making amends are in recovery, something comes first. We can be forgiven forever and still be in despair. Forgiveness is not enough; we need salvation, we need hope. Forgiveness is for the past, hope gives us a future that brightens our present.

The first three steps of recovery offer hope, the remaining nine provide cleansing, healing, forgiveness, and spiritual growth. Yet nothing begins without hope. Unless we admit our powerlessness (Step One), we cannot step into the hope of sanity (Step Two) in surrender to the arms of our Higher Power (Step Three). For it is God alone who supplies our hope and renews us. We cannot find it alone. Even if we gain forgiveness forever, without hope of new life in Christ we wither and die. As Saint Paul says, "In this hope we were saved" (Rom. 8:24).

O Lord of all hopefulness, I thank you that I am not hopeless. Encourage me and stimulate me to yearn for the good you hold out to me. Amen.

"I came that they may have life, and have it abundantly."
JOHN 10:10

A millionaire died, and his will instructed that he was to be buried sitting in his gold-plated Mercedes (with the air conditioning running), a five-dollar cigar in his mouth, and a scotch and soda in his hand. This bizarre request was granted, and as the funeral crowd left the graveside, one of the grave diggers looked down and said, "Man, that's really living!"

Egyptian kings and queens were buried in greater wealth and luxury than this. Grand tombs have been erected to grand people throughout human history, and all were as dead as those in potter's field. Princes and paupers all die the same death. Each of us in our own way tries to hang on to the things of this world that give us security and status. No one escapes death, and no one escapes the desire to escape it.

We who are addicted (or afflicted) are well aware of this bind. We use whatever we are addicted to, to try to escape. We flee from pain. We deny our weakness. We minimize our sickness. We grasp at any crutch to lean on except one—God. Yet only through God can we ever truly experience life and hear ourselves shout, "Man, that's really living!" For the Twelve-Step way is real life, not a phony staging of life propped up in a car sitting in a grave.

Almighty Deliverer, save me from attachments to status and earthly security. Take me to your life of real living in you. Amen.

For God sent the Son into the world, not to condemn the world, but that the world might be saved through him.
JOHN 3:17

In the ancient world ships often included in their crews a powerful swimmer. In case of a shipwreck within sight of land, this person would swim ashore, carrying a line, and he would fasten it securely to something on shore so the rest of the passengers could follow in safety. Such a swimmer was called *archegos*.

Jesus was given the same name by the writer of Hebrews: "Looking to Jesus the *archegos* and perfecter of our faith" (12:2). Most Bibles translate *archegos* into our English word *pioneer*, and indeed, Jesus is our pioneer and trailblazer. Yet pioneering can imply a sort of rugged individualism that goes out and beyond weaker souls who may not dare follow. Pioneers often do not pay much attention to those left behind, adrift, aground, or alone.

"Lifeline swimmer" seems a better translation. Jesus is our strong swimmer; his power fixes our lifeline on the shore so that we can pull our way to safety. Our salvation is secured by the efforts of Christ, yet we must pull our way to him on the rope he offers.

We who are within the company of the recovering addicted know that we cannot go it alone. We often run aground and get stuck. We know the distress and fear of being adrift, "dead in the water." We need "strong swimming" not only in Christ but in the Christ who lives in our fellowship. We need help. Yet we have to choose it and use it. The recovery lifelines are plentiful; our part is to grasp them, hold on, and pull for shore. Each of the Twelve Steps is such a lifeline, and so are the slogans, our sponsors, regular meetings, reading, meditation, and prayer.

Dear Lord of my salvation and recovery, give me the courage and trust to accept your lifelines and come to your safe shore. Amen.

"You are the salt of the earth. . . . You are the light of the world."

MATTHEW 5:13–14

After many years in an institution, a mental patient was discharged. But he was very unhappy. "You're cured," said his doctor. "Some cure," the healed man spouted. "When I first came here, I was Abraham Lincoln. Now I'm nobody!" He was feeling like the woman who received a gift of lovely handkerchiefs with a card that said, "We wanted to give monogrammed handkerchiefs, but nobody could remember your name."

To feel unknown, unimportant, unnoticed is no laughing matter. We only laugh at such stories because laughter helps ease our own pain of being alone and abandoned—a "nobody." In the old South, people of low rank were called "no-count." To not be counted—even as "one"—to be a zero, is pure torture to the soul.

The good news of Christ's gospel is that we are not zeros; we are above counting or measurement. We are seen by our Lord as so precious as to be infinite in worth. How far from zero can we get! We need not overdo our value, of course, even if Christ is extravagant in his love; yet we are far from nobodies.

Recovery lives to recover worthwhile and valuable persons. The church exists to carry out Christ's salvage operations. Both work for important people—you and me. After all, we are the world's salt and light!

O most holy and living Lord, to know you value me so much raises my estimate of myself from nobody to somebody you love. That's plenty good. Amen.

> *"Give, and it will be given to you; good measure, pressed down, shaken together, running over, will be put into your lap."*
>
> LUKE 6:38

Our Lord and our program never cheat us. The more we give ourselves to our health and recovery and the more we give to others in our walk together, the more God will give us in "good measure, running over" right into our laps. We don't merely get back what we give; we get more, much more! The measure we get is always more than the measure we give. Our Twelve-Step cups "runneth over."

Not only do we always get more, what we get is usually a pleasant surprise; we stumble upon serendipity. The word comes from an ancient Persian tale of the three princes of Serendip. The three went on a treasure hunt. Even though they never found what they were looking for, they continually found treasures of greater worth.

Those of us who enter the Twelve-Step treasure hunt become familiar with serendipity. How many times have we started out looking for one thing and found something better? We hope for control and find abstinence. We yearn for sobriety and find serenity. We strive to cope and learn to live. We obsess about others and learn to value ourselves. We strain to accomplish one thing and discover that we have many choices. We try to get well and get "weller than well." We yearn to be more self-disciplined and learn to relax and "let go." That's how it goes in recovery with Christ. What a wonderful surprise!

Dear Lord of good surprises, stimulate my free spirit of happy expectations. I know you have more serendipity waiting for me. Amen.

"But he who endures to the end will be saved."

MARK 13:13

A young unmarried woman began dating a young man who was interested in marriage. She told her mother, who asked what his religion was. "He's an atheist, Mother," her daughter replied. "This is dreadful. How can a good Catholic girl live with an atheist? You'll have to sell him on the faith," her mother urged. After the first date, the daughter gave this report: "Things went beautifully, Mother, I sold him on the Blessed Trinity." Following the second date, she proudly reported that she had sold her suitor on baptism and Holy Communion. Just when success seemed at hand, the daughter came home from her third date completely crushed. "I oversold him, Mother; he's going to be a priest."

Not all our efforts pay off with happy results, at least from our point of view. Being a Christian in recovery has many unpleasant and disappointing moments. Each of the Twelve Steps calls us to an honesty that frequently hurts. Our egos can be deflated. Things often don't turn out the way we hoped. Yet each hurt, each unpleasant self-revelation, and even each disappointment become part of the larger picture of our life.

Recovery demands change. Change always brings some pain. But "no pain, no gain" is a law of life. While strain and struggle build muscles, moving through grief, anger, resentment, guilt, and many other hurts builds, cleanses, and heals each step of the way—as long as we keep stepping.

Blessed Jesus, I know I cannot avoid pain and hurt, help me to endure to the end with you. Amen.

And he went up into the hills, and called to him those whom he desired; and they came to him.

MARK 3:13

Frequently Christian believers are disturbed to encounter atheists and agnostics. This can be painfully plain at Twelve-Step meetings. As Christians we feel strange and stifled when someone challenges our open use of the name of God or Jesus Christ. Often we clash head on with recovering people who resent our open faith. We yearn to be as open about our religious vocabulary as we are at a prayer meeting. We can. We have that right.

Happily, the wisdom of our programs offers a way through this problem in a simple phrase: "My Higher Power, whom I choose to call _____." To the Christian attending a Twelve-Step meeting, the consistent use of this phrase *before* filling in the blank with "God or Jesus Christ" can be a great joy. We choose God. We choose Jesus Christ as our Lord and Savior, our Higher Power. The choice is completely free—without pressure or coercion. Jesus calls us to him. We come to him. He did not force us to come; he gave us complete freedom of choice.

Why not offer the same freedom to atheists and agnostics? Jesus does. If they choose to fill in the blank our way some day, it will be an occasion for rejoicing. Until then, we have a perfect right to fill in the blank our way. Jesus will keep on calling others to fill in the blank with his name. He loves everyone—even unbelievers. He believes in them, even if they don't believe in him.

Lord Christ, help me to be as open and courteous to others as you are, especially to nonbelievers. I will openly bear witness to you, but I will not force you on anyone. Amen.

"The kingdom of God is at hand; repent, and believe in the gospel."

MARK 1:15

The short Gospel of Mark is considered by most scholars to be the earliest written record of Jesus. Mark reveals a Jesus who begins his ministry making an announcement, "The kingdom of God is at hand," followed by a commanding appeal, "Repent, and believe in the gospel." That same message is still directed at us. Jesus tells us something we constantly forget: God is near, so near that he is here. He is not in a far-off heaven or in a forgotten time. Heaven is wherever God's kingdom is—and that is here and now. Jesus proclaims that we don't have to wait around or go searching for God's rule and power. We are there already!

This should be good news. But is it? Do we want God that close at hand? If we can't leave him in a faraway place, it could be "bad news" for our old ways. "Believe the good news of God's presence and power," says Jesus, "but *repent* first." To repent is to change—literally, to turn around and change direction. Similarly, "convert" means to change from one way to another (in the same way that electrical convertors change AC current to DC current).

To recover from addictions and live a new life means change from beginning to end, and it never ends. To repent or convert means to reorder and rearrange our lives. Doesn't the fact that God is here now make change urgent?

Lord Christ, when I know how near you are, how can I keep on my selfish road and refuse to walk with you? Please help me alter my course and change my direction to yours. Amen.

"This is my commandment, that you love one another as I have loved you."

(JOHN 15:12)

Henry Ward Beecher once wrote: "We ask the leaf, 'Are you complete in yourself?' and the leaf answers, 'No, my life is in the branches.' We ask the branch, and the branch answers, 'No, my life is in the root,' and it answers, 'No, my life is in the trunk and branches and leaves. Keep the branches bare of leaves, and I shall die.' So it is with the great tree of being. Nothing is completely and merely individual." Why not seek complete recovery in ourselves? We don't know why. We just know it does not work. Saint Paul said, "None of us lives to himself" (Rom. 14:7).

We may not want to go to meetings, work and walk the Twelve Steps, and share our life with others, but we must. There is no other way to recover and keep on recovering. We cannot hold on to God's presence alone. We cannot recover alone. We are like bees. A beekeeper cannot keep a bee, only bees. The production of honey requires many bees. The production of sobriety and serenity requires many people.

The famous singer Marian Anderson was asked why she says "one does" and "we do" instead of "I do." She said, "Because the longer one lives the more one realizes that there is no particular thing that you can do alone. There are so many people—those who wrote the music, those who made the piano the accompanist plays, the accompanist who lends support to the performance. To go out without any of these, to stand on your own—even the air you breathe is not your own. So, the 'I' is very small indeed." Isn't it the same in recovery?

Lord, thank you for all those who enrich my recovery: those who gave me the Twelve Steps, those within the Big Book, my sponsors, my group, my friends—my life. Amen.

"And do not fear those who kill the body but cannot kill the soul."

MATTHEW 10:28

Many years ago, a ship was caught in a violent storm at sea. The terrified crew members lashed themselves on board to keep from being swept away by the wind and waves. Suddenly they heard a horrible crashing sound below deck. A cannon in the hold had pulled loose and was banging into the sides of the ship, tearing holes in the keel each time it lurched in the storm. At the risk of their lives, two sailors untied themselves and managed to get below to secure the loose cannon. They knew it was far more dangerous than the storm.

So it is with recovery. The outside storms and problems of life are not the real danger. Relapses, slips, and anxious moments come from below deck—inside ourselves. Outward circumstances have influence and can affect us, but how we respond from within is far more powerful. We can neither control nor determine most circumstances, but we can choose our response.

A woman in the Twelve-Step community was once asked how she managed to keep her dignity and poise in the midst of her tragic and chaotic life. She said, "You see, I'm in a partnership. I went into a partnership with God. I agreed to do the work, and he agreed to do the worrying. I haven't had a worry since. He's kept his bargain, and so have I."

Lord, please help me keep my inner resources well and strong so I can face the storms outside. Amen.

"There is joy before the angels of God over one sinner who repents."

LUKE 15:10

Rich's department store in Atlanta has become an institution. Part of the folklore about this store concerns its return policy. The only recorded failure of the store to accept a return was when a little boy wanted to exchange his baby sister for a football helmet! Rich's just doesn't ask questions about returns and takes back twice as much as the average department store. It accepts altered clothing, items many years old, even goods purchased from competitors. Generosity is still store policy.

The Twelve-Step program's policy is even better. So is God's. No questions asked. No arguments. No sales slips necessary. You don't have to be a previous customer. You don't have to even be on the premises. You don't even have to return anything! Just bring yourself along, and you just might get a new self in exchange.

Recovery is more like a repair shop. It has no new merchandise to sell. In fact, it has nothing to sell at all—it only has recycled and salvaged goods that are much better than brand-new. Eugene O'Neill could be describing Twelve-Step salvation in *The Great God Brown*: "That is the secret for today; man is born broken. He lives by mending. The grace of God is glue." Doesn't that sound like us?

O Redeemer, keep taking me back. O Healer, keep repairing me. Then help me help others find you. Amen.

"Jesus perceived the thought of their hearts."

LUKE 9:47

A man once picked out six of his friends at random. He sent each of them a telegram that said: "All is known, flee at once." All six left town immediately. How would you respond if you received that wire? Well, of course, we know that "all is known" by God. We are aware that Jesus perceives our thought. We are an open book to him. Most of us do not like to think we are so transparent. Yet we are to God. Most of us would want to "flee at once" from him, spurred on by our shame and our burden of guilt and self-reproach.

Yet to run from God is futile. There is nowhere to run. We've tried that escape route before, but it doesn't work, because he still knows. We might as well give up—we're caught. Then what happens? If God knows, what then? Punishment? Prison? Put-down? Never! God wants us to be free! He wants us to be well! He loves us! We may *want* to run, but we don't *need* to. It's unnecessary. Why? Because "If our heart condemns us, God is greater than our heart. And knoweth all things. Beloved, if our heart condemns us not, then have we confidence toward God" (1 John 3:21–22).

Yes, all of us are guilty, yet we need not remain in shame. God is greater than our shame and self-contempt. We may live in self-imposed condemnation, but God in Christ directs no condemnation our way at all. He is judge not tormentor. When we accept his love and his cleansing forgiveness and stop condemning ourselves, then we can face God and life with confidence.

Thank you, Lord Christ, for your cleansing and accepting forgiveness. I accept your judgment upon me at the same time that I accept your noncondemning love. Amen.

And the Word became flesh and dwelt among us, full of grace and truth.

JOHN 1:14

A new young missionary with a Ph.D. was sent to join an old seasoned missionary to a primitive tribe. The old man had to interpret for the younger one. The newly arrived minister addressed his new congregation in these words: "Truth is absolute as well as relative. The gospel is absolute as well as relative. The gospel is absolute truth, but its application is relative to immediate needs and aspirations." The old missionary translated this gem of profundity: "He says he's glad to be here."

At almost every meeting and after many sermons, we are overwhelmed with complicated ideas and need a translator. For fifty years folks have been trying to explain, interpret, and improve on the Twelve Steps. Literally thousands of libraries have been filled trying to figure out the gospel. Underneath both is the simple truth of faith, hope, and love.

Thank God, in meetings or in church, Christ says, "I'm glad to be here!" That thought alone is enough. To feel the pleasure and presence of God in our program and in our religion is a blessing. Having someone be with us is a comfort. Having someone delight in our presence is a joy. To be in the company of those who want us stimulates our faith, our hope, and our love. Isn't the welcome we feel at meetings like that? Isn't the hospitality we encounter in church that way too? (And if not, Christ may be absent too.)

My dear friend Jesus, how grateful I am that you choose to be with me and that you are glad to keep company with me. Amen.

*And he said to them, "You have a fine way of rejecting the
commandment of God, in order to keep your tradition!"*

MARK 7:9

A certain man loved to go to revivals. He loved to get up
and testify. He made his witness over and over again, pub-
licly admitting his past sinful life. He had done it all—lied,
cheated, stolen, pushed dope, spent time in jail, broken
all the Ten Commandments and then some! It was his custom at the end of his long recital of wrongdoing to smile
and say, "I thank God through all those wicked years I never
lost my religion." You have to wonder what his religion was!
Whatever it was, his sins were more exciting and interesting than his religion.

Sometimes our own catalog of misdeeds can also become
our primary ritual, our tradition. Jesus said that we have
a "fine way of rejecting the commandment of God" so that
we can hold on to our tradition. Saint James defines true
religion in a quite different fashion, ignoring our interest
in our mistakes and focusing on our service: "Religion that
is pure and undefiled before God and the Father is this:
to visit orphans and widows in their affliction, and to keep
oneself unstained from the world" (James 1:27).

Christ measures our actions of love as well as our faith.
What we do is as important as what we say or think. What
actions we perform are our religion, no matter what we call
them. The Twelfth Step of recovery is the corrective to our
fascination with the group and our recovering buddies. It
calls us to act not just talk. One of our best sayings is to
"walk the walk" not just "talk the talk." Indeed, we are called
by Christ to "walk the talk."

*Dear Lord, help me to break away from just talking and enjoying
the life of my group and to go out and help those who need me
the most. Amen.*

"They all alike began to make excuses."

LUKE 14:18

The great Christian philosopher Kierkegaard once described the church in a vivid metaphor. It could also be a description of recovering people. It is a parody, yet it has truth in it. He describes us as a gaggle of geese! We waddle in to church (or meetings), listen to how much God loves us, bow our heads, and agree with the pious words and slogans we hear. We hear that God has given us new life and new power and wings! We nod "Amen." We hear how we can use our wings to fly and fulfill our destiny of being "new creatures" in Christ. We say to ourselves, "How true." We thrill at the inspirational message, and then we waddle back to a big meal and sit around talking about the wonderful words we heard and how we *intend* to start using our wings "one of these days."

We say, "We've got to make those Fourth and Fifth Steps soon," "We've got to find a sponsor one of these days," or "Boy, those Sixth, Seventh, Eighth, and Ninth Steps sure look hard; we'd better wait till we've got more time in the program." Sound familiar? Unfortunately, Kierkegaard's story goes on. When we keep on eating words of inspiration without exercising our new wings, we get "fat and juicy and are then slaughtered and sold by the pound in the marketplace!"

Recovery in Christ is strenuous. We are in a struggle — a life-and-death contest between disease and health. We belong to a team in training, straining to gain more lift and power to our wings. We are not in a "feed lot" to take our ease and lose our will to fight or ability to fly. It's our choice.

Inspire me, O Lord, with your words, but move me to exercise and "work out" each day on your program. Amen.

"Let your light so shine before men, that they may see your good works."

MATTHEW 5:16

A brand-new preacher came to town. He was very young, yet brilliant. He thrilled the congregation with his first sermon. The next Sunday, everyone returned to hear his next message. To their dismay, they heard the same sermon he had preached before! The same thing happened on the next two Sundays. Finally, a committee called on the clergyman and demanded an explanation: "Is that the only sermon you have?" they asked. The preacher answered, "No, I have several more sermons, and I'm working on still more. But you haven't done anything about the first one yet."

Most important matters bear repeating. It's amazing how we can hear something over and over and never truly "get the message." Our program of recovery lives on repetition. We know that practicing is the best way to learn. A cartoon in a recent magazine showed some parents arguing about their son's new musical endeavor: "OK," the stunned father yells, "so he'll grow up to be a tuba virtuoso! But can't he just go take lessons? Does he have to practice?"

It's amazing how many Christians know their lessons but fail in their practice sessions. We are strong on words and weak on action. Our recovery depends on continual learning *and* doing, doing and then learning more. We are in a "practicing" group with "practical" action to take, rehearse, improve on, and implement—again and again, one day at a time.

Dear Lord, teach me to listen and learn; above all, help me practice what I hear. Amen.

> *"For every one who exalts himself will be humbled, and he who humbles himself will be exalted."*
>
> LUKE 14:11

A minister printed a motto at the top of the Sunday worship bulletin: "Life is a love, not a competition." That afternoon his telephone rang without ceasing. His angry callers all complained about this impractical and naive saying. "You are deluded and mistaken," the callers said. "Life is most definitely a competition, and you have it easy being able to indulge yourself in such sentimental mush. The real world is dog-eat-dog and survival of the fittest."

Many who call themselves Christians actually cannot conceive of life being "a love." Competition is the name of the game they play. Yet Jesus did not follow the competitive path. He called us away from self-centered striving and grasping. He was quite clear that we give way to others and take the last place, not the first. Maybe we should listen to Jesus, even when he sounds impractical.

What is life like in the fast lane? What is scratching and clawing our way to the top like? Pretty uptight and anxious, isn't it? Our ulcers, heart attacks, strokes, and even cancers are some of the results of the stress of competition and the drive to "get ahead." We would do well to follow the path of letting others win and move ahead once in a while and see what rewards come from patience, consideration, and "life as a love."

Actually, sound scientific research has proven that we get things done much better and faster through cooperation. We know in recovery that equal and respectful sharing really works better. Perhaps Jesus is not so impractical either.

Jesus, keep me living a life of love, not blind competition that blocks me off from others as I strain to be first. Amen.

"For my yoke is easy, and my burden is light."

MATTHEW 11:30

A rabbi once stunned his congregation by declaring that Moses was not really much of a leader! This statement really got attention. The rabbi went on to explain: "If, when Moses led the people out of Egypt, he had turned right instead of left, we would have the oil, and they would have the desert."

Naturally, this was a device to attract audience attention and interest. Moses was a great leader. He was perhaps one of the world's best, and that is precisely because he led his people into the desert wilderness: it was in the desert that God was found. It was in the wilderness on the stark, stony mountain that God's law was revealed. It was through forty years of hardship and wandering that the people of God were formed, toughened, and unified. It was in the desert wilderness that Jesus too found his strength and purpose.

This is also true for us. Our own personal wilderness, our dry places, our barren lives often bring forth revelation, insight, strength, and courage. When things are easy and go well for us, we may fail to see God or reach the spiritual depths we find in tough times. It is often said that as Western civilization has become more wealthy, it has also become less spiritual. Easy times produce easy marks. The gospel and the Twelve Steps are tough and produce toughness; yet both promote caring love. The strength of recovery and faith is like a soft and resilient rope, not a brittle, harsh chain. Christ calls us to share his gentle yoke—a bridle that is tough yet tender.

Thank you for all my past deserts and barren places, Lord, and help me see your helping hand everywhere. Amen.

"Peace! Be still!" . . . *And there was a great calm.*

MARK 4:39

Henri Nouwen, a Christian writer, has contributed deeply to our well of spirituality. Going against the grain of our noisy world, he says:

There was a time when silence was normal, and a lot of racket disturbed us. But today, noise is the normal fare, and silence, strange as it may seem, has become the real disturbance . . . perhaps we should say that we can't stand the sound of silence.

We are surrounded by noise pollution: stereos, TVs, horns, jets, lawn mowers, chain saws, and sounds from all sorts of people and machines. We are used to noise. Even in offices we must have background music, and we are frequently put on hold listening to music. In the sacred precincts where holy silence should envelop us, our church services must have "fill-in music," preludes, and postludes to occupy any silent pause.

It is wise to consider that three of the world's great religions began in the silent desert of the Middle East. Israel discovered God in Sinai; Mohammed, in Arabia; and both Jesus and Paul went to the desert to listen and learn. The great monastic orders of the church still find God in silent contemplation—in the still, small voice of God within.

When outside noise and distractions are missing, we can hear softer sounds—birds, wind, insects, and the sound of our own soul. Recovery also seeks to recover our sensitivity to God within us. But we can't hear if the static and noise all around us keeps us from hearing the whispering voice of peace.

Dear Christ, help me to be still, silent, and sensitive to your soft voice. Amen.

Once a man was driving late at night and foolishly picked up a hitchhiker. Afraid he had made a terrible mistake, he automatically felt for his wallet and found his pocket empty and then thought he had put it on the dashboard. It was not there either. Certain his passenger had taken it, he pulled over to the side of the road and yelled at the hitchhiker to hand over the wallet and get out of the car. The startled hitchhiker handed over a billfold and the driver drove on.

After arriving home, he began to tell his wife of the attempted theft, but she stopped his tale to tell him, "Did you know that you left your wallet at home this morning?"

Poor hitchhiker. Being falsely accused or judged wrongly is so common. We are so fast to assume guilt in someone else. Many of us have been so judged. At least two slogans remind us to "Live and let live," and "There but for the grace of God go I," and both help us not to be harsh judges . . . of others or ourselves. Thank God, most of the time such mistakes can be rectified by "humbly admitting," our misjudgements, and the quicker the better. It is not easy to admit a mistake, but it is the key to humility and honesty, which are keys to recovery. When we plead guilty to a mistaken judgment, it will cleanse our soul and gain us a new friend in the process.

Jesus reminded us that we can look a splinter in our brother's eye and fail to see the log in our own! He says, "Judge not, lest ye be judged." He knows that our tendency to condemn others and set up ourselves as superior or right is the cause of great injury and destruction among us. Our prejudging or prejudices are our most dangerous enemies.

And when Jesus heard it, he said to them, "Those who are
well have no need of a physician, but those who are sick; I
came not to call the righteous, but sinners."

MARK 2:17

For thousands of persons recovery in Christ was like
being in a hospital, flat on our backs, helpless and open
to the mercies of doctors and nurses. When we are desperately ill, we submit ourselves to their care. When we are
"just in for a checkup," we can be rather stubborn and
uncooperative. It's amazing how compliant we become as
we become helpless and afraid.

When our burdens become too much, we allow someone else to help. What is sad is that so many of us waited
so long. We don't have to become bedridden patients before
we wake up to the fact that we are sick. More and more
of us are seeking and asking for help earlier and earlier.
Thank God the average age in recovery will soon be under
thirty!

The embarrassing facts of our lives are these: We are out
of control. We are sick. We are selfish. We are foolish. Yet
in admitting our sickness, foolishness, and pride, we then
can let the Twelve Steps and Christ take us on as "outpa-
tients," patients who really want to get well *before* we are
flat on our backs. When we surrender to the skillful hands
of the "company of the recovering," our trust begins our
healing.

Dear great Physician, I submit myself totally to your care and to
the rehabilitation program of the Twelve Steps. Amen.

"Jesus wept."

JOHN 11:35

A famous old story tells of a rabbi who was deeply depressed, fatigued, and physically weak. Yom Kippur, the Day of Atonement, was approaching. This is the high holy day of repentance and restoration, when Israel's sins are atoned for and its brokenness healed each year. The sad rabbi was standing in the doorway of his house when a cobbler came by and shouted, "Do you have anything that needs mending?" The rabbi said it was like the voice of God. He immediately saw what needed mending—himself.

We often fail to realize our own need for healing. Once we are aware, we can begin to seek help, but awareness is not enough. We also need to know that we *can* be helped, that others like us have been helped, that there is hope. We are not alone.

A psychiatrist once took a teenage patient who had attempted suicide several times to a very depressing play about very depressing people. A friend asked, "Why take this poor child who is already so full of fear and sadness to this hopelessly despairing drama?" The doctor said, "This sad story opened my patient up. She virtually danced out of the theater that night. She finally saw that there are *other* persons she could identify with. If I'd taken her to a bouncy musical, she would have sunk further into her own hopeless despair."

Isn't it strange how recovery can be like that? The cheery, bouncy, and jovial folks around us can actually drag us down because they seem so unreal. Somehow the tears and sorrow of the cross and the shared pain we experience in our program has a healing power that pulls us up and connects us to life again.

Holy Jesus, your tears and your pain draw me close to you in my own sadness and suffering. I know that I never cry alone. Amen.

Were you a slave when called? Never mind. But if you can gain your freedom, avail yourself of the opportunity.

1 CORINTHIANS 7:21

William Booth founded the Salvation Army. For this he should be honored and praised, for the Salvation Army is a true arm of God's mercy and kindness in this world. When General Booth was eighty years old, he was asked for his secret of success. He said:

I will tell you the secret. God has had all there was of me. There have been men with greater brains than I, men with greater opportunities; but from the day I got the poor of London on my heart, and a vision of what Jesus Christ could do for the poor of London, I made up my mind that God would have all of William Booth there was. And if there is anything of power in the Salvation Army today, it is because God has all the adoration of my heart, all the power of my will, and all the influence of my life.

God has a way of creating greatness in us. The greatness of people like William Booth and the power they exercise in life come directly from the measure of their surrender to God.

As we submit and surrender our out-of-control lives to God in Twelve-Step recovery, we stand on the brink of greatness—the greatness of God. Yes, God will heal us. But if we truly give "all the adoration of our hearts, all the power of our wills, and all the influence of our lives" to God, he will accomplish more than just our healing. He will use us for his purposes in ways that will astound us. All this from our surrender. All this from our capitulation. It is true. God's miracles are performed by his willing slaves.

O Christ, I submit myself totally to you. Use me as you will. Amen.

But he gives more grace; therefore it says, "God opposes the proud, but gives grace to the humble."

JAMES 4:6

Who is the truly spiritual person? Someone said that the truly humble are truly spiritual. But what is humility? When you are truly humble, you are invariably unaware that you possess humility. Also when you are "spiritual," you are unselfconscious about the spirit within. People who take credit for their own humility immediately become proud of being humble, an impossibility. A person in whom God dwells displays a naturalness and an innocence that disavow any special gift at all. A true saint is transparent. Honesty and humility exist without thought or effort and therefore prove their existence without awareness or display.

As we recover from our pride and destructive illnesses, we realize that what we seek is not self-justification and self-salvation but God. God is the only answer to our condition. He must replace any phony, contrived, or prideful ploy we use. Only he can drive out our hypocrisy and dishonesty. Only he can replace our old center with his own life of love. We will lose our sense of self-concern and give up our need to assert our will when God has taken over. Then we will be humble, but we won't know it or care. We will only live for Christ:

When I survey the wondrous cross
Where the young Prince of Glory died,
My richest gain I count but loss
And pour contempt on all my pride.

Were the whole realm of nature mine,
That were an offering far too small;
Love so amazing, so divine,
Demands my soul, my life, my all.
(1940 Hymnal)

O Christ, melt me down into your spirit so that you become my everything. Amen.

"We are unworthy servants; we have only done what was our duty."

LUKE 17:10

The famous evangelist Billy Sunday was once asked, "What must I do to go to hell?" Billy Sunday answered, *"Nothing."* A defeated politician said to his supporters after his election loss, "I had the solid support of all those good people who didn't go to the polls."

We hear of the "silent majority" and the hidden uninvolved. The old saying "Idleness is the devil's workshop" is important to hear and heed. Recovery is an active process. Today we hear a debate about whether we are "recovered" or "recovering." Actually we are both. We truly do make gains and recover bit by bit and can look back and say, "I'm recovered" from that. Yet so much is yet to be done. There is always more to recover from; in that sense we are always "recovering." It takes a lifetime.

If we think we are more "recovered" than "recovering," we may delude ourselves into thinking we can ease up or even do nothing. This sort of complacency is the major factor in "slips." We can never become cocky. The Twelve Steps are never fully achieved but always there ahead of us. The gospel of Christ is never fully realized, but always calls us to follow Jesus anew each day.

Dear Savior, recovery is your saving gift to me. Help me to know that I am saved, am being saved, and will be saved. Help me also to realize that I am recovered, am recovering, and will continue to recover. Amen.

"God was in Christ reconciling the world to himself."

2 CORINTHIANS 5:19

A prison chaplain was making the customary visit to a prisoner on death row. The condemned man was to die in two hours. The chaplain sat down in front of the doomed prisoner, and both remained silent. Then the convict looked up and spit in the chaplain's face. The minister just sat there, not saying a word. Finally he asked the prisoner, "Got any more spit?" The man looked at him in wonder and then broke down in tears. They stayed together to the end. During the next two hours a wayward child of God found his way back to his Father's arms and found out that he could turn his face away from the wall, be reconciled to God, and be healed.

A great psychologist described life as a process in which two great forces work: the demonic and the divine. The demonic is whatever rips, shatters, tears, pulls apart, and separates. The divine is the love of God himself, healing, mending, restoring, joining, and putting together what is apart. This divine mending is called reconciliation and is the pathway of recovery. The Seventh, Eighth, and Ninth Steps are the "amendment" steps of reconciliation; they constitute the highest point of recovery. For we allow all that has fallen apart to get glued back together; we meet the depth of the healing cross of Christ, and we become whole persons in him through his conquering love.

Christ, you have given the ministry of reconciliation to us, help me be a reconciler. Amen.

Making a whip of cords, he drove them all, with the sheep and oxen, out of the temple.

JOHN 2:15

A woman with a fiery temper died. As her casket was lowered into the grave, a storm suddenly arose. The wind howled; lightning flashed and struck a nearby tree. Her husband quickly looked up to heaven and said, "She has arrived."

In recovery we are cautioned about anger. There is no doubt in the world that anger can be a problem. It can also be a blessing. Anger can move us; it can stir us up and get us stimulated to action. Its energy has great power. When anger agitates us, we act. Yet the problem is not the energy of anger, it's *how* it is expressed and put into action. Christians should show their anger in ways that fit the Christian gospel. We have every right—even the duty—to be angry at injustice, immorality, evil, and waste. To suppress our "righteous indignation" at such things is to fail to express our faith.

Saint Paul says three things about anger in Ephesians 4:26. First he says, "Be angry." Go ahead, feel your anger, be stirred up. That's OK. But, second, he adds, "Do not sin." Do not express your anger in sinful, cruel, and un-Christian ways. Third, he says, "Let not the sun go down upon your wrath." Make sure your anger is resolved and exhausted before the day is over. Stored-up anger turns sour. Anger won't keep; it spoils like milk. It turns into the corroding acids of resentment and hatred when it's held on to. Good advice for recovery—we don't need acid in our lives.

Holy Jesus, when you cared deeply, you were deeply angered. Teach me to get angry over the same things you cared about. Amen.

*Teach me to do thy will, for thou art my God! Let thy good
spirit lead me on a level path!*

PSALM 143:10

Education is essential to recovery. Everyone who is making a solid recovery has become a reader and a listener. The Twelve Steps, our literature, meetings, and Scripture are sources of learning. Books, lectures, tapes, workshops, television, and movies are also arenas of enrichment. If we don't learn, we don't recover. If we don't learn, we cannot find true happiness. Timothy Dwight said:

The happiest person is the person who thinks the most interesting thoughts. Education may not increase wealth, but it enriches life; it increases the wealth of mind and hence brings happiness.

A recovering person has an interesting mind. Recovering minds must be kept full, because empty minds become bored, lazy, and weak. A recovering mind, however, is disciplined. *Discipline* comes from the word *disciple*, or "one who follows." As disciples of Christ, we also follow the discipline of the Twelve Steps, a proven program full of sound learning. As disciples of the Twelve Steps we are taught God's will—led by God's "good spirit" and onto a "level path" where we can finally stand upright, steady, and strong.

Lord of learning, may I always be filling my mind with interesting thoughts as I follow you. Amen.

"You shall love your neighbor as yourself."

MARK 12:31

In New York a social worker who was beginning a half-way house for recovering addicts received a request from a woman who wanted to help. In her letter she confessed her many inadequacies and hoped she could be accepted in spite of her shortcomings. The social worker wrote back:

Dear Madam. Your truly magnificent shortcomings at the present time are far too great. Nothing would be able to stop you from inflicting them on unsuspecting victims of your humility. I advise that you learn to love yourself a great deal more before you squander any love on anybody else.

On the surface the social worker's response seems cruel and rejecting. Actually it was full of compassionate wisdom. No doubt others with good intentions and low self-esteem had come across this social worker's path. It is often said in recovery, "You can't really love anyone else unless you love yourself." How can we give love if we don't possess it? Removing our shortcomings is not the way to self-esteem; accepting God's love for us *in spite of shortcomings* is. When we know we are loved, we can love ourselves, and then others. Empty tanks cannot fill others.

In recovery it is essential to work on "self-recovery" before we undertake "other-recovery." The first eleven steps are prerequisites to the Twelfth Step. We need to "get our act together" before we start working on someone else's. Otherwise, we are beggars trying to share wealth we do not possess.

O Lord of love, help me to accept your love for me, and love myself, so I may share out my abundance and not inflict my poverty on others. Amen.

*"Come, follow me." At that saying his countenance fell,
and he went away sorrowful; for he had great possessions.*
                                            MARK 10:21–22

A young man spied a beautiful young woman strolling
in a park. He began to follow her. She stopped and con-
fronted him. "Why do you dog my footsteps?" she
demanded. "Because you are so beautiful. I am madly in
love with you and wish you were mine." To this she replied,
"But you have merely to look behind to see my sister who
is far more beautiful." The young man quickly spun around
but saw no one. "You have mocked me," he said, "and have
lied," to which she answered, "If you were so madly in love
with me, why did you turn around?"

Isn't that just like us? We have roving eyes and impetuous desires. We promise undying devotion one minute and
turn our heads toward every passing attraction the next.
How about our promise to follow Christ? How about our
promise to walk the Twelve Steps? To attend meetings? To
make Twelfth-Step calls? To help the helpless? Sure, we
mean it at the time, and then we are distracted. Something
else looks better.

God knows we are fickle, weak, and easily led astray. He
knows we slip and slide and wander and hide. That's why
he gives us a fresh twenty-four hours every day! We can
start all over again, renew our promise to him, and recom-
mit ourselves to our program—again. Each time we restart,
we gain strength and resolve. Our loyalty and love grow,
and our fickleness falters one day at a time.

*Oh Christ, keep me fixed and steady on your Twelve-Step path. If
I stray, lead me back each day. Amen.*

"The gate is wide and the way is easy, that leads to destruction."

MATTHEW 7:13

A story is told of a man who died and opened his eyes in the next world. What he saw was beauty and luxury beyond any on earth. He found that his every wish and whim were immediately fulfilled without his asking. All he had to do was think of something he wanted, and an attendant would appear and grant his wish. After a while he became restless and bored. "If only something different would happen," he said to himself, "if only just once there would be a refusal." Finally, the monotony became unbearable; he summoned the attendant and said, "I want something that I can't have unless I earn it." "Sorry," the attendant replied, "that's the one wish we cannot grant here." "Very well," the man said, "then let me out of here. I would rather be in hell." At that, the attendant said, "And where do you think you are?"

The easy way is hell, a place for "spoiled children." The path of immediate gratification and instant pleasure is a prison. We are made to create, work, and achieve. Boredom is hellish for us. Our Twelve-Step path is far from easy. The road of Christian discipline is also a strenuous effort. Recovery in faith provides no easy chair. It can never be boring. We are required to "work the steps" and to "labor for love." It is a heavenly path.

Thank you, Christ, for labors of love, for hard tasks to accomplish. Save me from boredom and laziness. Amen.

"O men of little faith!"

MATTHEW 6:30

Psychologists maintain that a mentally healthy person can tolerate uncertainty and change. Our ability to adapt and live with the unknown and unexpected is our strongest survival tool. People in mental hospitals cannot live with unanswered questions. They must have the correct answers for everything—even if they have to create their own fantasy world of answers.

Living with uncertainty is the hallmark of spiritual health as well. This is called "faith." The author of Hebrews defines faith "as the assurance of things hoped for, the conviction of things not seen" (11:1). Faith is trust in God's providence and care. It's an attitude that declares "I don't know what God is doing, but I do believe that whatever it is, it's good." Christians don't need answers because we have the presence and love of God in Christ. How could we need answers when God is with us to comfort and assure us in the midst of our ignorance and confusion? We are like little infants being held in the strong, safe arms of our parent. We don't need to know it all. We're OK. We can rest in the "everlasting arms"; we are content.

A recovering Christian is like the old woman who was told by a census taker that he was there "because every ten years the government tries to find out how many people live in the U.S.A." The old woman replied, "Lordy, honey, I sure don't know." We sure don't have to know how recovery works—it just does.

Jesus, you have so many surprises in store for me. I'm ready for them as long as you are with me. Amen.

I consider that the sufferings of this present time are not worth comparing with the glory that is to be revealed to us.

ROMANS 8:18

It is interesting to learn that the word *travel* comes from the French word meaning "suffer." Our English word *travail* is close. Some travel can be a travail: packing, standing in line, crowding into planes and trains, going through security and customs, not to mention jet lag, confusion, intestinal distress, and aching feet. There definitely is suffering in travel. Yet for those who know its value and benefits, the suffering is soon forgotten. Reaching our destination, enjoying new discoveries, experiencing delightful events and people—all of these add up to satisfaction and pleasure.

The Twelve Steps are a journey. Christian faith is a pilgrimage. Recovery in Christ is full of "suffering," but no pain can compare to the joys that we find as we travel the King's highway. Jesus walked and stumbled along the way of the cross to Calvary to his Easter destination. We are assigned the same itinerary.

Recovery has its hazards, but it sure beats the alternative, which is to stay in darkness. We are on a tough road and the trip is hard, but it leads to "the light of life."

Dear Lord and my traveling companion, keep me with you on your road even though I suffer, for when I am with you, I have already "arrived." Amen.

"Many that are first will be last, and the last first."
MARK 10:31

A writer once wrote a tremendously popular book. A decade later, he decided to bring out a revision. When his new book appeared, all he changed was the preface, which said:

Wherever in this volume appears the word "is," substitute "is not" and wherever the words "is not" appear, substitute "maybe," "perhaps," or "God knows."

People change, don't they? But even though change is inevitable, *some* things remain constant.

The gospel is everlasting. The Twelve-Step path of recovery is as good today as it was fifty years ago. People may show all kinds of change, but the healing love of God stays with us. God may alter his approach and his method in order to reach us better, but his purpose is always salvation and love. We can't ever get too confident about a changing world, but we can be sure about love, especially the love of Jesus. Above all, we can be certain that if God brings about change, it's got to be good, even if it doesn't always feel good to us. How do we know what God is changing? Listen to Jesus.

O Christ, in your unchanging love, you move me to change my life. Keep me attentive and obedient to your demands of love. Amen.

*For men shall be lovers of their own selves, covetous,
boasters, proud.*

2 TIMOTHY 3:2

Our worst enemy is not a thing; it's a "who." It is you and
me, a person. Another way to put this is that selfishness
is the root of all evil. The self-centered, egocentric human
being is the most dangerous enemy of life. We live in a glass
room, each one of us. The great Harry Emerson Fosdick
explains:

A person completely wrapped up in himself makes a small package indeed.
The great day comes when a man begins to get himself off his hands.
He has lived, let us say, in a mind like a room surrounded by mirrors.
Every way he turned he saw himself. Now, however, some of the mirrors
change to windows. He can see through them. He begins to get out of
himself—no longer the prisoner of self-reflections but a free man in a
world where persons, causes, truths and values exist, worthful for their
own sakes. Thus to pass from a mirror-mind to a mind with windows is
an essential element in the development of a real personality. Without
that experience no one ever achieves a meaningful life.

Moreover, without that experience no one can recover from
addictions in Christ. Our program of recovery will guarantee that we will be put into the hands of God. He will
package us as windows of clarity and love. We are saved
from our worst enemy.

*Take me off my hands, Lord. I know I am my own worst enemy.
Open me as a window to the world with an open door to you. Amen.*

"Blessed are the pure in heart, for they shall see God."
MATTHEW 5:8

On a rainy Saturday afternoon, a father came up with an idea to entertain his bored eight-year-old daughter. He tore a large map of the world into small pieces, mixed them up. and told her to put them back together like a jigsaw puzzle. To her father's surprise, the girl completed the puzzle in a few minutes. "How did you do it, dear?" he asked. "It was easy," she said. "At first I couldn't fit all the lines, dots, and colors together on the map. Then I saw part of a man's face on the back of one of the pieces. So I turned all the pieces over. When I got the man on the back together, the world on the front took care of itself."

This child had her priorities right. When individuals are put together, "the world takes care of itself." When the person of Jesus Christ no longer seems a puzzle and begins to come together with our program for us, our world gets taken care of. To see God, Jesus says, we need pure hearts. Anything that is pure is one hundred percent itself, unpolluted and containing no additives or foreign matter. The pure, clear, and simple sight of a child who can see a person's face in the midst of a puzzle is close to what Jesus had in mind. No one recovers alone. No one recovers without other people. We belong to a recovering fellowship. We belong to a Christian community. When we see God in both, our hearts will have become pure.

O Christ, help me see your face on the other side of my confusion and help me get you in focus first. Amen.

But he answered them, "You see all these, do you not?"
MATTHEW 24:2

A famous psychiatrist told the case history of a woman who was plagued with feelings of inferiority and inadequacy. She had been shy from infancy. Her entire family was outgoing, even boisterous. Her father was a bouncy, talkative extrovert, as were her mother and two sisters. The father worried about her shyness and tried to coax her to become more expressive. One day he brought her a present. It was a beautiful little glass elephant on a gold chain. He put it down on a table and told his bashful child, "I've brought you a present." She was dumbfounded. Her mouth dropped open, and her eyes widened as she stared in rapture at this gorgeous present. It shone like the sun to her not only in its own beauty but also because it was a symbol of her father's love. She just sat staring at this sacrament of love for several minutes, unable to respond. When she was finally able to move, she jumped up and ran into the other room to tell her mother. When she returned, however, she was devastated. Her beautiful elephant was around her sister's neck. The father announced sternly, "You didn't want it, so I gave it to your sister."

It's no wonder that the shy little girl became a neurotic, fearful woman without feelings of worth. Listening and sensitivity can bring life. Inattention and hasty insensitivity can stifle and kill. This father didn't realize his cruelty. Neither do we. We can't understand if we don't take time to listen, even to the joy and wonder of another's silence. Listening is not done with our ears alone—our heart is needed, too.

O Christ the compassionate, teach me to listen with my heart. Amen.

"Whatever you wish that men would do to you, do so to them."

MATTHEW 7:12

The Golden Rule has been called the core of Jesus' teachings. It has been called the Mount Everest of morality. Many civic clubs use it as their motto. Yet Freud said, "It is a good thing that we do not love our neighbors as ourselves, because otherwise we would murder them." If we look at the Golden Rule as our primary guide, we are indeed in trouble. Freud is right. If our desires are to direct us, we are all at our own mercy! Most of us in recovery realize that the quality of our own self-regard and self-love can be rather shoddy.

If it's up to us, our compulsiveness will ask for alcohol, food, drugs, gambling, and activities that enslave and destroy. If how we get treated depends on you and me, our sights are often much too low. Fortunately, biblical sayings belong in a biblical context. The Golden Rule depends on God first! Our love, devotion, worship, and dependency on God in Christ create new selves that are of higher quality than our old separate and selfish selves. When we stand in the grace of God's love and are filled with his honor and goodness, then we have something to base the Golden Rule on. It has no gold in it at all without God in it.

Direct me, Lord, with your gold in me, before I apply the Golden Rule. Amen.

When the wine failed, the mother of Jesus said to him,
"They have no wine." . . . Jesus said to them, "Fill the jars
with water." And they filled them up to the brim. He said
to them, "Now draw some out, and take it to the steward
of the feast."

JOHN 2:3, 7–8

Suppose that you have accepted the invitation from Christ to go to the banquet. With hope and trust you begin to drink in the relief, support, and peace of your Twelve-Step program. Then you run dry. You find yourself in a flat, stale place. You experience the pain of relapse, and you slip backwards. In discouragement and panic you feel like the old wine that ran out—exhausted and helpless. No more left. What now?

When did the miracle of water-turned-wine take place? When there was nothing left, at the precise point of exhaustion, when all was poured out! Christ transforms the stale water of our lives into the very best wine when we obey his command to "now draw some out." When we dip our buckets into what seems an empty well, lo and behold, a miracle! With the steward of the feast we marvel, "You have kept the good wine until now!" (John 2:10).

When we are down and out is when Christ can turn our emptiness into a full, rich, and sparkling *new* wine of life. In our times of depletion and poverty, Jesus changes us.

O, Lord of life's banquet, transform my old wine into a new and sparkling one. Use the nowness of my need and fill my emptiness with your very best. Amen.

> *But a Samaritan, as he journeyed, came to where he was;
> and when he saw him, he had compassion, and went to
> him and bound up his wounds.*

LUKE 10:33

Two men were riding on a sleigh during a blizzard. They were almost frozen and afraid they would not reach warmth and safety. They came upon another traveler in the storm who had fallen in the snow and was almost dead. One pleaded that they stop and help. The other refused. The first man decided to stay and help even though the delay could mean his death. His companion left him behind. Working feverishly, he massaged the unconscious man's body. After several hours of labor, the man responded and began to function. The two men got up and walked in the snow together. The vigorous work of massage had saved both men. As they walked on, they came upon the man who had refused to stay and help. He was frozen to death.

The energy we spend is never wasted. Each meeting, each encounter with a fellow sufferer, each time we stop to help restore a frozen brother or sister, we assist our own salvation. We *need* each other. We need the stimulation and inspiration of our company. Together we survive. Alone, we freeze and die.

The Twelve-Step path to recovery is never lonely, and it is *never* "every man for himself." We are a family of fellow searchers who rely on each other for warmth and safety. Though we might hear our groups called "selfish programs," that's not really true. They are "self-full programs," full of selves helping selves. Didn't Jesus call our attention to our need to help each other in the parable of the good Samaritan?

O Christ the compassionate, keep me from staying isolated. Spur me on to revive others and thereby revive myself. Amen.

"My sheep hear my voice, and I know them, and they follow me."

JOHN 10:27

A profound description of humanity is found in an old legend about the great war in heaven. Satan, the rebel angel, was cast out of heaven with all his allies. Satan, one of the original archangels, began a rebellion to overthrow God himself. There were three groups in the war: the angels of Satan, the angels of God, and a small group of angels who could not make up their minds. These "undecided ones" became the human race.

This ancient tale tells a truth about us. We can't make up our minds about who we will follow and give our loyalty to. The angels of Satan are still everywhere, denying God's rule and living without any loyalty to him. Then there are most of us. We struggle and strain to be on God's side. We listen to God and respond to him, but not all the time. Much too often we obey the orders of the rebel.

Our programs are at the mercy of ourselves, the "undecided ones." We try and then we don't. We get with it, and then we coast. But though we are not dependable, we *are* loved. We are not much, but we are all God has to work with. He calls us each day to follow him, one day at a time. He never gives up on us.

Strengthen my loyalty to you, O Christ, and keep me close to your side. Amen.

But there are also many other things which Jesus did; were every one of them to be written, I suppose that the world itself could not contain the books that would be written.

JOHN 21:25

When the Italian traveler, Marco Polo, came back from China in the fourteenth century, he told stories of the wonders he had seen and the marvelous cities he had visited. Because these things were beyond the comprehension of the people of his own city, they began to accuse him of lying. They even ridiculed him. When he was dying, they asked him to confess his lies, since he was soon to face God. Marco Polo's last answer was, "I never told the half of it."

When those of us who have seen the wonder of recovery try to explain the many marvels we have witnessed, it too is hard for others to believe. Someone who has never seen or experienced the honesty, love, healing, and peace of our program just can't comprehend it. Yet we "never tell the half of it." Recovery in Christ from addiction and the continued life of the Twelve Steps are true miracles of spiritual resurrection. If we were able to tell all the wonders of the new health we have found, it would be hard for "an outsider" to believe it.

Yet we have nothing to prove. Like Marco Polo, we know the truth. Later, when others traveled to China, they realized he was not a liar. When new travelers join us on the Twelve-Step road to recovery, they become believers who experience it for themselves. That's always the best way to learn.

O Christ of wondrous miracle, teach me to simply believe and live my own program and point the way to you, so others may make their own discoveries. Amen.

"Even though you do not believe me, believe the works."
JOHN 10:38

A cold, rigid woman asked advice from her lawyer. "I hate my husband. He is making my life miserable. I want a divorce and more than that, I want to make things as tough as possible for him. What do you advise?" The lawyer replied, "Begin by showering him with compliments. Indulge him in every way. Give in to his every whim. Then, when he realizes how much he needs you and wants you, start your divorce proceedings. That will tear him up." Six months later, the lawyer met the woman and asked, "Are you following my advice?" "I am," she answered. "Are you ready to file for divorce?" he asked. "Are you crazy?" replied the woman, indifferently. "We're divinely happy. I love him with all my heart!"

Even love begun as an act cannot continue to be phony. Real change begins with acts, rather than ideas. In recovery we say, "Fake it till you make it." Wisdom teaches us that you can act your way into a new way of thinking better than think your way into a new way of acting. Great men and women have become great by conforming to the expectations and roles of a high office. Our transformation and healing are accomplished by acting out the Twelve Steps. The steps call us to a higher and better plane of living; even if we step upon each step with hesitation, they will support us and actually change us.

Dear Christ, you are my model and offer me my role. Help me to become what I do in your name. Amen.

*And Mary said, "Behold, I am the handmaid of the Lord;
let it be to me according to your word."*

LUKE 1:38

A wise person maintained that we can only do four things
with our life: (1) run away from it, (2) run along with it, (3)
take hold of it, or (4) surrender to it.

We often take the first option. We run away and hide. We
evade and avoid the challenges and burdens of responsible living. There are times when we all want to pull the covers up over our heads. Running away works, until we run
out of places to hide.

Frequently also, we take the second road—we run along
with the pack. We stick with the herd and do what "everyone else" is doing. Company gives us courage, the false
courage that comes with numbers. But while the mob
instinct is strong, we lose our souls and integrity in the
crowd.

We like to think we use the third way: we take hold of
life and manage our affairs with purpose and strong will.
We flex our muscles and dig in with determination to master and control our lives, until we keep stumbling over our
addictions.

Finally, with the grace of God, we stop running away, stop
running along, and stop trying to run everything, and just
stop and surrender to our Lord and to our program. Then
we let Christ, our Higher Power, run us. To be run by Christ
is to run with power and purpose because *he* impels us and
propels us with his love.

*Are you running my life, Lord Jesus? If not, please stop me and
make me let you take over. Amen.*

"You know how to interpret the appearance of the sky, but you cannot interpret the signs of the times."

MATTHEW 16:3

Two men who went up in a balloon were enveloped by thick clouds and soon lost their bearings. Finally the clouds parted, and they saw they were close to the ground. A man was standing under the balloon, and one of the men called down, "Where are we?" The person on the ground looked up, looked around, looked up again, and said, "You're in a balloon!" One balloonist asked the man on the ground, "Are you a politician?" The man yelled up, "Yes! How did you know?" The balloonist said, "Only a politician could give you an answer so quickly that is so logical and yet tells you so little about where you are and where you want to go."

We could say similar things about economists, preachers, psychologists, and professors. Yet most of the time we miss the obvious by complicated thinking. How many of us refused to recognize that we were "in a balloon" of addiction and insisted on hundreds of other reasons for our troubles. At the least we minimized, rationalized, excused, or evaded the truth that we were addicted and out of control. We also avoided the answer to our need: "God as we understand God to be." We Christians see and know him in Christ Jesus. He'll tell us where we are and where we want to go.

O Christ, give me sight to see your presence always. Give me the desire to seek you. Amen.

"What do you seek?"

JOHN 1:38

A minister held up a sign at the beginning of the sermon. It read: "GODISNOWHERE." He asked the congregation what it said and most responded, "GOD IS NOWHERE." Then the minister asked, "Didn't some of you see this message: 'GOD IS NOW HERE'?" Everyone did, of course, after being told.

What a true picture of our attitude about God! The same letters can carry different messages. It all depends on how we see it. We often believe God is absent. Less frequently we assume he is here with us. If we expect God to be away, he usually is—for us. Yet if with hopeful expectation we feel sure of God's presence, he's here! God is present as we expect him to be. We miss him when we jump to negative conclusions.

Life can be blessing or curse, problem or opportunity. It all depends on what we habitually look for: the good or the bad, God or no God at all. It's up to us. We have the choice of faith. We can always choose the way of the psalmist who said, "I believe that I shall see the goodness of the Lord in the land of the living!" (Psalm 27:13)

Dear Christ, help me see through your eyes, to look through the eyes of optimistic faith. Amen.

The Lord . . . sent them . . . two by two.

LUKE 10:1

There is an old parable about a man lost in a dense forest who suddenly meets another man. "Now I will find my way out with this other traveler," he thought. "Tell me, sir, which way out of the forest?" he asks. The stranger replies, "Friend, I do not know. I too need to find the way. But one thing I do know: do not take the way I have been taking. That will lead nowhere. Let us both look for a *new* way out *together.*"

This story describes us all. Whatever path each of us takes before recovery keeps us lost and frustrated. As long as we search a way out alone, we stray deeper into the forest. But when we join with another person or two or more, and we all search together for a new way, we find it. That way, of course, is "the way, the truth, and the life" of recovery in Jesus Christ. The gospel path of recovery will always place us in the company of other guides and teachers and continually be new and sure.

The old paths still beckon us back into the forest. We can still get lost if we allow old habits to claim us. We can never get complacent and think we can find our way alone. The lonely path "will lead nowhere." The path of Christ always takes us somewhere worthwhile.

Dear constant Companion, keep me close to your path and the Twelve Steps so that I may find new life with others. Amen.

"Fear not, I am the first and the last."

REVELATION 1:17

The legendary Knute Rockne knew the power of fear. Today we call it "psyching out your opponent." Notre Dame was facing a critical football game against a vastly superior Southern California team. Rockne recruited every brawny student he could find at Notre Dame and suited up about a hundred "hulks" in the school uniform. On the day of the game the Southern California team ran out on the field first and awaited the visiting Fighting Irish. Then, out of the dressing room came an army of green giants who kept on coming and coming. The USC team panicked. Their coach reminded them that Rockne could only play eleven men at a time, but the damage was done. USC lost. They did not lose to the hundred men. They were beaten by their own fear.

The Bible knows what an enemy fear can be. The phrase "fear not" appears at least a hundred times in Scripture; it could well be the most frequent declaration in the Bible, and for good reason. Fears and anxieties are dreadful foes to recovery and serenity. Only the confidence we place in the strong, solid Twelve Steps and in Christ's love can save us from "fruitless fears and worldly anxieties." As Saint Paul wrote, when we "know God is for us, who can be against us?"

O Christ, help me to see clearly that you are always with me. Teach me to fear less and trust more. Amen.

"You cannot serve God and mammon."

MATTHEW 6:24

A novice painter had just completed a truly lovely landscape. Her family lavishly praised her work, but a wise uncle shook his head from side to side as he looked at the painting. "You don't like it?" asked the young artist. "Oh, I like it all right, but it will not last," was his reply. "Your picture has two centers of interest—see, a large tree there, and a snow-capped mountain there. In time, people will be confused about the focus of your picture's subject, and even you will begin to dislike it. No work of art endures when there is more than one center of interest."

Recovery that is not similarly single-minded cannot endure. As recovering Christians, we cannot live with two "centers of interest." Our Twelve-Step path and our faith are one center—not two competing subjects of attention. Recovery is salvation, and salvation is recovery. There is no conflict. God is the author of our healing. Our health integrates the Twelve Steps and the gospel. Our healing will suffer if we separate the two.

We cannot live with divided loyalties. Our focal point pulls together the surrounding background and details to illuminate the major subject. That subject is Jesus Christ, who is the spotlighted center of our life's painting, whose light gives beauty and meaning to the entire landscape of our lives.

O Christ, the center of my life, help me to always keep you as my major interest. Amen.

"Whoever receives one such child in my name receives me."
MARK 9:37

Three generations of women—a grandmother, a mother, and a little girl—went to a restaurant. The waitress took the grandmother's order, then the mother's, and then she asked the little girl, "What would you like, honey?" The mother immediately interrupted and said, "Oh, I'll order for her." Politely ignoring the mother, the waitress repeated her question, "Just what would *you* like to eat, dear?" Glancing over her shoulder to see how her mother was reacting, she answered, "A hamburger." "How would you like your hamburger, with mustard, catsup, pickles, and the works?" asked the waitress. With glee she answered, clapping her hands, "The works!" The waitress shouted out grandmother's and mother's orders, then bellowed, "And a hamburger deluxe with all the works!" The little girl turned to her mother in utter amazement and said, "Mommy, she thinks I'm real."

This waitress is in the ministry. She sees people as unique and special. She listened to a little girl and treated her like a real person. This kind of attention is life-giving. When we are in the company of another who looks at us, listens to us, responds to *us*, and conveys interest and enjoyment in our presence—a miracle takes place. We become real. We never realize what a gift of grace we can be until we have received such life-giving attention ourselves.

How many times have we experienced such genuine interest from another in Twelve-Step meetings? How often have we given it *to* another?

Dear Lord of listeners, please teach me to give the gift of life to others' souls by listening to them and rejoicing in their reality. Amen.

Phillip Brooks said, "It is almost as presumptuous to think you can do nothing as to think you can do everything." Often we think in our recovery that we are completely unable to do anything at all. The truth is that we are powerless over our disease or our addictive compulsion, not everything. We still have choices. We must stop trying to control what is out of control and turn that over to God in Christ. Yet there is a lot left over that we can do. We have some power, some ability. We can read the scriptures, we can go to meetings, we can worship, we can meditate, we can pray, we can help others, we can choose to adopt a positive attitude.

Quite simply, God does not expect us to do what we cannot do. But he knows that he has blessed us with abilities. Above all, we can choose to stick it out. We can choose to persevere and commit ourselves to the path of health and recovery. Our determination is determined by ourselves and no one else. Josh Billings said, "Consider the postage stamp: its usefulness consists in the ability to stick it to one thing till it gets there. I think that is the way it works. We never give up. Jesus was quite clear in his story about the persistent woman who kept on knocking on the judge's door late at night, until he got up and answered her request. St. Paul urges us to never grow weary in our prayers and to pray in and out of season. Being insistent and persistent is the course that God in Christ has set before us. Knowing what we can do and trusting that God-given capacity will give us encouragement in our limited abilities that added to God's unlimited power will bring a bountiful harvest, if we never give up on ourselves and God.

"Why do you see the speck that is in your brother's eye, but do not notice the log that is in your own eye?"

MATTHEW 7:3

One Saturday a new clergyman came to town and asked a small boy the way to the post office. When he received his instructions, the preacher thanked his little guide and said, "You seem to be a bright young fellow. How would you like to listen to my sermon tomorrow so that I may show you the way to heaven?" The boy replied, "You're going to show me the way to heaven? You don't even know the way to the post office!"

Jesus has a way of getting right down to the bone. He sees where we cannot. He knows we are like birds unaware of the air or fish unaware of the water. We are too close to our own environment—we don't see our own faces. We need others to hold the mirror of truth up to us. Jesus tells us that we are like people with huge chunks of wood sticking out of our eyes, trying to find little wood chips in the eyes of others.

When we see how ridiculous we are when we judge others, how futile and foolish our judgmental ways really are— maybe we can begin to laugh at ourselves. When we see how pompous and proud we are of being right, we might allow ourselves the glorious relief of being wrong. Most recovering "winners" can readily admit they are "losers" and laugh about it. Real recovery laughs a lot.

Dear Christ of truth, hold up your mirror of reality to me, and ease the pain of my discovering with my own laughter. Amen.

"Seek first his kingdom."

MATTHEW 6:33

We can be programmed by the power of suggestion. Positive or negative impressions can capture our attention. Curiously, we have a quirk in our nature that responds to "don'ts" with "do." Tell a child *not* to do something, and you often guarantee its doing.

A famous baseball pitcher has a vivid memory of such a hang-up. Facing a batter he didn't know, the pitcher called for a conference with his manager, who said, "Our scouts tell us that this guy is hitting high outside pitches. Keep it away from that area." As he was leaving the mound the manager repeated, "Now, remember, don't pitch to the high outside corner." The pitcher retells what happened, "'High and outside' flashed in my mind. Where do you think I threw the ball? Of course, I delivered high and outside and the batter hit a home run."

Realizing what a problem is does not remove it. To concentrate on what is wrong perpetuates and reinforces the problem. What is wrong needs to be replaced with what is right. That's what it means to have a "right mind." Our pitcher needed to focus on "low and inside," because that's where he needed to go. In recovery, we need the same focus, and the Twelve Steps give us positive direction. Saint Paul captures this eloquently: "Whatever is pure, whatever is lovely . . . think about these things" (Phil. 4:8).

O Lord, direct my sights toward positive goals. Amen.

*For he who was called in the Lord as a slave is a freed-
man of the Lord. Likewise he who was free when called is
a slave of Christ.*

1 CORINTHIANS 7:22

There is glory and joy in surrender to God. When we
surrender to other masters we are crushed, shamed, and
defeated. When we give our lives over to God in total submission, we are glorified and find victory. An unknown poet
knew the honor of our defeat at God's hands:

> Make me a captive, Lord.
> And then I shall be free.

When we give up our will and our way totally to God,
we can face him with nothing: nothing more, nothing less,
and nothing else—but his will. Richard Baxter, the great
English Puritan, died with these words on his lips: "Lord,
what Thou wilt, where Thou wilt, and when Thou wilt."
When we take into our lives God's complete and total control, we become what someone has called "God-
intoxicated." Yet our being is not flooded by toxic poison
when God takes over, we are given a transfusion of health
and recovery. There is no other way but the way of surrender, submission, and giving ourselves up to him. It's
terribly hard, yet completely necessary.

*My dear Lord and Master, I am your obedient servant in every way.
Use me as you will. Amen.*

"I am the bread of life."

JOHN 6:48

Edwin Markham wrote these familiar words: "I sought my soul, but my soul I could not see; I sought my God, but my God eluded me; I sought my brother, and I found all three." A Hindu proverb says, "Help your brother's boat across, and lo! Your own has reached the shore."

Railway tickets carry the words, "Not good if detached." This is true for the separated or detached person too. Ants, bees, termites, and other insects live and thrive in communities; maybe that's why 80 percent of all living things are insects. God has given us a herd instinct, yet human beings seem to be the last to learn that survival and progress depend on being in relationship and cooperative union.

The United States is one of the best examples of unity within diversity. Working together and living with a common bond also supports our Twelve-Step groups. Recovery is real because it is a mutual and cooperative effort. The unity of each group is essential. Naturally, each individual person is important, but the power and strength come from being surrounded by the care and love of many.

We are one though many. Saint Paul said, "We who are many are one body, for we all partake of the one bread" (1 Cor. 10:17). Christ is the one bread who feeds us all and together we "pass the bread" to our companions in Christ.

Dear Christ, you surrounded yourself with friends. Help me to keep in union with my group for support—for me and others. Amen.

And he healed many who were sick with various diseases, and cast out many demons.

MARK 1:34

A preacher spoke one Sunday about the existence of demons and the power of alien and hostile influences in our lives. He identified our demons as depression, hatred, greed, jealousy, and the like. He made a convincing case for this kind of demon possession. We can indeed become "possessed" by despair, hate, and destructive urges. After the sermon a man took exception with the preacher, "I don't agree with your ideas about demons. I'm over fifty years old, traveled the world over, and I've never run into a demon." The preacher replied, "Maybe that's because you're going in the same direction."

Did we not cooperate with our demons of compulsion? Did we not go along with our addiction? Whenever the impulse to drink or use drugs or lose ourselves to our condition itched, didn't we scratch it? We placed ourselves into the hands of urges and powers beyond our control. If we did resist, we eventually said, "Why fight it, I'll join it." We even protected our addiction. In short, were we not invaded or possessed by our addictive demons?

When we start "going in the same direction" as God, our demons are expelled and driven out, but they are always ready to come back in if invited. When we take a look at the character defects and destructive habits, thoughts, and feelings we once had, we know many still live in us. Only God can exorcise our demons, past, present, or future.

O holy Jesus, drive my demons away. Deliver me from self-pity, despair, hatred, and selfishness. Amen.

"Do not marvel that I said to you, 'You must be born anew.'"

JOHN 3:7

Recovery and the Christian faith share an attitude of "making the most of it." Both see possibilities in disaster. Both "make lemonade out of lemons." Both have a way of "turning the tables" on misfortune. Here is an example from the life of the great preacher Henry Ward Beecher. He received a note from an usher with just one word on it: "Fool!" Beecher knew who wrote the note and didn't want to embarrass him and drive him away from the church. He turned to the congregation and described the paper he had received; then he said, "I have known of people who write notes and forget to sign their name, but this is the first time I have ever known of someone signing their name but forgetting to write the note." He turned an unpleasant attack into a humorous moment.

A woman once stained a handkerchief with ink. Her friend, an artist, sketched the petals of a rose around it. The handkerchief became so beautiful and precious that it was framed as a reminder of what an artist can do with mistakes. Our life in recovery is like that. Christ and our program take our imperfections, stains, mistakes, and blemishes and paint beautiful roses around them all. All we need do is give ourselves, "warts and all," to our master Artist, and we shall "be born again."

O Christ, I give myself to you to transform, renew, and reconstruct. Amen.

"Father, forgive them; for they know not what they do."
LUKE 23:34

A young mother had just bought a beautiful party dress for a very special occasion. She laid it out carefully on her bed before taking her bath that evening. When she reached for her dress, she saw that it was torn and slashed into shreds! Her little girl, in anger, not wanting her mother to leave the house, had ripped and cut her mother's dress. Instead of reacting in anger, the mother fell across the bed, her torn dress in her hands, and sobbed. The little girl realized what she had done and tugged at her mother's arm, calling out, "Mommy, Mommy." Her mother ignored her as she continued to cry. Finally in desperation, the little girl screamed, "Mommy, please!" At last her mother rose and asked, "Yes, what do you want?" Her daughter pleaded, "Mommy, please take me back!"

This is the heart of healing. This is the soul of forgiveness. The church calls it redemption, reconciliation, and atonement (at-one-ment). The little girl knew where she needed to be—back. She needed to be back in relationship, to be at-one-ment, with her mother again. She didn't say, "I'm sorry" or "I won't do it again" or "I did it because." All that mattered was to be in her mother's arms. Apologies, promises, or excuses could come later.

Of course, God never hides his face from us or ignores us. But like the little girl, we have to change our selfishness and pride to concern and desire for companionship. We do cause God pain. We do grieve him. Yet all we need do is move toward him, and he will take us back.

O forgiving Lord, teach me to move through my shame and sorrow into your arms and into the arms of others I have hurt. Amen.

"I pray you, have me excused."

LUKE 14:19

The word *alibi* goes back to the Romans, and in those days it meant "to be in another place." For lawyers it still means pretty much the same. Fishermen have lifted the "alibi" to a high level. After a long, unproductive day on the lake, a fisherman will say: "Well, whaddya expect with the water as muddy as it is?" The same fisherman, after another unproductive day, will say: "That crystal clear water looks great on picture post cards, but it sure spooks the fish."

Benjamin Franklin said, "He that is good for making excuses is seldom good for anything else." Someone else said, "He who excuses himself accuses himself." As we recover we remember all the alibis and excuses we used to use to rationalize what we were doing. There always seemed to be a reason, some circumstance or person we could blame. Maybe we learned excuse making in school when we had our parents give us a note: "Please excuse Mary because . . ." We got used to "getting off the hook" and got accustomed to self-justification.

However, in recovery there is no room for alibis. Excuses are not allowed. Only the truth is admitted. Complete honesty and self-responsibility are required. Like a private in the army our response should be, "Yes sir," "No sir," and "No excuse, sir." Our life as recovering Christians is one that needs no excuses—just performance and willingness to do better.

Lord Christ, I have no excuses. Cleanse me and shed your loving truth upon me and set me free from guilt. Amen.

"Our Father, who art in heaven . . ."

MATTHEW 6:9

The disciples of Jesus asked him, "Teach us to pray." He gave them the Lord's Prayer. We say it by heart, yet we will never exhaust its power or fully fathom its meaning. Prayer is the heart of faith. Prayer has been called "the worthiest art," the "best resource," "the sublimest joy," "an education." The saints prayed often. Saint Ignatius Loyola devoted seven hours a day to prayer. John Wesley blocked out whole days for prayer and fasting. Saint Paul advised and practiced prayer "without ceasing." Jesus himself spent days and nights talking with God. Yet prayer is still a great mystery—a necessary one. It is our connection with God.

The great theologian Richard Niebuhr was once asked, "What is your theology of prayer?" He replied, "I don't have a theology of prayer. Prayer is not something you talk about. Prayer is something you *do*. Prayer is not the consequence of theological thought. It is the basis for all theological thought." Niebuhr's answer keeps prayer a mystery still.

Whatever prayer is—adoration, asking, telling, pleading, praising, interceding, confessing, thanking, or listening—it is between the human soul and God. It is a dynamic interpersonal relationship between Creator and created. It is natural and normal, like breathing. Archbishop Temple said that when we pray, miracles occur. "Couldn't what you call 'miracles' be nothing more than mere coincidence?" a skeptic asked. "Yes, I suppose so," said Temple, "but I have noticed that when I pray coincidences occur in my life, and when I don't pray the coincidences stop." Our lives are not mere incidents or accidents; they are "God-incidences" vitalized by prayer.

Lord, I believe in God-incidences, not co-incidences. I know my life is not accidental or incidental, but important to you and to others. Amen.

> *"When he saw him, he had compassion, and went to him and bound up his wounds."*
>
> LUKE 10:33–34

Someone was recently reflecting on how few Twelfth-Step calls are now being made. "There was a time when someone called in distress and we'd argue over who would go and help. Sometimes two or three of us would make the call." Maybe we just don't hear much about recovering persons going out in the dead of night to "sit up" with a fellow sufferer. But without Twelfth-Step outreach to our anguished brothers and sisters, we all suffer and wither.

Mother Teresa of Calcutta could be our Twelfth-Step partner and inspiration when she said,

Christ has no body now on earth but yours, no hands but yours, no feet but yours; yours are the eyes through which Christ's compassion looks out on the world; yours are the feet with which he is to go about doing good; and yours are the hands with which to bless us now.

Do we love those who have yet to come to our meetings? To our church? Love cannot exist with good feelings that remain in one place. A song in *South Pacific* reminds us: "Love isn't love till you give it away."

Dear compassionate Jesus, get me on my feet and on my way to show my love by giving my time and effort to help others in pain. Amen.

"If any man would come after me, let him deny himself."
MATTHEW 16:24

The gospel gift that is the greatest blessing is that we have been set free from ourselves. Christ has not delivered us merely to love ourselves, but to free us from self-obsession. The cross does not free us *for* the ego trip but *from* it. Our recovery lifts the burden of our own selves.

The great Albert Schweitzer gives us the antidote to pride, this dead-end.

Open your eyes and look for some person, or some work for the sake of humanity, which needs a little time, a little friendliness, a little sympathy, a little toil. See if there is not some place where you may invest your self.

If there was ever a place for self-investment, it is the Twelfth-Step place. Every meeting presents an opportunity to escape from the prison of self and give a little to others. The core of health and recovery is freedom from the prison of the self. Every other person we meet is our potential deliverer and rescuer.

O holy Jesus, draw me out of myself to the freedom of sharing and caring for others. Amen.

"Judge not, that you be not judged."

MATTHEW 7:1

Nonjudgment has been called the art of not criticizing people. It is easy for the wise, difficult for the clever, and impossible for the self-righteous. Criticism is difficult for the wise because wisdom does not indulge in cleverness or self-righteousness. Wisdom refrains from finger-pointing and faultfinding blame. The wise person is too wise to render snap judgments or resort to name calling or to labeling people.

An old fable tells of a Persian king who wanted to discourage his four sons from criticizing others. At his command the eldest son made a journey in winter to see a mango tree. When spring came, the next oldest was sent on the same errand to the tree. In the summer, the third son was sent. The youngest went to the tree in the fall. The king called them all together to describe the mango tree. The first son said it was like a burnt old stump. The second said it was a beautiful, lacy green. The third said its blossoms were as beautiful as the rose. The youngest said its fruit was like a pear. "Each of you is right," the king said, "for each of you saw it in a different season. Remember this lesson: Judge not, for you may not know the whole truth."

This is good advice for recovering Christians. Saint Paul cautions us to not judge even ourselves: "I do not even judge myself. . . . It is the Lord who judges me" (1 Cor. 4:3–4).

Jesus, please keep me from being stupid in my certainty. Deliver me from blame and judgment and keep me open and positive. Amen.

"And I tell you, you are Peter, and on this rock I will build my church."

MATTHEW 16:18

A little city girl was visiting her grandfather's farm for the first time. When she went into the barn, she exclaimed, "Oh, Grandpa, what a funny-looking cow—but where are the horns?" Her patient grandfather explained: "Well, honey, some cows are born without horns, others shed their horns, and some are cut off so they won't hurt others. There are lots of reasons why some cows don't have horns and some do, but the reason this cow doesn't have horns is that she isn't a cow. She's a horse!"

Getting names right is important. Identification is important. We are quick to label and stick the wrong names on others. To put labels on others where they don't belong can be embarrassing and destructive. During a recent census in England, a census taker asked a woman how many children she had. She said, "Well, there is Wilbur and 'Orace and Ethel." He interrupted, "Never mind names; I just want numbers." Then she angrily replied, "They haven't got numbers; every one of them's got names!"

A Christian receives his or her name as a gift, as a special, unique identity. Traditionally we received our names at baptism. Now we get them at birth. As recovering persons our name is primary, and our disease is secondary: "My name's Phil, and I'm an alcoholic." We are persons who happen to be addicted, not "drunks," but persons first and foremost.

Lord of my life, help me claim my own name and uniqueness and resist labeling myself and others. Amen.

"But they all alike began to make excuses."

LUKE 14:18

A woman went to O'Malley's Travel Bureau and asked about a trip. "Madam, perhaps you'd be interested in a safari to Africa," the agent suggested. "Oh, no," she said, "I couldn't stand the smell of the animals." "Well, perhaps a visit to India and the shrines?" he offered. "No," she said, "India is full of disease and Hindus. I couldn't stand that." "Well, how about a trip to the Emerald Isle—to Ireland— it's so beautiful now." He smiled. "No, indeed," she snorted, "I understand that Ireland is cold and damp and full of Catholics." "Well then, madam," the Irish agent replied. "how about going to hell? I understand it's hot, dry, and full of Protestants."

Some of us can remember that we had many excuses for not going to our meeting. Sometimes we hear prejudice about Twelve-Step groups. Every so often we are seen as "those kind of people." Yet the great surprise for most of us is how many wonderful human beings are in recovery. On the whole, any church would be blessed and enriched beyond measure with them. Most of us have met the cream of the human crop at our meetings of fellow sufferers. Why? Maybe we are survivors, or maybe pain has tenderized us.

Dear Christ, help me always look for you among those who are not necessarily of "good reputation" but who are real and honest. Amen.

Every good endowment and every perfect gift is from above.

JAMES 1:17

A great Christian pastor had a friend who lost his little boy to the dread disease cholera. The boy's father said, "Well, Padre, it is the will of God. That's all there is to it. It is the will of God." The minister answered, "Suppose someone came up to your boy and stuck a syringe full of cholera germs into his arms, what would you think of that?" The father answered, "Nobody would do such a damnable thing. If I caught him I would execute him on the spot for murder!" "But my dear friend," the pastor said, "isn't that what you accused God of doing? Didn't you just call God a murderer when you said it was his will? Call your little boy's death the result of mass folly, bad drains and sanitation, carelessness and ignorance—but don't call it the will of God!"

God wills that we have life. God intends for us to be healthy. God works and moves his energy toward salvation. Whatever pain, suffering, and disaster befall us are not God's desire. Whatever hell we have been through up to this point in our recovery, we did not go through that hell because God willed it. An ancient prayer reflects this fact of God's love and care:

O merciful God, and heavenly Father, who hast taught us in the Holy word that thou dost not willingly afflict or grieve the children of men; look with pity, we beseech thee, upon the sorrows of thy servant for whom our prayers are offered.

Our suffering and sorrow are *never* God's doing. Whoever and whatever is to blame for our pain, it is not God.

O Christ, you gave your life and will to the Father. Help me to know that he wills only good for me. Amen.

"You will know them by their fruits."

MATTHEW 7:16

A Christian minister spoke at a Rotary Club meeting. When he finished, he sat down next to a rabbi and asked, "Rabbi, was I too Christian for you today?" He said, "Oh no, the more Christian you are, the better you'll treat the Jews." This is true of most religions. The more we each live up to our religious ideals, the better we'll treat each other.

Compassion, caring, sensitivity, and love for others are what make humanity humane. We can talk to each other forever, but it's how we treat each other that creates true humanity. The way human beings know how to act is best seen in the example of the supreme human: Jesus Christ. His love and caring for the worth of all people is the model for us all. Jesus is what love lived looked like. He can give us that same love.

Our greatest medical problem is not hardening of the arteries but hardening of the heart. When we become defensive, aggressive, and private, we will set our hearts in concrete. When we stop caring and stop crying over other's pain and suffering, we are already encased in cement. Whatever and whoever we seek in our Higher Power, if we don't see love and compassion there, we are gazing at evil, not God. Love is the core of all life. Without it we perish. Without it we can never recover.

O Christ the compassionate, give me the gift of love alone, and then I will possess everything. Amen.

"Come away by yourselves to a lonely place, and rest a while."

MARK 6:31

A man was rushing through an airport crowd and pushed by two men, who called out to him, "What's your hurry?" He slowed up enough to say "Washington, D.C. plane!" only to have them reply pleasantly, "It's all right, mister; we're your pilots." All had a good laugh together.

Our age has been called the age of sprinting, squinting, and shoving. Everyone's in a hurry. Jesus calls us to follow him in action but also to inaction—to "rest a while." God created rest in creation and devoted a holy day to rest and relaxation. In fact, God himself rested on the seventh day and made rest itself holy.

We modern people have trouble resting, relaxing, and seeking serenity in solitude. We tend to soothe ourselves with people, activity, and noise. Yet we are also meant "to be still." Jesus invited his disciples, "'Come away by yourselves to a lonely place, and rest a while.' For many were coming and going, and they had no leisure even to eat" (Mark 6:31). The way we "grab a bite" and eat on the run, it is no wonder we have stomach disorders. We need to listen to the song that says, "Slow down, you move too fast." A little boy who was asked what he liked about his trip answered, "The toll booths; that was the only time the car stopped still long enough to see anything."

Please put my brakes on, Lord, and make me rest and relax for a while each day. Amen.

"By your endurance you will gain your lives."

LUKE 21:19

A father kept bringing work home night after night. When his daughter, a first-grader, asked him why, the father explained that he had so much to do at the office that he couldn't finish all his work there, so he brought it home. "Well, then," she asked, "why don't they put you in a slower group?"

Gandhi said, "There is more to life than increasing its speed." Recovery is a process that cannot be rushed. "Easy does it" reflects an element of recovery that is essential. We cannot force solutions. We cannot strain ourselves or rush ourselves. A hurried and anxious program actually regresses back to control, and overcontrol is the enemy of our progress. Strain and serenity just don't go together.

A woman said to her pastor, "I needed to talk to you yesterday, but when I phoned you were not in your office." The minister replied, "I'm sorry, but yesterday was my day off." The woman retorted, "A day off? You know the devil *never* takes a day off." Smiling the pastor said, "That's perfectly true. But if I didn't take a day off I would be just like him." There is nothing serene about the devil. Contentment, confidence, and an unworried, unhurried approach to life comes from God. Our Christian life in recovery is not a chore but an experience to savor and enjoy. Recovery cannot be stuffed in or gobbled up; it must be slowly digested and enjoyed.

Lord Jesus, please slow my steps and give me patience and trust. Amen.

[Jesus said], "What do you think?"

MATTHEW 17:25

An elderly woman became tired of her old apartment. After much searching she found a new place. While she was preparing to move she thought of the joy and relief she would have in her new apartment. Her mind was already dwelling in her new home, and she didn't notice her annoying old place at all. Just before she was to move, she took a look at her old place and saw its real value and advantages. Somehow the old place looked better. She was seeing her old apartment with a fresh mind. So, she decided to stay. "Why," she exclaimed, "I didn't have to move into a new apartment. All I had to do was move into a new mind!"

Saint Paul describes this transformation from within: "Do not be conformed to this world but be transformed by the renewal of your mind, that you may prove what is the will of God, what is good and acceptable and perfect" (Rom. 12:2).

Most of recovery has to do with "moving into a new mind" of health and wholeness, through the saving power of Christ.

Dearest Jesus, transform and renew my mind, so that I may see you and love you. Amen.

"By this all men will know that you are my disciples, if you have love for one another."

JOHN 13:35

A great philosopher once said, "It is our duty to seek our own perfection and others' happiness, not our own happiness and others' perfection." This has also been called giving love instead of getting love. Getting love has been called "cat love," because a cat does not caress you when it rubs itself against you; it is caressing itself. Self-gratification is not love. Erich Fromm describes love as self-giving:

Love means to commit oneself without guarantee, to give oneself completely in the hope that our love will live in the loved person. Love is an act of faith, and whoever is of little faith is also of little love.

In recovery, freedom from addiction is found in the faith we place in God. The risk of surrender, "to give oneself completely," is the core of a new health and hope. The more we trust, the more we risk and the more we love. The more we love, the more our love bears fruit. There are no guarantees in the risky business of loving others, but it is never wasted. Saint Paul describes a love that "does not insist on its own way; it is not irritable or resentful; it does not rejoice at wrong, . . . bears all things, believes all things, hopes all things, endures all things" (1 Cor. 13:5–7). Such love comes from the risk we take when we "let go and let God."

Dear Lover of my soul, teach me to love deeper, better, and freer. Amen.

"Be of good cheer. I have overcome the world."

JOHN 16:33

In the Middle Ages, devils were thought to be the major cause of misfortune and misery. The specific demons thought to be responsible for depression and despair were called "blue devils." Three hundred years later the American writer, Washington Irving, abbreviated "blue devils" to "the blues." From that time on "the blues" has become a common expression for low moods of discouragement. We frequently say we are in "a blue funk." Very few of us still think we are dealing with devils, however.

Whatever is the actual cause of depression, moods of sadness are a familiar companion to recovering persons. We usually become discouraged when we push too hard, too fast, and too often. We become impatient and forget we have a new program every single day. If we did poorly yesterday, today is always brand-new. We become sad when we expect too much and when we think our progress is too slow.

As recovering Christians, however, we know that recovery is a lifetime journey that never ceases, and that we have all eternity, one day at a time, to receive God's healing. There are no deadlines. We get a fresh start each day. Now that is a guaranteed fact—given us by Christ. He encourages us, "In the world you have tribulation; but be of good cheer, I have overcome the world"—with all its "blue devils."

O Christ, you are familiar with despair, but you triumph over sadness with your joy. Keep me close to you, especially when I have "the blues." Amen.

"Which of you by being anxious can add a cubit to his span of life?"

LUKE 12:25

An inspiration for our slogan "Easy does it" is the late, great Satchel Paige. He explained his lengthy baseball career with six simple rules he lived by:

1. Avoid fried foods which angry up the blood.
2. If your stomach disputes you, pacify it with cool thoughts.
3. Keep the juices flowing by jangling around gently as you move.
4. Go very light on the vices, such as carrying on in society, as the social ramble ain't restful.
5. Avoid running at all times.
6. Don't look back, something might be gaining on you.

We are familiar with his sixth rule and know that death will catch up to us all. Yet his first five rules are worth meditating on and trying on for size. The first five rules have to do with life and how we live it. There is serenity there.

Those of us who are recovering Christians can benefit from such a relaxed life-style. Stress is being blamed nowadays for much sickness. Following Paige's advice would be a good antidote to our strenuous existence. And it sounds a lot like Jesus: "Therefore I tell you, do not be anxious about your life, what you shall eat, nor about your body, what you shall put on" (Luke 12:22).

Lord, help me to walk more gently and with a relaxed step. Amen.

He who believes in the Son has eternal life.

JOHN 3:36

An American airman was shot down over a South Sea island in World War II. He immediately went into hiding, because his information identified the natives as head-hunting cannibals. He became sick and delirious. He was discovered by the islanders, yet he was nursed back to health. Not only was he treated kindly, he learned that there was no jail, no poverty, no divorce, no crime, and practically no disease. The chief said, "There is one doctor, but he spends his time fishing." When asked by the airman how these wonderful conditions had developed after years of savage cannibalism, the chief said, "Your ancestors sent us missionaries. We are Christians. We have taken Christ seriously."

Wouldn't it be wonderful if we could say the same thing? If, after years of addiction, failure, and frustration, we began to take Christ and the Twelve Steps seriously we would all be transformed. We would stop eating ourselves alive or allowing our sickness to cannibalize us—and be healed. When Christ is taken seriously and taken at his word, miracles happen. We are no exception. It all depends on our seriousness. Recovery is not fun and games, it's serious business. It's about survival.

Oh Lord, keep me from playing games with recovery and help me to take you and my health seriously. Amen.

> *Whoever believes in him should not perish but have eternal life.*

JOHN 3:16

A boat was returning from a Caribbean cruise. On deck a boy was playing with a man's dog, throwing a stick on deck for the dog to retrieve. One toss went too far and went over the rail into the sea. The dog jumped overboard after it. In distress the dog's owner begged the captain to turn the ship around and rescue the dog. "Stop the ship for a dog! I can't do that," said the captain. "Then you will stop it for a man!" shouted the dog's owner, as he jumped overboard. Of course the ship stopped, and both man and dog were rescued.

God has done that for us. He has jumped overboard to save us all. We are never too insignificant for his rescue operation. A saying declares, "If you were the only person left on earth, Christ would die for you." Every soul is important to God. A great educator in his appeal for educational funds said, "If all the money expended results in the salvation of one child, it will not be in vain. Exaggerated? Not if it were *my* child."

Each of us belongs to God. We are each his precious child. His loving salvation is for every one of us. No one is left out. Saint Paul tells us: "For as in Adam all die, so also in Christ shall *all* be made alive" (1 Cor. 15:22).

O Christ, keep my faith firmly fixed in you. May my life be all yours forever. Amen.

He destined us in love to be his sons in Jesus Christ, according to the purpose of his will.

EPHESIANS 1:5

A family was taking a trip to a local resort. Their six-year-old daughter was gathered into the car without knowing any of the plans. She asked, "Daddy, when we get where we are going, where will we be?" This is the question of life. Where is our destination? What is our destiny?

A man was shocked to read his own obituary in the local paper. Angrily he called the editor, "I'm calling about the report of my death you published in your paper last Friday." The editor replied, "Yes, sir, and where are you calling from?" Traditionally we head for heaven or hell. Yet that goes beyond our first real stop: death. Death is the destiny for all life. Yet something screams at us, "But we cannot be destined to die! My destination is life!"

Recovery in Christian faith declares that our destiny is not a matter of chance but a matter of choice; it is not a thing to be waited for, it is a thing to be achieved. Our destiny is to walk the Twelve Steps of life. Each step is a choice of life—one day at a time—for in each day's life we find our destination. Our destiny is not to reach a destination that is described in time or space. We are not going to a place, we are called to be with a person. We are invited to be children of God. Our goal is not where we will go, but who we will be.

Where are we going? Wherever God's children go, and that's got to be good.

O Christ, wherever you are I choose to be. That alone is my destiny—my only destination. Heaven is with you, hell without you. Amen.

"I tell you, my friends, do not fear those who kill the body, and after that have no more that they can do."

LUKE 12:4

A psychology professor who had no children would often scold his neighbors for spanking their children. "You should love your kids, not punish them." One day the professor put in a new cement walk. He worked long hours troweling and making it perfect. Just as he was finishing, he saw a little boy making handprints and writing in the cement. He rushed over, grabbed the boy, and started to spank him. A neighbor leaned out the window and shouted, "Watch it, professor! Don't you remember? You must love the child." The psychologist yelled back, "I love him in the abstract but not in the concrete!"

Someone recently said, "Today, in the midst of our superabundance of love-talk, there is a super-absence of love-action." Love is *not* love when it does not act. Love is only love when it is done, not just felt or talked about. Love is an active verb that demands "concrete" expression with deeds of love. Love can be demonstrated without words. The gift of love always is delivered by actual gifts and giving. Love requires "putting your loving where your mouth is." If any action speaks louder than words—it is love.

Recovery is constructed around acts, with deeds and active steps of love for God, neighbor, and self. In fact, recovery is impossible without love.

Dear Lord, you always showed your love in action, all the way to the cross. Help me act on my love for you and others. Amen.

"He who humbles himself will be exalted."

LUKE 18:14

Buddha said, "It is the wise who say always, 'It is Thou, it is Thou, O Lord,' but the ignorant and the deluded say, 'It is I, it is I.'" Recovery is basically escaping the prison of self—the cage of "me." When we wake up out of our ignorance and delusion and learn we are sick and out of control, then wisdom places us in God's hands and care. Many of us have remarked, "I learned that I was like everyone else and decided to join the human race." Too many of us felt somehow that we were superhuman and could defeat our addiction "all by ourselves." Then we realized we are not superstars or heroes—only God could reach us, and he couldn't reach us if we didn't stop being our own gods.

Walt Disney said that being famous "doesn't command the obedience of my daughter. It doesn't even seem to keep fleas off our dogs—and if being a celebrity won't give one an advantage over a couple of fleas, then I guess there can't be much in being famous." Thank God our Twelve Steps knock us off our high horse and remove us from thinking we are celebrities and somehow too exalted to get fleas on us. Saint Paul said not to think too highly of ourselves (Rom. 12:3). Getting better for many of us means getting down off our lofty perch and joining the rest of the "flea-bitten" world.

Jesus, save me from arrogance and pride. Give me your humble spirit. Make me accepting and human. Amen.

"Should we pay them, or should we not?"

MARK 12:15

A guest preacher in a rural church arrived at the church early and went into the sanctuary. He noticed a small box on the wall near the door. He thought it was one of those boxes to receive offerings for the poor, so he put fifty cents into it. At the end of the service, his host took him to the church entrance. He explained that their church was so small and poor that they didn't have any money to pay the preachers. What they did was put the little box by the door to receive contributions. He said, "You've done better than most—there's fifty cents in it today." The minister went home and told his family about this incident. One of his children said, "Daddy, if you had put more in, you would have got more out."

Recovery revolves around the word *invest*. To "in-vest" is to have a vested interest. Investment is involvement. Sometimes we invest or deposit a lot; sometimes very little. A tip is a small donation. A sacrifice is a total offering. When we show the greatest improvement in recovery is usually when we make major investments of time and effort. Tips and small deposits usually bring in small achievements. Recovery is not a gamble or good luck. Recovery is a thoughtful and sacrificial investment in our life and health. The more we put in, the more we take out. We receive *quid pro quo*—something for something.

Lord, you gave all in your sacrifice. Help me to give more and more of myself. Amen.

"And whoever would be first among you must be slave of all."

MARK 10:44

A great saint once said, "If a man were given all the material things of the world, all the cattle, lands, lakes, he would be unhappy unless he could share them with someone he loved." Leland Stanford lost his only child, and although he was the U.S. senator from California, he felt he had lost everything because he was childless. He built a million-dollar home, but it meant nothing. One night he dreamed his son appeared to him and said, "Father, never say you have nothing to live for—live for humanity, live for other people's children." Soon Stanford University was built in Palo Alto, dedicated to the education of children for generations to come. The Stanfords also began devoting their time and money to serving the poor, homeless, orphaned, and sick. A loss was turned into a blessing for thousands.

The Greek word *idiot* originally referred to anyone who used his or her possessions for selfish purposes instead of the common good. Twelve-Step programs are sometimes referred to as "selfish programs." This can be misunderstood. The Twelve Steps are indeed for the "self"—for each and every "self" that deserves healing. Yet it is a program that serves and helps each self by helping and serving all! We are not "idiots" but those who serve the common good. Jesus calls us to our own personal "salvation of self" by our devotion and service to and with others. Recovery is for no *one* person; it is for all. Yet as each one is healed, all are given new bits of health.

Dear Savior, stir me to active service for others. Teach me to give and help. Amen.

"Son, go and work in the vineyard today."

MATTHEW 21:28

A psychologist asked three thousand persons: "What have you to live for?" She was shocked to find that 94 percent were simply enduring the present while they waited for the future. All were waiting for "something" to happen—waiting for children to grow up and leave home, waiting for next year, waiting for a vacation or trip—all waiting for tomorrow without realizing that all anyone ever has is today. Yesterday is gone, and tomorrow never comes.

Recovery is not a waiting room. It is an exercise gymnasium or a factory for productive results that runs around the clock. Our health is accomplished by doing, not waiting. We used to wait, to dream, to wish, and to resolve to do better "tomorrow." Recovery is for today's action, not tomorrow's wishful thinking. The recovering Christian is not one who waits or one who draws back—but one who follows. Today is our arena, and action is our call.

The Twelve Steps are all calls to action. Each is a repetitive goal. Each is done only by doing, not by waiting or hoping. The steps are also signs along our journey. Each keep us headed in the right direction. Not every step can be taken today, but there is always at least one that is there to be our daily step. Some may have to wait—but Steps One through Three can be taken several times each day.

Jesus, you gave me this day. Don't let me wait, but plunge into the present. Amen.

"Think not that I have come to abolish the law and the prophets; I have come not to abolish them but to fulfill them."

MATTHEW 5:17

A well-known comedian told the following story from his childhood. He was in a restaurant just finishing a large, satisfying meal when an old wino came in and ordered twenty-six cents' worth of food. He savored every bit. When it came time to pay the check, he simply said he didn't have the money. The owner hit him with a bottle, cutting his face, and then started to kick him. The comedian said, "Leave him alone! I'll pay the twenty-six cents!" The wino managed to get up, and leaning on the counter, said, "Keep your money, sonny, you don't have to pay. I just did."

The wino paid with his bruises and his blood. So did we. We all paid for every binge, every drink, every obsessive act. We thought we could escape payment, but no one ever escapes. Our codependent loved ones also paid as they rescued us, covered up for us, lied for us, and paid our way, and then *everyone* wound up paying. There is a better payment plan, however.

The Twelve Steps help. Every step is a small installment payment on our debt. Yet as Christians in recovery, as we attempt to pay our own way and cover our debts and make our amends, we know we cannot even come close to settling the score. We know the ultimate payment plan. Our Savior has paid with his life; he submitted to the cuts, lashes, and kicks of his tormentors. Jesus paid for us the way the wino did, with his bruises and his blood. From the cross he gently looks at us in our poverty and says, "You don't have to pay, I just did."

Thank you, Jesus, for fulfilling the law and taking my punishment upon you. Amen.

The mother of Helen Hayes told her daughter, "Achievement is the knowledge that you have studied and worked hard and done the best that is in you. Success is being praised by others, and that's nice too, but not as important. Aim for achievement and forget about success."

Often we describe being in recovery as "working the program" or "working the steps." This description is a blessing, I think. Work is good. Work is normal. Work is necessary. It is good to know that recovery is not easy. Most valuable work is hard. It requires effort and energy and attention to detail. Yet work is so rewarding. In my life's work, the ministry, the work and ministry are enough.

Many times I have felt failure. Yet every time, the sense of failure was because I did not please another. Failing in someone else's eyes soon became a self-judgment as well. I did not gain approval, I did not receive praise. My grades were other-dependent, even co-dependent. Thank God, he delivered from my seeking approval outside of Him. When a priest in Episcopal Church is ordained, one vow is "to be a God-pleaser and not a pleaser of man."

Recovery does not depend on applause or pats on the back. On the contrary, sometimes criticism from others may indicate that we are doing something right! I appreciate Helen Hayes' mother. Achievement is what we know we have done. Success is what others proclaim to us. I am grateful also to my first bishop who said, "God does not ask for your success; he only asks for your faithfulness." If we are faithful, we will have all the success we need. Working the program is up to each of us and a faithful devotion is enough and God will grant the success.

> *"And in praying do not heap up empty phrases as the Gentiles do; for they think that they will be heard for their many words."*
>
> MATTHEW 6:7

Sometimes we just can't help losing. The more we try, the worse it gets. One foot gets in our mouth, soon only to find the other one there as well. A former governor of New York, Al Smith, was making his first inspection of Sing Sing prison and was asked by the warden to speak some uplifting words to the inmates. The governor began, "My fellow citizens." Then he realized that prisoners have forfeited their citizenship. He tried again, "My fellow convicts." But that came out all wrong. Finally, he stammered, "Well, anyhow, I'm glad to see so many of you here." Unless those inmates had a wonderful sense of humor, the governor probably failed to lift their morale.

We have times like that. Things just keep going downhill. Such moments may be more serious than embarrassment. Worse, these moments may become more than momentary; they may seem permanent. When we keep finding ourselves in scary places or deep water, too often we try to get out of our fix all by ourselves. When we need help, we need to yell "HELP!" When we need saving, we need a savior. Such salvation is always at hand—our Twelve Steps and Jesus Christ our Savior. All we have to do is ask.

Prayer is a very special way of asking. Calling our sponsor is another. When we begin to stumble, it's so much easier to regain our balance than to fall and get back up. Our program is like the balancing pole in the hands of a high-wire walker. It works best when we need our balance, not after we have fallen.

My Lord and Savior, keep me alert to my urge to cover up my embarrassment and to try to get unstuck by myself. Teach me to ask for help. Amen.

"For this I was born, and for this I have come into the world, to bear witness to the truth."

JOHN 18:37

An old fable tells the story of a proud lion who was convinced he was the sovereign lord of all he surveyed. He strutted around the jungle asking, "Who is the king of the jungle?" The little mouse answered, "You are, sir," and the donkey said, "You are, sir." So did the monkeys, deer, and hippos. When the lion roared his question to the elephant, the elephant wrapped his trunk around the lion, whirled him about his head, and crashed him into a tree. The lion got up, dizzy and dazed, and wobbled back to the elephant and said, "You don't have to get sore just because you don't know the right answer."

Isn't that just like us? We are sure we are in control. We are certain we are the king of our jungle. We insist on our delusions of grandeur even when we are thrown down and crushed. We rationalize, excuse, deny—even forget—the truth. Finally we "hit bottom" and meet our "moment of truth." Then the reality of our sickness becomes all too obvious. That's when the truth of the First Step shines like a lamp on our path: "We admitted that we were powerless."

Our Lord came "to bear witness to the truth," a truth about you and me. We desperately need a new king, a new sovereign, a new Lord, a new life. Our healing begins in the spirit of this old hymn:

> Redeemer, come! I open wide
> My heart to thee; here, Lord, abide!
> Let me thy inner presence feel:
> Thy grace and love in me reveal.
> So come, my Sovereign; enter in!
> Let new and nobler life begin.

Hold your mirror of truth up to me, Lord. Open my heart to receive your kingship and begin a new and noble life in you. Amen.

Thanks be to God through Jesus Christ our Lord! So then, I of myself serve the law of God with my mind.

ROMANS 7:25

The great American Christian Jonathan Edwards was a man who knew the Third Step. He wrote a prayer that says, in part:

I claim no right to myself—no right to understanding, this will, these affections that are in me; neither do I have any right to this body or its members—no right to this tongue, to these hands, feet, ears, or eyes. I have given myself clear away and not retained anything of my own. To God this morning I have given myself wholly . . I purpose to be absolutely His.

When Florence Nightingale was asked how she managed to be successful, she said, "I have only one explanation. As far as I was able or aware, I have kept nothing back from God." Such total dedication, such glorious consecration to God, is inspiring—but humbling and discouraging to struggling souls just beginning their pilgrimage. Yet we must remember that we surrender "one day at a time"; we take the Third Step daily. We must also remember that whatever we surrender is blessed. We start off with small sacrifices and end up with total surrender. If we give anything up and over to God, we are making progress. An unknown writer said:

> I saw the bundle of faults and fears
> I ought to lay on the shelf;
> I had given a little bit to God,
> But I hadn't given myself.

Giving ourselves is always available, always welcomed, always possible—always our Christ, when we are ready.

Jesus, you always receive my surrender, but don't force it. Thank you for your graciousness. I do surrender, freely and as completely as I can. Amen.

"For which of you, desiring to build a tower, does not first sit down and count the cost, whether he has enough to complete it?"

LUKE 14:28

A story is told of a knight who returned to his castle at evening. He was a mess. His armor was dented, his helmet out of shape, and his face bloody, and his horse was limping. The lord of the castle asked, "What has befallen you, Sir Knight?" The knight answered, "O, sire, I have been laboring in your service, fighting and harassing your enemies to the west." "You've been *what*?" cried the nobleman, "but I don't have any enemies to the west!" "Oh," said the knight. Then he said, "Well, I think you do now."

Jesus reminds us to "sit down and count." In other words, before we act on impulse and dash off in the wrong direction, we'd be wise first to think. Christians have a plan—a plan carefully prepared by God and laid down in the gospel of Jesus Christ. Within this plan God has provided caution signs and warnings to keep us from making errors in our haste.

Recovery also has a plan in the Twelve Steps. The Fourth Step prepares us for the Fifth and *then* for the rest. Christians in recovery are not at the mercy of compulsions and impetuous acts. We have guidelines that "sit us down to count," to add things up and to make lists. We know how easy it is to blunder enthusiastically into the wrong territory, but Christ and Recovery both provide thoughtful and careful directives. The Fourth Step is the first detailed and disciplined move in the right direction.

O Christ, help me to take my Fourth Step carefully, deliberately, and honestly. Help me to put "first things first." Amen.

"Mary has chosen the good portion, which shall not be taken away from her."

LUKE 10:42

A minister once asked a person he was counseling if he had any trouble making decisions, and he answered, "Well, yes and no." The word *intelligence* comes from two words — *inter*, meaning "between," and *legere*, meaning "to choose." An intelligent person is one who has learned to choose between good and evil, truth and falsehood, love and hate, gentleness and cruelty, humility and arrogance, and life and death. A Southern preacher said, "God always votes yes, the devil votes no, and your vote decides the election." A Christian vote is *always* positive.

Recovery demands a clear choice for life. To live one must say yes to recovery and health and no to compulsiveness and disease. We have the power to choose which way we want to go. We cannot recover by wanting recovery — or even by choosing the right road. Yet we *begin* the process of recovery with our desire and our choice. We need a lot more help along the way, but no step among the twelve can be taken without our consent. God calls us; he never compels us. However, once we answer his call and choose his way, he gives us the power and courage we lack. Our entrance into new life is our own responsibility, and then our recovery becomes God's own doing. But the first move is our choice.

Jesus, make my choices positive ones. Increase my intelligence. Amen.

Beloved, let us love one another; for love is of God, and he who loves is born of God and knows God.

1 JOHN 4:7

When early printers, using hand-set type, received an order to print a collection of Alfred Tennyson's poems, they immediately ordered hundreds of extra letters *L* and *V* for their presses. They knew Tennyson. He used the word *love* so often in his poetry that the average set of type could not possibly supply all the necessary letters. The life of recovery requires the same saturation with love.

We look back sometimes in anger and resentment. We nurse old hurts and rejections with thoughts of revenge. Such thoughts are "recovery wreckers." The third movie in the *Star Wars* series was originally called *Revenge of the Jedi*. Prior to its release this title was promoted, but someone saw something wrong. If the Jedi were knights of goodness and peace, they could not be motivated by revenge. George Lucas, the director, agreed. He retitled the film *Return of the Jedi*. Recovery is a return, not revenge. Recovery is resurrection saturated with love. Saint Paul describes it: "If your enemy is hungry, feed him; if he is thirsty, give him drink. . . . Do not be overcome by evil, but overcome evil with good. . . . Owe no one anything, except to love one another. . . . Love does no wrong" (Rom. 12:20–21; 13:8–10).

Jesus, saturate my life with love, and help me live a life with it. Amen.

"God, be merciful to me a sinner!"

LUKE 18:13

A study was made of delinquent boys in prison. They were all asked this question: "Why are you here?" Invariably the answers were like this: "Because the cops tricked me," or "I was picked up by mistake," or "Somebody ratted on me," or "I got caught." One prison official said, "My hardest job is to convince the young delinquent that he has done anything wrong."

For some people guilt and responsibility are nonexistent. When bad things happen in life, something or someone *else* is always blamed. Most of us used to be like that. We had an alibi or excuse for everything. Evading responsibility and avoiding blame became our way of life. We were so sick we could not stand the thought of anything being on our conscience—we denied any shame. Yet we were touched by God. He touched us in our remorse and shamefulness. Until we felt the pangs of our guilt and took responsibility for our actions, we could not face or find health. The road to health is honesty; the way to be cleansed is to admit openly our sin and failure.

When we face ourselves and see our own part in our misery, our burden of guilt can be removed. But we can't lay down a burden we refuse to carry or even see.

Make me honest, Lord. Don't let me blame others for my mistakes. Amen.

"Pray for those who persecute you."

MATTHEW 5:44

The famous evangelist Billy Sunday always made it a practice to pray for specific people in each city he was to preach in. Before going to one city, he wrote his usual letter to the mayor asking for a list of names of those in need of special prayers. The mayor responded by sending him the city directory! Nothing could be truer—we all need prayer.

Why is prayer recommended in the Eleventh Step? Is it for the people we pray for? Is it for us? When we pray, what happens? Usually our mood changes. Our thoughts focus on God. One thing is true for a sincere prayer: it is practically impossible to pray for someone and also hate at the same time. If resentment and ill will rise up in us, we stop praying.

If we approach God in humble petition and in earnest concern for ourselves or others, our prayer is never wasted. We cannot kneel in prayer without benefit to ourselves. George Meredith wrote: "Who rises from prayer a better man, his prayer is answered." It is impossible to pray without being bettered; therefore, all prayer is answered. The prayer itself *is* our answer. Whatever joins us to God is a moment of betterment. That's why the Eleventh Step urges prayer: it's so we will get better. The best cure for all our troubles is prayer. When we pray for others who have hurt us, whom we dislike, envy, or fear, a miracle happens inside us. We begin to love, and then Christ heals us from our resentments and drives out our demons.

Teach me to pray without ceasing, Lord. I need to pray to be healed. Amen.

"I will not leave you desolate; I will come to you."

JOHN 14:18

In his book *Passion*, Kark Olson describes Joe, the drifter:

There was nobody to care whether the drifter lived or died, no one to say in the morning, "Joe, it's time to get up. Take your bath and shave while I'm getting breakfast." There was no one to say, "Joe, your shoes need laces; here's a pair," or to say, "Good-bye, have a good day." Nobody tried to make Joe respectable. He was altogether outside the pale of respectable fellowship. He knew only one world, the world inside the bottle, and he shuffled in search of a drink as fast as his flopping shoes could move him.

The only comfort Joe had was alcohol. We know how that feels, don't we? Would we accept the caring comfort of a loving spouse or parent or friend? We can now. Now that we are breaking the power of our addiction, we can move toward those who love us, awaken us, feed us, encourage us, and wish us a good day.

Recovery in Christ offers us better strength and comfort than the welcome arms of addiction—a new, nonaddictive way to life. The Twelve Steps give us consolation and comfort beyond our expectations. The word *comfort* originally meant "to strengthen," not to make life easy. Christian recovery gives us strengthening comfort in the loving fellowship of fellow sufferers who care whether we live or die. The prophet Isaiah declares, "Comfort, comfort my people, says your God" (Isa. 40:1). No one is a drifter in Christ's sight. We are never "outside the pale." Our Lord is our home. What keeps us from "shuffling in search of his embrace as fast as our flopping shoes can move us"?

Christ, you are my comfort, for you alone are my strength and salvation. Amen.

"He who believes has eternal life."

JOHN 6:47

A fable tells of a scorpion who went up to a turtle about to cross a wide river. The scorpion said, "Mr. Turtle, would you let me ride upon your back across the river?" The turtle said, "Oh, no, you'll sting me, and I'll die." The scorpion denied it and said: "I wouldn't sting you, Mr. Turtle. You are my friend. If I sting you, we would both drown." Mr. Turtle agreed, and he swam into the river with the scorpion on his shell. Halfway across, the scorpion stung the turtle on the head. As they were sinking, the turtle cried out, "You promised! Why did you sting me?" The scorpion answered, "I had to: You see, it's my nature to sting. That's all a scorpion will do."

This is a parable of our pain. How many times did we trust alcohol, food, gambling, some action, or some person and get stung, again and again? Recovery is based on trustworthy people, trustworthy programs, trustworthy steps, and a trustworthy God. We must use our heads and "consider the source." God can help us because it's his nature to help and to heal. He will never betray or sting us. Why trust anyone else?

Teach me to trust only what can be trusted, Lord. Teach me to trust you. Amen.

The apostles said to the Lord, "Increase our faith!"
LUKE 17:5

What does success mean? When does it come? This list may be familiar: Einstein couldn't speak until he was four; Isaac Newton was rated a poor student; Beethoven was called a hopeless magician; Thomas Edison was judged too stupid to learn; Walt Disney was fired for having no imagination; and Winston Churchill failed the sixth grade and was expelled from school. Nevertheless, each of these geniuses woke up and started achieving. They were "late bloomers," but they bloomed. Failure did not defeat them.

Recovery is like the old story of two frogs that fell into a container of cream. Naturally they tried to get out but couldn't make it. One frog gave up trying, sank to the bottom, and died. The other frog thrashed about, keeping his long legs paddling in the cream, and made a great stir. Gradually the frog began to feel solid footing. His legs, whipping like eggbeaters, got traction, and finally he leaped out of the bucket. He had churned the cream to butter.

Success in recovery may not take place right away, but it will come as surely as butter comes from cream—if it is churned. We work "the steps," and by constant repetition and stirring we make it to the top.

Dear Lord, increase my efforts. Keep my energy high. Don't let me stop trying. Amen.

"Do you believe that I am able to do this?"

MATTHEW 9:28

Faith and trust are words that describe a relationship of confidence in God. Martin Luther made an interesting shift in words regarding faith. The usual word for faith in Luther's day was *fides*, which meant belief and agreement with certain propositions. To have *fides* was to believe something was true. Luther substituted *fidicia* for *fides*. *Fidicia* means personal trust. For Luther, trust was the essence of faith — not believing that something is true, but believing in a person. Faith is a relationship that involves an investment of trust. Today many banks are called "trust" companies, "fiduciary affairs" describes our trusted investments in the bank. In the same way, our recovery "banks" on our trust of the program.

If a friend invites you to dinner, you trust that he or she is not going to poison you. This is how the Twelve Steps work. We gain the benefits of recovery by trusting that our meetings, sponsors, and step work all are trusted friends! We receive the healing power of our recovery program if we trust in it and invest ourselves personally in it. It is more important to allow the wisdom of the program to nurture us in trust than to have to be convinced that it makes sense. Sometimes the aid and help our program offers is not always apparent or even sensible. In recovery we are like a child caught in a smoke-filled room on the second floor. Our father on the ground outside shouts, "Jump, and I'll catch you!" We protest and cry, "But I can't see you." Our program answers, "But I can see *you*, and that's all that matters. Jump!"

Lord, to trust in your care is my strength. Thank you for never letting me down. Amen.

"Blessed are those who have not seen and yet believe."
JOHN 20:29

A famous entertainer tells of her visit to a navy hospital during the Second World War. She came upon a sailor who had lost his eyes. She asked, "Is there anything I can do for you?" He replied, "Can you sing?" She answered, "Well, not too well, but what would you like?" He said, "Can you sing 'Smiling Through'?" When she came to the line, "Those two eyes of blue come smiling through," he stopped her. "Tell me," he said, "what shall I say to them when they ask me the color of my eyes? Shall I say they *are* blue or they *were* blue?" She said, "You must say they *were* blue." He said, "Oh well, it doesn't matter. I intend to be a minister, and you don't need eyes to see God."

Only the sight we receive in faith "sees" God. The eyes of belief, trust, and hope have sharp vision, eyes that recognize God in Christ, eyes that see God in recovery and in the Twelve Steps. What we can observe is not just what is on the surface. Deep within life is a reality that is greater than what is plain and apparent. In our recovery we can "see" through the eyes of experience. When people say there is no God they are like a six-year-old saying there is no such thing as falling in love—they just haven't experienced it. Recovery is like that: seeing and knowing God as we experience him.

My eyes are often dim, Lord. Help me see through your eyes. Give me faith to see through. Amen.

"For I was hungry and you gave me food, I was thirsty and you gave me drink, I was a stranger and you welcomed me."

MATTHEW 25:35

Where is God? How do I recognize the divine presence? An old Russian story tells us. A shoemaker dreamed that the Lord was coming to visit him. He washed the dishes, scrubbed the floor, cleaned the shelves, and decorated his little shop until it was spotless and beautiful. He set the table with his best and sat down to wait for his guest. He looked outside and saw a poor barefoot beggar in the cold. He felt sorry for him and called him to eat and warm himself and gave him a pair of shoes. Then he saw an old lady bent over with a heavy load of firewood. He gave her food and helped her carry the load. A child came to his door, lost and afraid. He fed and comforted the child, found its mother, and took it home. Now it was dark. The old shoemaker cried. Had the Lord forgotten to come? Then in the silence a voice he heard:

> Lift up your heart, for I kept my word
> Three times I came to your friendly door;
> Three times my shadow was on your floor,
> I was the beggar with bruised feet;
> I was the woman you gave food to eat;
> I was the child on the homeless street!

An old proverb says, "God often goes about in worn-out shoes." God is present in the needs of humanity. We cannot see God if we ignore each other; the power of our program of recovery is that we share concern for one another. When we help one another recover from our addictions we are in God's presence.

Activate my love and compassion for others, O Christ, so that I may be with you. Amen.

"So you have sorrow now, but I will see you again and your hearts will rejoice, and no one will take your joy from you."

JOHN 16:22

Two ancient sayings remind us of the power of an aching heart. One is an inscription found on sundials: "Without the shadow—nothing." The other is from an unknown author: "The soul would have no rainbow had the eyes no tears." Nothing is more familiar to the recovering Christian than sorrow and grief. The knowledge of repeated failure, of continual mistakes, of past broken promises—all are a heavy load of mournful shame and sorrow. Yet our grief is not to be given permanent stature; our tears are to be cleansing showers, not an endless flood.

Saint Teresa had a comforting bookmark with this inscription to help heal her griefs:

> Let nothing disturb thee;
> Let nothing dismay thee;
> All things pass:
> God never changes.
> Patience attains
> All that it strives for.
> He who has God
> Finds he lacks nothing.
> God alone suffices.

God is the anchor that always holds, the solid foundation that never weakens, the companion who never leaves us. Our Lord, Jesus, knows the agony of the broken heart. He knows our pain, and when we hold his hand, he understands and holds us safe and heals our hurt. His hand is always within reach. All we have to do is grasp it.

Dear Christ, I know your open hand is always stretched out to mine. Help me clasp your open hand. Amen.

And Jesus answered him, "It is written, 'You shall worship the Lord your God, and him only shall you serve.'"

LUKE 4:8

A certain city was planning a citywide evangelism campaign. A committee of ministers was looking over possible guest preachers. The name of the great Billy Graham was offered. A young minister stood up and asked, "Why Billy Graham? Does he have a monopoly on the Holy Spirit?" There was silence. Then an elderly minister spoke up, "No, he does not have a monopoly on the Holy Spirit, but the Holy Spirit has a monopoly on him."

None of us have all, yet some of us may have given all. Our recovery groups are filled with the Spirit of God, yet in each group there are some whose dedication and commitment to the program is complete. Such persons won't claim total knowledge or wisdom or even confidence—yet we can see for ourselves that their consecration to recovery and God is total. They don't have a monopoly on the program, but the program monopolizes them!

True health and recovery lie in allowing ourselves "to be taken over" and so merged into recovery that the Twelve Steps monopolize our lives. When this happens, nothing can compete with recovery. Yet we become as free and as whole as it is possible in life, because God becomes our life.

O Lord, take me over completely and monopolize my life. Amen.

"Every one who is of the truth hears my voice."

JOHN 18:37

For many years a professor started his first class by putting two figures on a blackboard:

$$\frac{4}{2}$$

"What's the solution?" he would ask. A student would say six. Another would say two, but the teacher would ignore them. Finally several would call out eight, and he would shake his head. The professor would then point out, "All of you failed to ask the key question. *What is the problem?* Unless you know what the problem is, you cannot possibly find the answer." Without a plus sign, a minus sign, a multiplication or division sign, the numbers cannot be computed.

Our life in recovery is exactly the same. We need to spend most of our time defining our problems and taking stock of our situation. That's why we make and take our inventories—so we can discover what's going on. Until we know what's happening and what we need to know, we are stymied. Problems are usually more complicated than we realize. Life and recovery are complex. As H. L. Mencken said, "For every human problem there is a solution that is simple, neat, and wrong." We never know all we need to know. Self-discovery is an adventure into an ongoing mystery. God is our problem and our solution, and there is nothing simple and neat with him. But he is always right.

Keep me humble, Lord. Don't let me get too proud and cocky. May I keep on learning. Amen.

"Give to every one who begs from you."

LUKE 6:30

Two of our most basic urges are the urge to get and the urge to give. Very few of us are all getters or all givers. Each drives us at times. Sometimes our need for serenity, food, status, possessions, and security is the strongest. Other times our need to reach out, to share, to assist, to lift up is supreme. The urge to give is the most mysterious, however. It makes sense to "have and hold"; it doesn't seem logical to give up and give over and give way to others. Yet givers recover, and getters get sicker.

When our urge to get is more powerful than our yearning to give, we are imprisoned by our own survival needs. When survival is all we care about, then we will surely perish, because survival is selfish and has no room for other survivors. Yet if others don't survive, we also die. In order to get, we must give! If no one gives, no one gets. Jesus said, "It is more blessed to give than to receive." Which urge will set the tone of our lives? If we cannot give up and let go, then we cannot "let go and let God." We don't *get* well; we are given wellness. We don't achieve health; we receive it. The mystery is we can't have recovery if we don't give up and surrender to it.

Give me your generous spirit, Lord. Make me a "giver" not a "getter." Amen.

"Give us this day our daily bread."

MATTHEW 6:11

It takes 1–3 minutes to have a dream; 45 seconds for the blood to circulate around the body; 2½ hours to play a football game; 4–6 months to make a Swiss cheese; one year to make a piano; 36 hours to read the federal budget; 130 days to grow an artichoke; several years to build a skyscraper; and a lifetime to recover from our addictions! Someone once asked Will Rogers, "If you only had twenty-four hours to live, how would you spend them?" He replied, "One at a time."

Our recovery is not only a lifetime proposition, it is given to us in little "lifetimes" called days. By living "one day at a time" we actually live a lifetime. We only have our lives in days, each day a fresh new opportunity to experience life now. Now is eternity. We can never touch the future or return to the past. Today is forever. Today is a lifetime. Fear and anxiety are always focused on a dreaded future event. Acceptance and serenity focus on what is now before us. We cannot live anywhere or any time but now—so why not relax and enjoy it? We are not convicts "doing time"; we are fine persons "having the times of our lives."

Today is your gift to me again, O Christ. Help me stay in the present tense. Amen.

"Can the wedding guests mourn as long as the bridegroom is with them?"

MATTHEW 9:15

If you had a bank that credited your account each morning with eighty-six thousand dollars, carried no balance over to the next day, allowed you to keep no cash in your account, and every evening canceled whatever was unspent, what would you do? Draw out every cent, of course! We all have such an account, and its name is Time. Each day we get eighty-six thousand seconds. Every night we have no balance left. Nothing carries over. There are no overdrafts. But we get a fresh, new supply every twenty-four hours.

An old grandfather clock had this inscription:

> When, as a child, I laughed and wept,
>   Time crept.
> When, as a youth, I dreamed and talked,
>   Time walked.
> When I became a full-grown man
>   Time ran.
> And later, as I older grew,
>   Time flew.
> Soon I shall find, while traveling on,
>   Time gone.
> Will Christ have saved my soul by then?

This is an interesting message, except for one flaw. At a special moment in history, on a hill outside Jerusalem, Christ already saved our souls. As a child, youth, adult, and aged person, our salvation is already accomplished by Christ once and for all time. His savings account is as full as our new account each day.

Dear Lord of time. Thank you for your generous gift of this day that I must spend and not horde. Amen.

The Lord is my shepherd. I shall not want.

PSALM 23:1

Right after World War II, Europe was flooded with homeless, hungry children. Thousands of insecure and frightened little ones were housed in refugee camps. They were lovingly cared for and adequately housed and fed. However, they could not sleep. They were restless and were never able to relax. A psychologist had an idea. After the children were put to bed, they were each given a slice of bread to hold. If they wanted more to eat, more was provided, but this particular "bedtime bread" was not to be eaten—it was just to hold. This slice of bread produced a miracle. The children went to sleep, subconsciously feeling they would have something to eat tomorrow. That assurance provided calm and restful sleep.

Our God gives such assurance. He places bread in our hands tonight. It will be there tomorrow. What we have to hold on to are the Twelve Steps, the Big Book, the Bible, and Christ himself. We need not worry. We will be taken care of. God will provide. He will take care of tomorrow.

In the Twenty-third Psalm we hear, "The Lord is my shepherd, I shall not want." Other translations say, "The Lord is my shepherd, therefore I shall lack nothing." Our recovery is based upon trusting God, resting in his arms, and knowing we will be nourished and fed. We can rest in peace with bread of trust in our hands.

Dear Lord, may I lie down in trust in tomorrow. Amen.

He makes me lie down in green pastures.

PSALM 23:2a

Most of us have been in the hospital. Perhaps everyone has been sick in bed at home. When we are sick, weak, and exhausted, we lie down. Sometimes we are forced to lie down. Nature has a way of making us rest and recuperate. In the Twenty-third Psalm we are startlingly likened to sheep, and God is the shepherd who makes us lie down. Why? One reason is to rest, of course. But we must also stop grazing in order to digest our food. Sheep will not eat lyng down; neither will they chew their cud standing up. Taking in spiritual nourishment works the same way.

We cannot inwardly digest what we spiritually feed on unless things are allowed to "settle down." Recovery doesn't mix well with an upset stomach or spirit. We all need moments of retreat from the unsettling and hectic world for rest and spiritual absorption. We cannot be uptight and upright all the time. We must heed the call to "be still, and know that I am God" (Ps. 46:10).

Holy Jesus, I thank you that I can lie down and digest your words and gain strength to rise up again and serve you. Amen.

He leads me beside still waters.

PSALM 23:2b

Sheep are terrified of moving, rushing water. One reason is that they are terrible swimmers. They are helpless in the water. Their thick coat of wool absorbs water and drags them down and under. Unless it is still, sheep are afraid of water. Shepherds know this and never attempt to get sheep to drink from a fast-flowing stream. They will even make small dams to trap tranquil pools of water so that their sheep may drink without fear.

We are often the same. Pools of calm water speak to us of peace. Gentle water, clear water, safe and serene water calls us. Raging floods terrify us. One of the most effective scenes that we can picture in our minds to aid our meditations is "still water." A little lake in a peaceful forest, a cool mountain spring bubbling gently from a moss-covered woodland glen, a calm sea with soft, lapping waves—all of these convey serenity, safety, and contentment. When we think of images like these, we can surrender ourselves to God's peace, absorbing the gentle strength and relaxing power of God himself as he comforts and reassures us of his presence.

Thank you, Lord, for the still, quiet peace of your pool of love. Amen.

He restores my soul.

If we watch the sheep in a pasture, we will see them do an interesting thing. Sometime during the day, each sheep, entirely on its own, leaves the flock and trots over to the shepherd, one at a time. The shepherd tenderly caresses the nose and ears, rubs the neck and head, and whispers in its ear. Calmed, encouraged, and reassured, the sheep goes back to graze with the rest.

We also need such daily affirmation and reassurance from God. When our souls are restored, they are revived and stimulated. We need the caress, the rub, the "pep talk" from our shepherd. Unless we hear an "encouraging word" we become fearful and frantic.

Recovery is a place to find assurance and acceptance. Our new life of health doesn't happen automatically. We need the constant and daily support of our group, the continual uplift of our meetings and the encouragement of our fellow members and sponsors. We simply cannot make it alone, and we must have the concrete "pat on the back." We need to know we are safe, that we are doing well and that we can count on the encouragement of our entire "recovering flock." Without this reassurance, we are lost sheep.

Good Shepherd, thank you for your loving words of reassurance and restoration. Amen.

He leads me in paths of righteousness for his name's sake.
PSALM 23:3b

On a plaque at a shrine these words are inscribed: "I come here to find myself. It is so easy to get lost in the world." We truly do need help in this confusing life. Getting lost is a real danger for us. Recovering Christians are well aware of the many times they wandered astray. A real weakness of sheep is their lack of direction. That is, sheep have no homing instinct, no internal radar or guidance system. Horses, cats, and dogs can find their way. Sheep have no rudders or compasses. They also have poor eyesight. No wonder sheep wander.

We are much like weak-eyed, confused, and disoriented sheep. We need guidance and the right path. The right path is the Twelve Steps. When we know that we cannot trust our own sense of direction, we begin to make the right moves. Recovery is not for self-confident, self-contained pioneers. Recovery is for blinded, rudderless sheep—who know their weakness and who do not even attempt to make a move without the sure, guiding hand of the shepherd. We cannot find our own way; we must depend on our program for guidance.

Dear Lord, thank you for your sure steps and secure hand to guide me in my blindness. Amen.

Even though I walk through the valley of the shadow of death, I fear no evil; for thou art with me.

PSALM 23:4a

There have been many "valleys of shadow" for the recovering person. All the shadows are not death. There is loneliness. There is disappointment. There is despair. We walk into shadows in ways. When we experience such dark places, these words buoy us up with courage: "I will fear no evil; for thou art with me." As God's sheep we follow our Lord into many places of danger and gloom— yet if he is with us, we have no fear of evil. His presence is the shield and protection we need to keep evil away.

When we enter any dark and dangerous place, we cannot enter alone without fear. However, when we have the hand of Christ in ours, when we hold the hands of others as well, we can plunge into even the darkest waters. So much of our walk in recovery is unknown. Our progress each day seems so cloudy, extra dark. We don't know what to expect. It takes more courage than we can muster to recover alone. Thank God, we don't have to! In fact, solo recovery is impossible. We walk together. We walk with God. With God and with each other we can walk anywhere, and not even know the outcome in advance—because we are together. When we walk side by side, when we walk in the midst of others, we can relax and trust our Leader, Christ.

Wherever Christ is, we are sure all is well. When we are with him, we are all well. Amen.

Thy rod and thy staff, they comfort me.

PSALM 23:4b

We build roofs to shield us from the weather. We build walls and fences to protect us from intruders. We dig storm cellars to provide safety from tornadoes. We also save money, invest in insurance, and install alarm systems—all for protection. However, as God's sheep, we cannot build or erect anything of our own making. We must rely completely on the Shepherd and on his rod and staff. We have no weapon of our own.

The rod a shepherd carries is really a club, about two or three feet long. This club was what David used to kill a lion and a bear as he protected his flock. The staff a shepherd carries is about eight feet long with a curved crook at the end. It is used to reach sheep who have fallen off a path. The crook reaches around the chest of the sheep and lifts it back to safety. In the same way, God can wield a heavy club to beat off our foes and he can reach down where we have fallen with his long staff and pull us back onto safe ground.

It is great comfort to know God is our protector. He is our body guard and ever-watchful sentry. James Montgomery expresses our confidence in our guardian God:

> God is my salvation, what foe have I to fear?
> In darkness and temptation, my light, my help is near;
> Though hosts encamp around me, firm in the fight I stand,
> What terror can confound me, with God at my right hand?

Praise and thanksgiving to you, O Lord, for your constant care and protection of me. With you as my guard, I am not afraid. Amen.

Thou preparest a table before me in the presence of my enemies.

PSALM 23:5a

It was dangerous for sheep to graze in the pastures of old Palestine. The danger was not just from wild beasts and high cliffs. The pastures grew more than grass. Poisonous plants that were fatal to sheep grew alongside the paths. Some plants had sharp thorns that would puncture the soft noses of the sheep and cause serious infection and sores. Each springtime the shepherd would take his pick and mattock and dig out these plants, pile them up, and burn them. Only by rooting out the enemy plants, could he make the pasture safe for grazing. The shepherd prepared the sheep's table.

As we enter our pastures of recovery, we also walk into dangerous ground—if we don't let our Shepherd prepare our table ahead of time. The first three steps prepared the table for us to take the Fourth and Fifth Steps. When we undertake any aspect of recovery, we rely on work that has already been done beforehand. In the Sixth Step we get ready to have our shortcomings removed. In the Seventh Step we ask God to remove them. We can't ask until we are ready.

Preparation always precedes participation. We cannot blunder into recovery. Recovery is a planned operation that depends on a step-by-step involvement, day by day. We cannot rush things. Our Shepherd is our guide. Our Shepherd is our host. He gets things ready. We wait until he has prepared the way. Our progress in our recovery requires patience and waiting to take the "next step." Our sponsors act as shepherds too. They will let us know when we are ready. They help prepare our table. To trust the program and our sponsors is the beginning of real recovery.

Help me, Lord, to know you are preparing the road ahead for me. Amen.

Thou anointest my head with oil, my cup overflows.

PSALM 23:5b

Recovery is healing. What we seek is "getting well." We are battered, bruised, and bleeding. We need medical attention. We need emergency care, first aid, hospitalization, and convalescence. As we think of ourselves as sheep, we realize that sheep get bruised, cut, and full of briars and thorns. Some days are bitter cold or blazing hot. Grazing, feeding, and enduring the day in the pastures is not always easy. We get hurt. We get tired. We get sick.

At the end of the day, the shepherd would stand at the door of the sheepfold and examine each sheep as it came in from the pasture. If there were any cuts or bruises, he would rub soothing oil on the hurt places. The oil would help heal the hurt. Also, as each sheep came in, the shepherd would dip down into a barrel of clear, cool water and give it a brimful cup of water to drink. He would anoint with oil and give a cup that ran over with water to refresh the tired body.

We can look to Christ in the same way. We get hurt often. We tire out often. Yet we will each get personalized attention. He will give us ointment and soothing medication for our damaged parts. He will give us life-giving water for our dry, parched souls. At the end of every day, our Shepherd is there to tend our wounds and soothe our pain and refresh us.

Lord, I am so grateful you are always there to nurse my wounds and give me water for my thirst at the end of each day. Amen.

Surely goodness and mercy shall follow me all the days of my life.

PSALM 23:6a

Positive experiences produce positive expectations. If we have gone through something that had good results, we look forward to a repeat or a re-run next time. It's only natural to trust our past as we look to the future. When we have a promising tomorrow, we have hope. Hope is the anchor of our life. It is faith in the future.

In the musical *South Pacific*, we hear these words, "I'm stuck like a dope, with a thing called hope, and I can't get it out of my heart." Yet hoping is not foolish. A hopeful person is no dope. Hope is a product of practical, learned experience. It is a healthy plant, not a wild, sickly weed.

Experience is not just the best teacher; it is the only teacher. As we look back at our hardships and tribulations, we can realize that, rather than being tragic and destructive, our difficulties have given us endurance, toughness, and patience. This patience is a direct outcome of experiencing and "going through" our trials. That's where hope comes from. That's where God sheds his love—right where we always need him the most. That's why we have hope. It makes sense. We are not dopes. We are wise and experienced.

Jesus, you always show me the way. You give me experiences to trust. Yo. give me hope. Amen.

And I shall dwell in the house of the Lord for ever.
PSALM 23:6b

In the *Wizard of Oz* Dorothy expresses our common desire when she closes her eyes and repeats, "There's no place like home. There's no place like home." The power of "going home" is enormous. The daily crush and anxiety in the rush-hour traffic heading home is always more intense than it is in the traffic going to work. Work is work. Home is home. Home is better, or should be. Some homes are not real homes. Some places of work feel more like home than where we live with our families. Yet we know that home is where we really should dwell, be at ease, feel relaxed; it is where we belong. We know that even the best job can't take the place of the best home.

Where we belong, where we are taken in, accepted, and included—that place is home. As Christians our true home is heaven with God and all the saints. Jesus assures us that we have a welcome prepared for us in our heavenly home: "Let not your hearts be troubled; believe in God, believe also in me. In my Father's house are many rooms; if it were not so, would I have told you that I go to prepare a place for you? . . . that where I am you may be also" (John 14:1–3).

Dear Lord, I look foward to my home with you. Thank you for opening the door and inviting me in. Amen.

Someone once said, "I'll say this for adversity: people seem to be able to stand it, and that's more than I can say for prosperity." Isn't this so true? I have known people who find prosperity or so-called success too much to bear and manage to mess it up. Yet on the other hand, I have seen so many in our recovery walk who stand all sorts of adversity, before and after entering recovery. I remember the words of Malcolm Muggeridge who said, "Everything I have learned in this world that has truly enhanced and enlightened my experience, has been through affliction and not through happiness."

This has been the experience of many. Suffering has a way of testing as well as toughening some of us. On the contrary, my experience has been that pain has tenderized me more than it has hardened me. My mother had one of these awful hammers with spikes on each end, which she used to beat and tenderize tough meat. In fact, that's exactly what she called that gruesome tool, a "tenderizer." Sometimes I feel I have been pummeled by such a weapon.

Thank God, in my case, the gift of pain has provided a sensitivity to it, not a numbness, nor a toughness. I think of pain with the old term, "passion," as in the "passion of Christ" and with him I have been granted more *compassion* or the capacity to suffer with others. Developing a more caring sensitivity to others in pain is another blessing of recovery in Christ. It was pain that got my attention, not pleasure. I recalled C. S. Lewis's words: "Pain insists upon being attended to. God whispers to us in our pleasures, speaks in our consciences, but shouts in our pains. It is his megaphone to rouse a deaf world."

"Blessed are the poor in spirit, for theirs is the kingdom of heaven."

MATTHEW 5:3

A clothing store advertised a going-out-of-business sale, and it really was closing its doors. The bargains were tremendous. On the morning of the sale hundreds of people were lined up waiting to get in. They watched in disbelief as a man walked past the entire line and started crowding in at the head. He was promptly sent to the rear by angry and impatient shoppers. As he stood at the end of the line, he said, "I'm going to try once more, and if they do that to me again I'm not going to unlock the store!"

The last thing this timid store owner demonstrated was the meaning of "the poor in spirit." What Jesus had in mind was being "poor" in the sense of being impoverished. Those who know they are poverty-stricken without God will inherit his kingdom. Those who do not presume to possess much of God's kingdom, can have it all!

"Letting God" is "letting go" of any idea that we are self-sufficient. Our blessedness depends on our dependency. When we acknowledge that apart from God we are spiritually bankrupt and are empty before him, we can be truly fulfilled—filled full with the riches of God.

It is no shame to "admit we are powerless over our addiction—that our lives had become unmanageable." That is the First Step to faith and to recovery! We are poor, but our Higher Power, whose name is Jesus, has all the riches we ever need.

Lord, please help me to acknowledge my poverty and need for your spiritual "welfare program." Teach me not to be "poor but proud," but "poor in spirit." Amen.

"He who has seen me has seen the Father."

The great Greek philosopher Thales was once asked to describe God. He agreed to try. He went to his home to study, and finally, after weeks of contemplation, he emerged to announce that he could not even begin to describe God. Tertullian, centuries later, referred back to Thales' failure as an example of the world's ignorance of God outside of Christ. Tertullian said, "There is the wisest man in the world, yet he does not know Christ, so he cannot tell you who God is. But even the most ignorant peasant among Christians knows God intimately and is able to make him known to others."

What is God like? Saint Paul exclaims:

O the depth of the riches and wisdom and knowledge of God! How unsearchable are his judgments and how inscrutable his ways! "For who has known the mind of the Lord?" (Rom. 11:33)

Yes, God is mysterious. But the mystery is not total. God is revealed in Christ. To see God, look at Jesus. To understand God's will and way, listen to Jesus. To follow God's plan, obey Jesus. As Christians we have a concrete, open, visible, tangible revelation of God. That display is Jesus our Christ, whose life, teachings, suffering, death, and resurrection all throw a spotlight on God. Our Higher Power is Christ, and Christ shows us the most we can bear to see of God.

O God, to know Jesus is to know you. Keep me close to him. Amen.

"Or if he asks for a fish, will give him a serpent?"
MATTHEW 7:10

Recovery is just another name for God. We become well and begin our life of wholeness entirely at the initiative of God. The action is all God's. He pitches. We catch. He pours. We receive. We are the vessels, the containers that lie open, ready, and receptive to God's filling.

Recovery is also another word for redemption, Christ's salvation. Our victory in our Twelve-Step program is Christ's victory. It is God who wills instead of us. To allow him to fill us so completely and to dominate our lives is fearful, but his life is the only real life in us. If we insist on our life, that life is a phony, a dying, false existence. Only Christ is meant to be our life.

We can rebel against God, but we will be defeated. We can endure life bravely and still find no peace in our courage. Or we can choose the will of God and make his will our own. All our prayers must accept God's will before we know or can even guess what it is. When we give God a free hand beforehand, we live and we will triumph because we have already submitted to his control. By giving up ahead of time we ensure our victory. We can then pray with Thomas à Kempis, who said: "O Lord, thou knowest that which is best for us. Let this or that be done, as thou shalt please. Give what thou wilt, how much thou wilt, and when thou wilt."

Dear God, you are my recovery program. Take me completely over. Amen.

"So you also outwardly appear righteous to men, but within you are full of hypocrisy and iniquity."

MATTHEW 23:28

In a Charlie Brown comic strip, Charlie is asked by Linus, "Charlie Brown, do you want to know what's the trouble with you?" Charlie says, "No." The two stare at each other. Then Linus says, "The trouble with you, Charlie Brown, is that you don't want to know what is the trouble with you."

That's everyone's problem. The threat of honest examination and the thought of admitting our flaws is never welcome. We all resist any criticism, any thought of our imperfection. To admit our "character defects" is to confront the most stubborn resistence we have to recovery. This Fourth Step is the beginning of real change, real healing.

We take the desperate steps of surrender in Steps One, Two and Three. Now we enter a new world of restoration and rebuilding. The Fourth Step focuses us to look at *ourselves* not our disease, at our character not our illness. Such a "fearless moral inventory" is hardly free from fear! It's full of it! Yet as fearful as we are, such a self-examination is the doorway to change and new health—it is the road of repentance, of changing course toward fuller recovery. The pain of examining the exact nature of our wrongs is as intense as our pride. The larger the ego, the tougher and longer the Fourth Step. Yet the greater the pain, the better the outcome and the more certain the victory of God over ego, and the more wonderful the restoration and reunion with God.

Dear Christ, I have so many flaws. I have such a warehouse of past wrongs. Please help me see them and confess every one. Look with me. Amen.

"One thing is needful. Mary has chosen the good portion, which shall not be taken away from her."

LUKE 10:42

God has no police force. He has no way to compel us to walk the road of recovery or to force us to follow the Twelve Steps. God gave us the power and privilege of choice. We are responsible. We are also accountable. The consequences of our choices are ours as well.

In Holman Hunt's famous picture *The Light of the World*, we see Jesus standing at an ivy-covered door that seems to have been closed for a long time. He holds in his hand a lamp. He stands and knocks. He seems to be there permanently, patiently knocking and waiting. As we look closer we see no knob, handle, or latch on the outside of the door. It can be opened only from the inside. The meaning is inescapable. God in Christ waits and knocks—he never stops. But the latch is on the inside. We must open the door ourselves. We must let him in.

This choice has been also pictured as an election. The Lord is always voting for us. The devil is always voting against us. Then *we* vote. Our vote breaks the tie. What attracts us to Christ is that he values us, appreciates us, and affirms us. What should repel us from evil is that Satan puts us down, depreciates and degrades us. How can we vote any way but with Christ? How can we let him stay outside? Our dwelling should be his campaign headquarters.

Lord, I fear my choices, but you make my decision easy. You are the sure winner. Amen.

> *"And about the eleventh hour he went out and found others standing; and he said to them, 'Why do you stand here idle all day?'"*

MATTHEW 20:6

A relationship is like a garden; it needs attention. A friendship lives only by stimulation, touching, and by "staying in touch." More marriages drift apart from neglect than from any specific actions or complaints. Relationships really rust out instead of wear out. Friendships fail when ignored and overlooked. Our Twelve-Step program is such a garden. It will not thrive alone and neglected. Recovery may last a lifetime, but we cannot wait forever to get involved.

In fact, Jesus doesn't offer us any excuses. He won't let us stand aside or be idle. In the story he told about the laborers who were hired to work in his garden, he made no room for neglect. He saw too much work to do! Naturally, he provides times for "resting on our shovels and rakes" but no time for prolonged laziness or unemployment. Christians in recovery are always involved in a "full employment" operation. Isn't that what it means to work the program rather than expect the program to work us? What is even more gratifying is to know that, as Saint Paul believed, "we are fellow workers for God; you are God's field, God's building" (1 Cor. 3:9). That should energize us and get us going!

Dear Christ, save me from the lazy neglect of my program and my relationships. Amen.

"All things are possible to him who believes."

MARK 9:23

Are recovering Christians converted? John Baillie defined conversion "as a personal crisis in which a man, leaving behind him a life of drift or of self-centered indulgence, completely surrenders to the highest he knows." That sounds a lot like "my Higher Power." The "complete surrender" sounds like the Third Step. When Christians surrender to the highest they know, who could that be but Jesus?

Conversion is not only a surrender of self to the "highest one knows," but also a discovery of more than was ever known before. The word *converted* comes from *con* meaning "with" and *verture* meaning "to turn." Conversion is "to turn with." Conversion is therefore a surrender to the highest, and a turning—a change of life. William James describes conversion as a change from a state of conflict and unrest to a condition of peace and happiness. The convert always describes this change as the result of coming into touch with "something more."

Our life in recovery is not a one-time event, measured by membership in a Twelve-Step group. Conversion is a continual and repetitive turning away from the compulsions and indulgences of the ego and a daily "turning with" God in Christ. We are being converted every day. Saint Paul says when we turn to look at Christ, "we all, with unveiled face, beholding the glory of the Lord, are being changed into his likeness from one degree of glory to another" (2 Cor. 3:18).

Change me, Lord, each day from my old self to the new person you want me to be. Amen.

And he told them a parable, to the effect that they ought always to pray and not lose heart.

LUKE 18:1

C. S. Lewis once said, "We can bear to be refused but not ignored. In other words, our faith can survive many refusals if they really are refusals and not mere disregards." God always hears us. God always answers our prayers. His answers are yes or no. When we complain that God does not answer our prayers, we really mean that we cannot tolerate a negative answer. Most of our prayers are selfish requests or misguided petitions that need refusals. God hears us only too well.

As a father may hear his son plead for a rifle and refuse it, knowing the child is too young to be trusted with firearms, so too our Father in heaven in the same wisdom may not give what we ask for. God gives what we need, not what we want. He may give us the very no we need to accept in order to wait until we are ready.

In recovery God is more open to "make me" prayers than "give me" prayers. He is much more interested in making us well than in giving us what we want. We would do much better to ask to be "made over" than "given unto." We need changing, not spoiling. After all, if we pray, the answer is really God's will not ours. He really does know best, and he really does answer.

Dearest Savior, please help me accept your no as the right answer as well as your yes. Amen.

Bear one another's burdens, and so fulfil the law of Christ.
GALATIANS 6:2

A Christian pastor once took in a ragged, hungry boy. He clothed him and fed him supper. After supper he knelt down with the boy and prayed for him. The boy asked, "Did you call God our Father?" The pastor replied, "Yes, my boy, yours and mine." The boy said, "Then we are brothers." The pastor said, "Yes, indeed we are," and gave him money to buy new shoes. A few days later, the shoemaker called the pastor, "I had a strange thing happen the other day. A boy came in and said his brother sent him for a pair of shoes. I asked him who his brother was, and he said you were." The pastor replied, "That's right, and he is your brother too, and if you like, you can also share in the cost of his shoes."

Perhaps nothing is more powerful in our recovery than knowing that God is our Father and that we are all brothers and sisters. Therefore, we are all connected and responsible for each other. Saint Paul thought that this was essential and that "bearing me another's burdens" is a requirement for Christians, "the law of Christ." Christians in recovery must obey the same law of mutual support. We are not regulated by the rule of self-reliance, but by the commandment to really show that we "love one another." If we don't share in the cost of our shoes, we'll all have bare feet and empty hearts.

Lord, help me obey your law of love and inspire me to help shoulder the burdens of my brothers and sisters. Amen.

"And you will be hated by all for my name's sake. But he who endures to the end will be saved."

MARK 13:13

Nothing pays off like perseverance. Leon Uris, who wrote *Exodus* and many other books, was once a Marine, and when he quit the Marines, he became a truck driver. He wanted to share his many exciting experiences, so he wrote a book. Yet he was no writer. He had failed English three times! But night after night, even after a long, hard day's work, he sat up writing. Many times he was exhausted and discouraged, but he kept on until his book was finished. It became a best-seller. He said, "The most important thing a writer needs is the perseverance to apply the seat of his pants to the seat of the chair."

Recovery is impossible without endurance. Not everything is enjoyable. A lot of our recovery in Christ is plain old hard work. Gritting our teeth and clenching our fists can strain our recovery if we *overstress* ourselves. However, *persistent* effort is essential.

Saint Paul tells us that "more than that, we rejoice in our sufferings, knowing that suffering produces endurance, and endurance produces character, and character produces hope" (Rom. 5:3–4).

Patience and perseverance always pay off. Hanging in there may not be fun or easy, but it is always worthwhile.

O Christ, you endured the agony of the cross for me. Help me learn the patience of your love. Amen.

"As for that in the good soil, they are those who, hearing the word, hold it fast in an honest and good heart, and bring forth fruit with patience."

LUKE 8:15

An American tourist was walking through the gardens of an English manor house. During his stroll he met one of the gardeners and asked him, "How do you get your grass lawns to look like this?" The gardener looked at him and said, "Well, sir, you see we just water them and mow them and roll them, and water them and mow them and roll them — and when we have done that for eight hundred years they look like this." The American's eyes grew wide, and he said, "Wow! I'd better get back to New Jersey and start rolling and mowing!"

When we begin our lifetime of recovery, many of us respond with the same impatience and alarm. When we hear, "Easy does it," we try to "Do it now." A few weeks often seem to be eight hundred years to us. Yet as Christians in recovery, we need to hear our Lord's message about the small seed that grows slowly and yet eventually becomes a great tree. True patience is not passive giving in to reality, but an active energy that works down deep into the rich soil of the gospel, fed by the nutrients of the Twelve Steps. Patience in recovery is a capacity for endurance based on confidence in God's good time.

Dear Lord, give me a willingness to work without depending on the quick and easy. Grant me patience with your plans. Amen.

> *"So have no fear of them; for nothing is covered that will not be revealed, or hidden that will not be known."*
>
> MATTHEW 10:26

A woman was seen rushing to catch a bus. She was carrying a heavy suitcase. As she strained to get on board, she was actually running before she finally made it. But she kept on holding the suitcase as the bus drove on. A man gently touched her arm and said: "Lady, you can put the suitcase down now; the bus will carry it for you."

Isn't this a familiar picture? We have a heavy suitcase full of worries and fears and keep clutching it tightly without putting it down. Of course, to be alive is to carry some anxiety. The inspired singer, the stimulated artist, the excited athlete, and the intense student all experience some stress appropriate to the occasion. But we don't have to carry unnecessary burdens.

As Christians we enter recovery with real concerns. We need not take on unrealistic or imaginary worries. We have plenty of reality to be concerned about. Each of the Twelve Steps addresses real life issues—not phantoms or fantasies. Furthermore, recovery is for work more than worry. Robert Frost said, "The reason worry kills more people than work is that more people worry than work." Isn't it a relief, then, that we are urged to "work the program" and not to worry over it? Jesus reminds us to have no fear—even what is unknown or hidden are blessings in disguise. In fact, the good news is that what we have hidden or what we don't know needs to be revealed, so that Christ can work his healing power on what is real. He doesn't work with delusions. Openness and honesty are what his program is all about.

Lord, help me to lay down my burdens, open myself to you. Save me from useless worry, so I can get on with your work. Amen.

When all things are subjected to him, then the Son
himself will also be subjected to him who put all things
under him, that God may be everything to every one.
                                    I CORINTHIANS 15:28

An old traditional hymn goes like this:

> God be in my head,
>   And my understanding;
> God be in my eyes,
>   And in my looking;
> God be in my mouth,
>   And in my speaking;
> God be in my heart,
>   And in my thinking;
> God be in my end,
>   And in my departing.

What would it be like if God was such a totality in our lives?
What would the main benefit be in having God in our
heads, eyes, mouths, hearts, and endings? Perhaps Leo Tol-
stoy has a hint:

> Where there is faith, there is love;
> Where there is love, there is peace;
> Where there is peace, there is God;
> And where there is God, there is no need.

When God is total, when he is so completely in our lives,
"there is no need." Nothing is necessary. Nothing is needful. All is supplied. All is satisfaction. When God is so
much, nothing else is needed. Our appetites are sated. We
are full. There is nothing we lack. Poverty vanishes. God
is all-sufficient. We struggle to describe this spiritual event
as "the priceless gift of serenity." Such contentment comes
to us as God increases his presence in us. As our incom-
pleteness is filled by his spirit, we realize that we have everything. What else could we possibly need?

Dear Christ, you are all I need. Help me desire you as all I ever
want. Amen.

"And you will know the truth, and the truth will make you free."

JOHN 8:32

A fisherman returned from a fishing trip empty-handed. He stopped at the local fish market on the way home. To the dealer he said, "Throw me five of the biggest trout you've got!" "Throw them?" asked the puzzled attendant. "What for?" "So I can tell my wife I caught them," the fisherman said. "I may be a terrible fisherman, but I'm not a liar." Not much. Anyone can see the deception. We use countless ways like the fisherman's to avoid the full truth. Mark Twain said, "Tell the truth. It will confound your enemies and astound your friends." More than that, it will save your soul.

Nothing is more important to recovery than honesty and the whole truth. The nature of our disease is to deny and delude ourselves. We cannot face reality, so we construct a complex web of rationalizations, excuses, alibis, and outright deceptions to hide the plain truth of our illness. Everything in recovery is to bring the full display of truth and honesty to bear on us.

What we fear is not the truth but rejection. We fear the emptiness of abandonment. We are terrified that if we are discovered we will be deserted. Thank God, our Lord does not work that way. He knows and embraces us anyway.

Thank you, Lord, for loving me even though you know the truth about me. Amen.

And Jesus answered them, "Have faith in God."

MARK 11:22

One of our favorite words is security. We speak about national security, office security, and social security. Billions of dollars are spent to try to ensure our safety by building up our weapons of defense. Yet we know that salvation and security are not the same. Being saved and being safe don't always go together.

The Twelve Steps of recovery are not safe, easy, or secure. They are dynamic, exciting, and scary. Recovery does not offer security; it offers life and health. Safety and security are a prison for the fearful. Growth and salvation are a free world open to vast possibilities among countless risks. Addiction offers security and a painless way. Recovery offers the liberation of choice and change and victory.

Our program of recovery in Christ is neither a sedative for nerves nor a flight from fear. We are pilgrims, always vulnerable and unsafe, exposed to every insecurity, yet always alive and alert to real dangers. We face fear not by hiding behind walls of security but by being open and easy targets who absorb and embrace every terror in Christ. Being nailed to a cross is not safe. Being part of a crucified and suffering Lord is not secure — but it is life beyond security. it is triumphant and glorious love. It is resurrection and new life everlasting.

Lord, I know there is no safety and security except the love and trust I have in you. Amen.

"And it shall be that whoever calls on the name of the Lord shall be saved."

ACTS 2:21

A delightful and true story of the power of God's word comes from the streets of New York. A street-corner preacher gave an old man a small pocket New Testament. The old man was tickled to get the little book. He was happy because the thin pages were just the right size for rolling his homemade cigarettes! He smoked his way through Matthew, Mark, Luke, and half of John. When he reached the tenth chapter of John he ran out of tobacco. To pass the time, he began to read. As he read about Christ, the Good Shepherd, he became filled first with shame and then gratitude. He surrendered to Christ. The old man smoked his way right into the kingdom of God.

The "roll your own" salvation of this old man is familiar to many of us. We tried to drink God out of a bottle. We looked for salvation in food. We searched for meaning in obsessive relationships to persons and things. Yet sooner or later, we all had to take a look and see where our God really lives. Deep, deep inside we finally meet the reality of our need for God and God alone. Nothing else will satisfy. No one else will heal. Each of us exerted tons of energy trying to fill our lives with everything else—but God. We now know there is no other. Only God is Savior. Only Christ is Lord.

O Lord and Savior, thank you for your presence and power in my life. Take me again each day into your care. Amen.

But Peter and the apostles answered, "We must obey God rather than men."

ACTS 5:29

In the sixties and seventies a popular quest was "finding yourself." People dropped out of schools, careers, and marriages. The search for the true self beckoned to countless individuals. What is so terribly sad is that when many self-seeking persons *did* find themselves, they were gravely disappointed. They found sinful, guilt-ridden, godless, cynical, selfish lives of despair and defeat. Many searches were successful, but the discoveries were tragic.

Recovery does not depend on finding your self; it depends on losing it. Real self-discovery is in losing ourselves by discovering God. Jesus told us to seek, not to seek ourselves, but God! We don't need more of us, we need more of God. The great composer Joseph Haydn was once asked why his church music was so joyful. He said, "I cannot make it otherwise. I write according to my thoughts. When I think upon God, my heart is so full of joy that notes dance and leap, as it were, from my pen. God seizes my hand and forces the cheerful from me, and I am lost in his rejoicing."

To be lost and completely seized by God is the core of recovery. We don't need to know all about ourselves; we need only be in Christ.

Holy Jesus, I submit myself to you. Take me and control me as you will. Amen.

Moved with pity, he stretched out his hand.

MARK 1:41

A famous surgeon once said, "If I am going to be a good surgeon I must know three subjects—physiology, mental therapy, and religion." He went on to explain that when he enters an operating room, he must remember that he is treating a human soul who needs more comfort than a pill. Fear and anxiety are the main enemies of a successful operation. He declared, "We doctors today need something more in our medical kits than we can buy at our corner pharmacy—we need a grip on God!" This doctor knows God to be love, and that love is the way of healing.

A newspaper reporter once watched a nun cleanse the gangrenous wounds of a soldier. "I wouldn't do that for a million dollars," he said. The nun quietly answered, "Neither would I," and went on mopping and cleaning the wound. Love cannot be bought or sold. Yet love can create life and bring riches beyond measure. What we receive from godly surgeons, nuns, and Twelve-Step friends can never be bought or ever repaid. What we give one another is love and caring that is free, yet so valuable that its cost could never be calculated.

Think and give thanks for our membership in our Twelve-Step fellowships. For whatever reason and by whatever means we managed to begin to follow the way, rejoice and be glad. We have found God's treasure house.

Increase love in my life each day, O Lover of my soul. Amen.

"You are my friends if you do what I command you."
JOHN 15:14

In the legend of Robin Hood there is the familiar story of Robin's first meeting with Little John. The two men were traveling through the woods. They first saw each other at opposite ends of a small footbridge that would hold only one man at a time. Each was too proud to let the other pass first, so they met in the middle. They exchanged words and began to fight. The incident ends with both men falling into the water below. Later, as they swam out to the bank together, they laughed at themselves and became the best of friends. From struggling enemies to embracing friends, these two demonstrate an important part of recovery.

Before our walk in recovery, we were opposed to God. We saw him as a threat to our freedom. We struggled with him, not allowing him to subdue us. Our will and pride would not let him pass. When we did finally fall off our log into the water below, we discovered that we were not subjugated or enslaved by our master but came up on the bank embracing and laughing with our friend. Surrender to God is not defeat but the victory of an eternal friendship. Saint Paul saw natural man as God's enemy without Christ, but in Christ we have now all become reconciled and friends forever (Rom. 5:9). Our struggle with God is worth it; it leads to friendship and freedom.

When I struggle with you, Lord, help me surrender to your love and friendship and let go of my pride. Amen.

Fight the good fight of the faith; take hold of the eternal life to which you were called when you made the good confession in the presence of many witnesses.

I TIMOTHY 6:12

On the Boeing 707 jet aircraft, a line of small blades is placed halfway down the upper wing. These little blades that stick up from the otherwise smooth wings are called "vortex generators." They are put on the plane for the purpose of creating turbulence in the airflow that passes over the wing. The plane designers had discovered that the Boeing 707 would not steer accurately when the air current was too smooth.

For whatever reason, our recovery does not steer accurately when everything is too smooth either. We seem to need a little roughness and turbulence in our program in order to make progress. Many recovering persons experienced their worst relapse and "slip" when everything was going smoothly. If we don't encounter rough seas or difficulties, we get cocky and complacent and can easily get off course and crash. Without struggle and strain we become easy and vulnerable prey to stupid errors. We need to stay alert. Saint Paul says, "We rejoice in our sufferings" (Rom. 5:3), because our problems and rough times produce endurance and toughness that sees reality as a struggle, not an easy, smooth highway.

Keep me off the smooth, easy road, Lord Christ, and keep me struggling with the Twelve Steps. Amen.

"He who finds his life will lose it, and he who loses his life for my sake will find it."

MATTHEW 10:39

In Africa, monkeys are hunted for their meat. An ingenious method is used to trap the animals. Large wooden vases are fastened to trees. Each vase has a single opening, just big enough for the outstretched hand of an adult monkey. Candy is put inside the vases because its smell lures the monkeys to reach inside. But their doubled-up fists are too large to go back through the openings. Rather than "let go" the candy to escape, most monkeys refuse to drop their treasures even when they see the hunters approach. They are trapped by their own foolish greed.

We have been in the same trap. Like greedy monkeys we were sure we could hang on to our addiction and still be free. Even when we saw the trap and the hunters came, we hung on to our habit. When we finally realized we could not have it both ways we "let go and let God." And then we found freedom.

Clearly we are not stupid, foolish monkeys. Obviously, our attraction to our "candy" was strong and even understandable. Even more to the point, we did not realize our plight or recognize our addiction: our minds were clouded. But once we see the trap and know we are caught, we would be monkeys, indeed, if we kept hanging on to our candy.

Jesus, please help me see my greed and help me let go and live. Amen.

"For where your treasure is, there will your heart be also."
MATTHEW 6:21

Jesus talked about money and possessions in at least one third of his parables. He usually concluded that money couldn't buy what really counts. In fact, the most important elements in life have no price tags.

It is interesting that Twelve-Step recovery charges no fee. A person's wealth, possessions, or station in life are irrelevant. There is a cost, however. We must invest ourselves. Our possessions are not important. We are. As Henrik Ibsen said:

Money may buy the husk of things, not the kernel. It brings you food not appetite, medicine not health, acquaintances, not friends, servants but not faithfulness, days of pleasure but not peace or happiness.

Jesus and the Twelve Steps can supply the kernel. Our Lord tells us that we will put our hearts where we place our treasure. He also directed us within to look at the treasures in our hearts and minds. Saint Paul knew that the greatest treasure our hearts could ever hold is the peace of God which passes all understanding, supplied by our knowledge and love of God and of his son Jesus Christ. Nothing can match such a treasure. Saint Paul expressed this wealth with poetic words of rapture: "O the depth of the riches and wisdom and knowledge of God! How unsearchable are his judgments and how inscrutable his ways! . . . For from him and through him and to him are all things. To him be glory for ever. Amen" (Rom. 11:33–36).

Jesus, you had no money and possessions. Please grant me the treasure of your heart. Amen.

Not that I complain of want; for I have learned, in whatever state I am, to be content.

PHILIPPIANS 4:11

Seneca, the first-century statesman and philosopher, gave us words that sound just like Saint Paul:

The great blessings of mankind are within us, and within our reach. Tranquillity is a certain equality of mind which no condition of fortune can either exalt or depress. A wise man is content with his lot, whatever it be, without wishing for what he has not.

Our stores and shopping malls constantly beckon us to "wish for what we have not," trying to stimulate our appetites for more and more. This is just good business and makes sense in a consumer economy.

Yet as Christians in recovery we already have everything that really matters. We have our Lord and Savior Jesus Christ and the program of the Twelve Steps. When we are so blessed, we really need nothing else. Why wish or want any more? Such blessings are like a powerful river that propels us forward. The river is our recovery program; the current is our Lord's serenity. Therefore, we are urged, in Emerson's words, to "place yourself in the middle of the stream of power and wisdom which flows into you and then you will be impelled to truth, to right and a perfect contentment." The wise words of Scripture describe this satisfaction: "There is great gain in godliness with contentment; for we brought nothing into the world, and we cannot take anything out of the world; but if we have food and clothing, with these we shall be content. . . . For the love of money is the root of all evils" (1 Tim. 6:6–10).

Lord Jesus, with you I have everything I need. With the Twelve Steps and your gospel I am content. Amen.

> *"Peace I leave with you; my peace I give to you; not as the world gives do I give to you. Let not your hearts be troubled, neither let them be afraid."*

JOHN 14:27

In our recovery almost everything depends on an attitude of trust. Above all, we must trust the elements that make up the program—especially the Twelve Steps. Trust in God brings confidence, which, in turn, creates hope. Why? We belong to God; he is working in us. As Frances de Sales said:

Do not look foward to the changes and chances of this life in fear, rather look to them with full hope that, as they arise, God, whose you are, will deliver you out of them, . . . Either He will shield you from suffering, or He will give unfailing strength to bear it.

God will either shield us or strengthen us. His hands protect us or empower us. We frequently choose to rely passively on God's protection as if we have no active part to play. We forget that he will strengthen us and give us power to prevail. He loves us and carries us when we are helpless, but he also expects us to help ourselves when we can. So, we can trust him to help us float, but we can also swim on our own with the strength he gives us. Saint Peter gave us these words of strength: "After you have suffered a little while, the God of all grace, who has called you to his eternal glory in Christ, will himself . . . strengthen you. To him be the dominion forever and ever. Amen" (1 Pet. 5:10–11).

Dear Lord, help me depend on your protection and expect to receive your strength. Amen.

> *"When the Spirit of truth comes, he will guide you into all the truth; for he will not speak on his own authority, but whatever he hears he will speak, and he will declare to you the things that are to come."*
>
> JOHN 16:13

One of the most beautiful and inspiring hymns ever written is a constant source of faith. "Lead, Kindly Light" was composed by Cardinal John Henry Newman, and it was the favorite of both Franklin Delano Roosevelt and Mahatma Gandhi. Its words are especially helpful for recovering Christians:

> Lead, kindly light, amid the encircling gloom,
>   Lead thou me on;
> The night is dark, and I am far from home;
>   Lead thou me on.
> Keep thou my feet, I do not ask to see
> The distant scene; one step enough for me.

As we follow the Twelve Steps, our recovery depends on walking one step at a time, one day at a time. Our daily prayer can be, "Lead, kindly light, lead, thou me on, one step enough for me." We don't need to see the "distant scene" or understand the program. All we need is to keep our feet on the path, trust God, and keep making one step, and then another.

He will lead us on. He will show us "things to come." The light Christ sheds on our path is "kindly"—a kind and gentle light that shows us enough and not too much. Such a kind light shines softly without glare and harshness and reveals what we can handle one step at a time.

Lord, in your kindness, lead me. I will follow and walk your path one step at a time. Amen.

And I am sure that he who began a good work in you will bring it to completion at the day of Jesus Christ.

PHILIPPIANS 1:6

Openness to the future is a mark of recovery. Confidence in what lies ahead creates an atmosphere of trust and hope that provides a rich soil for growth. Some of the most beautiful words ever written about the future are from Lyman Abbott:

I neither know nor wish to know what the future life has for me. I would not, if I could, stand at the open window and peer into the unknown beyond. I am sure that He whose mercies are new every morning and fresh every evening, brings into every day of my life a new surprise, and makes in every experience a new disclosure of His love, sweetens gladness with gratitude, and sorrow with comfort.

Whatever lies ahead, when we trust in God, will be good. Whatever comes, we are privileged to be walking with Christ. We are honored and blessed simply to be in step with him, as we walk the Twelve Steps of recovery. An old hymn says:

> I know not where the road will lead
> I follow day by day, or where it ends:
> I only know,
> I walk the King's Highway.

In recovery, we are on that highway, the Camino Real, the King's Highway of health and salvation. As Saint Paul assures us, our Lord not only places us on his road and gives us a "push start," he also keeps us going and actually keeps our motors running.

Jesus, walk with me always. Keep me from straying from your path. Amen.

For as we share abundantly in Christ's sufferings, so through Christ we share abundantly in comfort too.
2 CORINTHIANS 1:5

We are often troubled and frustrated, down and depressed. Those of us in recovery, however, know that our lowest point is often the beginning of life, not the end. We have learned that the lowest ebb is the turn of the tide. We have learned that when all seems against us, just when we thought we could hold out no longer, was the exact point when things started to get better. Grace Noll Crowell gave us these lines:

This too will pass. O heart, say it over and over,
Out of your deepest sorrow, out of your deepest grief,
No hurt can last forever—perhaps tomorrow
Will bring relief.

As certain as stars at night, or dawn after darkness,
Inherent as the lift of the blowing grass,
Whatever your despair or your frustration—
This, too will pass.

We can steer safely through any storm. Every storm blows itself out. All tempests cease. With our trust in God, we may be shaken or stunned by a storm, but like sailors lashed to a mast, we tie ourselves to Christ and come out safely into the sunshine of his calm sea. When we go through each storm, we can sail on the soft breeze of God's love. He always guides us through to a new day.

Lord, as I cling to you in storm or calm, I know you will pilot my ship to your shore. Amen.

He who does not love does not know God; for God is love.
1 JOHN 4:8

So much has been written, said, and sung about love.
We have filled libraries on the subject. Yet we still are shy
on the surface. We all experience some form of love, but
not all of us experience God's love. His love is there for
everyone. Sadly, not everyone knows it. It is the job of recovery to never rest while a single soul is unaware of God's
love. Saint Augustine said, "God loves each one of us as
if there were only one of us." A recent version of this passage from Saint Augustine runs, "If you were the only person left in the world, Christ would die for you." God's love
is beyond understanding.

Knowing that the source of our life and being is love and
loves us gives us life and hope and joy. Above all, he stirs
our own love and devotion to him. When we love God we
feel as if we have no love to give but his love, no life to give
but his life. We feel as if we are nothing, happy to be emp-
tied of self and of ego, content to be lost and swallowed up
in God. When we allow God to love us we are transformed,
converted, recovered. He becomes the fountain of our life,
our all-abounding grace. His love becomes our dwelling
place, our source, our center. There is nothing else.

God, you alone are my life. Your love is my sunshine. Amen.

"Therefore my heart was glad, and my tongue rejoiced; moreover my flesh will dwell in hope."

ACTS 2:26

Abraham Lincoln said, "Most folks are about as happy as they make up their minds to be." Anyone who has taken the time to observe the world's happy ones usually finds some common traits. People who have joy seem to share it and shed sunshine on others. If being happy is something we "make up our minds to be," then it seems we need to help others be happy first. We get as we give. In fact, if we don't give we can't keep. The nature of joy is to share it. As Sarah said in Genesis 21:6, "God has made laughter for me; every one who hears will laugh over me."

An old Christian saying is, "A sad saint is a sorry saint." We might add that a sad saint is a contradiction in terms. Being a Christian means being joyous. These words from the third-century martyr Saint Cyprian describe this well:

It is a bad world, an incredibly bad world. But I have discovered in the midst of it a quiet and holy people who have learned a great secret. They have found a joy which is a thousand times better than any pleasure of our sinful life. They are despised and persecuted, but they care not. They are masters of their souls. They have overcome the world. These people are the Christians—and I am one of them.

We have the same joy. We are Christians in recovery. We know the same secret. We walk his Twelve Steps, steps that help lead us through this "incredibly bad world" with joy. It's no accident that so much laughter is heard at our meetings. Even in our pain we can have "rejoicing hearts" and "glad tongues."

Jesus, keep teaching me your secret of joy, so that I may share it where it's needed most. Amen.

*If we are afflicted, it is for your comfort and salvation;
and if we are comforted, it is for your comfort, which you
experience when you patiently endure the same sufferings
that we suffer.*

2 CORINTHIANS 1:6

What is God like? There is no complete way to answer that question. Yet there are hints. We find them in Scripture, poetry, and song. One such description for our "Higher Power" came from an anonymous Christian in the first century:

God is presence, warm, all-enfolding, touching
   the drab world into brilliance, lifting
the sad heart into song, indescribable, beyond
   understanding,

Yet by a bird's note, a chord of music,
   a light at sunset, a sudden movement of rapt insight,
a touch of love, making the whole universe
   a safe home for the soul.

We have such hints in great beauty, truth, goodness, and love. Yet our best and most brilliant portrayal is Jesus.

To answer our question, What is God like? Like Jesus. Whatever answers we find as we look to Jesus will always supply more than we can ever digest. Whatever answers surface when we look at Christ will never be exhausted. Love, hope, and faith will shower us in joyous abundance. Our personal universe will become a safe home for our souls. We will never need more answer than this: Jesus. Then we will see him in sunsets and sponsors, hear him in music and meetings, and feel him in love and fellowships, for he lives for the believer in his gospel and in recovery. Saint Paul says he shines in our hearts.

Jesus, you are my answer upon answer—always more than I can ever need to know. Amen.

An absent-minded professor was taking a walk when he met another professor. After exchanging greetings and talking a bit, the first professor asked the other, "Bill, in what direction was I heading before we met?" His friend pointed. "That's good," said he, "then I've already had lunch."

We need help at times; even the most brilliant of us. It is so easy to forget the most obvious things in our recovery. So, we need little reminders from our friends. How easy it is to forget the slogan "I am responsible" and start blaming others? It is also common to forget to "Live one day at a time" and rush into the future. I suppose the easiest to forget is to "Let go and Let God" as we struggle to manage our lives without him.

A good example in my life was when I was writing *Letting God.* I had completed half the meditations and reached a road block. I could go no farther. I complained to my wife that I was stuck and all dried up. She slyly asked, "What is the name of your book?" I replied, "You know it's *Letting God.*" She smiled and said, "Why don't you?" Oh, yes! It crashed in on me. I stopped writing the book and let God take over the job. The last half was done in no time. I had forgotten. I stopped going to the real source of inspiration. It was so easy to forget. Thank God, my wife reminded me.

Don't we need reminders in our walk? The Big Book is full of them. The Bible is too. Our friends in Christ and in recovery often jolt us into remembering. I think it is wise to recall that Jesus said, "Do this in remembrance of me" (Luke 22:19).

Therefore it is said, "Awake, O sleeper, and arise from the dead, and Christ shall give you light."

EPHESIANS 5:14

A father knelt down beside his little boy's bed. It was time for the tender tucking-in and the familiar prayer:

> Now I lay me down to sleep;
> I pray the Lord my soul to keep.
> If I should die before I wake,
> I pray the Lord, my soul to take.

However, this night the words got mixed up and the child prayed:

> If I should wake before I die,

then he stopped to apologize: "Oh, Daddy, I got all mixed up." His father responded with some insight: "My dear son, that's the first time that old prayer was prayed right. My deepest desire is that you wake up before you die."

All the power and wisdom in recovery are in the reality of those words. By the grace of God we are all "waking up before our death." We have been guided by our Lord and Savior to a new birth, a dawning of a new day, a new life—before our certain death. We were all living perilously close to the edge of death. Now, praise God, we are awake, awake in time. We have another chance; we have a new chance; we have a new life. Every time we say our prayers, go to a meeting, work a step, get up for a new day, that old prayer is answered in a new way—a new "wake-up call" in Christ.

Thank, you Christ, for all your "wake-up calls" to me. Amen.

> *"But the hour is coming, and now is, when the true worshipers will worship the Father in spirit and truth, for such the Father seeks to worship him."*
>
> JOHN 4:23

A few years ago a major television network ran a series called *Battlestar Galactica*. It was a science fiction story set in the future relating the adventures of a crew of space warriors. Many teens were entranced by the story; however, the ratings were poor. The show was canceled. After the last episode was televised, one young viewer went to his room and wrote a short note that read, "Life without *Battlestar Galactica* is not worth living." Then he committed suicide.

That youngster's religion let him down. His god was false, subject to ratings and at the mercy of cancellation. Any idol or any power worshiped that is less than God is just as false and dangerous. Our gods of success, prestige, money, sports, sex, youth, health all are "cancel prone." Nothing less than God lasts. Our only hope is in a God who does not fail. We have such a god in our Lord and Savior, Jesus Christ. His series goes on forever and is always renewable, fresh, and exciting.

Saint Paul warns us, however, that we can easily be hooked by attractive lesser gods: "Therefore, my beloved, shun the worship of idols. . . . You cannot drink the cup of the Lord and the cup of demons" (1 Cor. 10:14, 21).

You alone, O Christ, are my God and my life. I have only time and effort to bow down and worship you. Amen.

And Mary said, "Behold, I am the handmaid of the Lord, let it be to me according to your word."

LUKE 1:38

A well-known Christian found the secret power of the Third Step without knowing it was part of our Twelve Steps of recovery. Once when in doubt and despair, he had reached the "end of his rope" and sat down and wrote the following:

To the Governing General of the Universe:
Dear Sir:

I hereby resign my self-appointed position as directing superintendent of my own life and of the world. I cannot level all the mountains of injustice, or fill in all the valleys of selfishness. There is too much of it in me. I hereby turn over to you for your disposition and use my life, my money, my time and talents to be at your disposal.

Your obedient servant

Why not write your name after "obedient servant"? When we resign our self-control to God-control, our doubt and despair has no place to go—God is capable of handling things. We are not. Yet when we are connected to God, he works through us to give us strength to cope and triumph. As Jung said: "The individual who is not anchored in God can offer no resistance on his own resources to the physical and moral blandishments of the world." We don't lose by giving up and turning over lives to God; we gain by joining ourselves to him.

Dearest Savior, stop me from the stupidity of trying to save myself and make me surrender to your rescue. Amen.

In this is love, not that we loved God but that he loved us and sent his Son to be the expiation for our sins. Beloved, if God so loved us, we also ought to love one another.

1 JOHN 4:10–11

Those of us who have failed time after time to control our addiction have, as a result of our failures, an image of ourselves as losers. We look at ourselves and are ashamed and disgusted. We are convinced that we are ugly and repulsive to others as well. How can we be worth loving? But when we begin to recover we also discover that our failures and our ugliness are irrelevant to God. We find out what Willie found out.

Willie was a little farm boy. He was the youngest of a poor farm family. In fact, this family was a share-cropping family, who had no more money than they needed for survival. Finally one year they had a few dollars left over and sent away for their first luxury to Sears Roebuck. They ordered a mirror. When the mirror arrived, each family member looked at himself with delight. When it was Willie's turn he didn't know what to do; his face was full of terrible scars. He had been kicked by a horse when a small infant. He was really an ugly sight. Willie turned to his mother and asked: "Mom, did you know I looked this way all the time?" "Yes, of course, I did." "And you still loved me?" "Yes, Willie, I still loved you, and I do love you. Your face doesn't make any difference. I love you because you're mine."

This is the answer we have from God in Christ. No matter how ugly we feel—no matter how ugly we actually are—God loves us because we are his.

Thank you, Lord, that my ugliness doesn't matter and that I'm yours and you love me anyway. Amen.

Submit yourselves therefore to God. Resist the devil and he will flee from you. Draw near to God and he will draw near to you.

JAMES 4:7–8

Someone once asked a man, "Can I possibly be a Christian without fellowship in a church?" His reply was this: "Yes, I suppose it's possible, but it would be like being a student without a school, a soldier without an army, a salesman with no customers, a parent without a family, a football player without a team, an author without readers, or a bee without a hive." We might ask if we can recover from our addictions without going to meetings and get the same answer.

Recovery is like a sculpture the artist works on for a lifetime. A chisel lies beside a block of stone. The Twelve Steps are the chisel; we are the blocks of stone, and God is the sculptor. The Twelve-Step chisels are useless unless placed in the sculptor's skillful hands. But not even God can sculpt us without a hammer and chisel and without our willingness to be chipped and shaped by him. In the same way we can become chisels and sharpeners in his hands. We can be instruments in the molding of others in recovery. We can help each other become works of art and healthy recovery.

Christ, be my sculptor. I am available to your shaping and molding. Amen.

*And when he had given thanks, he broke it, and said,
"This is my body which is for you. Do this in remembrance
of me."*

1 CORINTHIANS 11:24

So much of our lives is based on memory. What we remember and what we forget provide the ingredients of recovery. We tend to remember what we pay attention to. We have a choice of what we focus on. Our life does not depend on drifting and dreaming, but on conscious and deliberate decisions. We can actually choose a great deal of what we remember and forget. In spite of what psychologists call unconscious repression, we can choose to store in our memory banks what we want to keep. A recovering memory makes a conscious attempt to save what is valuable and discard what is trash. That's why we repeat the Twelve Steps and utter the slogans, over and over again. What we hang on to determines who we shall be.

An "unrecovered" memory collects trash, not treasure, hoarding hostility and grasping grudges. Remembering resentments becomes the obsession of the unrecovered mind. Such trash collecting ensures bitterness and is sure sabotage for recovery. On the other hand, the company of the recovering gathers and holds on to the peace, love, and joy of the program. When we choose to harvest and store what's truly valuable and helpful, we are immersed in step meetings, sponsor conferences, and books. Our program treasures won't jump into our memory by themselves!

Thank you, Jesus, for giving me the words to choose and hold in memory's treasure. Amen.

*For neither circumcision counts for anything, nor
uncircumcision, but a new creation.*

GALATIANS 6:15

If we believe we are ugly or evil, we will commit ugly and
evil acts. Most hardened criminals do not see much beauty
or goodness in themselves. A case in point was a twenty-
five-year-old inmate who was described as "particularly
vicious, venomous, and evil." He was also ugly. He had a
scar, inflicted by a razor in a fight, which began on his right
cheek, went across his nose and twisted down across his
lips to his chin. A prison official took an interest in this
young criminal and persuaded him to have plastic surgery
on his face. The operation was successful. In a few years
he was paroled. He settled down, got a job, married, and
has not been in trouble since. Today, statistics prove that
defaced and scarred convicts who receive plastic surgery
are not as likely to return to crime as untreated criminals.
How we look and how we see ourselves does make a
difference.

Tennyson said, "Oh that a man might arise in me, that
the man I am might cease to be." Our sickness or blindness cannot be helped only by increasing light and truth.
More awareness may only increase the harshness of our
self-hatred and shame. What we need is change, surgery,
and transformation. We need a new birth. Recovery through
the Twelve Steps provides such a beauty treatment. We are
remade and reconstructed. Our scars are removed. We
become beautiful inside and out by the grace of God in
Christ.

*O Christ, I thank you for changing my ugliness with your beauty.
Amen.*

> *"Repent therefore, and turn again, that your sins may be blotted out, that times of refreshing may come from the presence of the Lord."*
>
> ACTS 3:19

The great Queen Victoria would occasionally visit some of her most humble subjects. Once she visited the cottage of an elderly Christian widow. Later, the widow's neighbors teased her with, "Who is the most honored guest you've ever entertained, Granny?" She answered, "Her Majesty the Queen, of course!" The neighbors said, "Did you say the Queen? Surely, you are mistaken. Isn't Jesus Christ your most honored guest?" Her answer was strong and sure, "No! Indeed! Jesus is no guest in my house. He lives here!"

The secret of recovery is to know that we don't receive God as a guest. He is a permanent resident. He is head of the house. He is the heart of our home. There is nothing temporary about him; he doesn't come and go. He lives in our lives—to stay. Recovery is God. God is recovery. God is always. God is forever. The feet of God's permanent residence is expressed by this anonymous hymn:

> I find, I walk, I love, but
> O the whole of love is but my
>   answer, Lord to thee.
> For thou were long beforehand
> With my soul. Always thou lovest me.

My thanksgiving, Lord, is great and my gratitude strong, for you are always with me. Amen.

*"All mine are thine, and thine are mine, and I am
glorified in them."*

JOHN 17:10

Our English word *church* comes from the Greek word
kurike. The German *kirche* and Scottish *kirk* also come from
the same word, which means "belonging to the Lord."
Another word for Christian people is *ecclesiastical,* which
also comes from a Greek word *ekklesia.* The French *eglise*
and the Spanish *iglesia* come from this word, which means
"assembly." Christians therefore are an assembly of those
belonging to the Lord.

Are not our Twelve-Step recovery groups the same? We
derive our identity by meeting together. We gather ourselves
into regular assemblies. We devote ourselves to God, our
Higher Power. We give our "lives and wills" over to him.
We willingly join ourselves to God. He owns us.

As long as we continue to assemble and go to meetings
and as long as we remember that we belong to God, we
will keep recovering. However, if we stubbornly decide to
go it alone and quit submitting to God's ownership, we will
falter and fail. We are God's possession. We are God's
assembly. Recovery and Christianity are not solo flights on
independent courses. We are a group called "a fellowship"
that has the stamp of God's own belonging. Rather than
lose our freedom, we gain everything when we join the
assembly of God's own.

*Dear Lord, you called me to belong to you and to gather with my
brothers and sisters. Keep me from straying away alone. Amen.*

God is love, and he who abides in love abides in God, and God abides in him.

1 JOHN 4:16

A sign on a psychiatrist's office wall reads: "Specializing in people who have no idea who they are." Sometimes children have a better idea who they are than adults. A child was playing alone in her backyard. As she played in the sand, a neighbor called over the fence, "Where's your mother, Mary?" "Mom's asleep," came the reply. "Well, where is your little brother?" "He's asleep, too." "Aren't you lonesome, playing all by yourself?" "No," Mary answered, "I like me."

What a wonderful, healthy attitude. A sense of self-esteem and of our personal worth is a powerful ingredient in recovery. Who are we? People who like themselves, that's who. Or at least, we want to.

Where does self-esteem come from? Love of self comes from God. Knowing that we are loved creates self-regard and self-respect. Saint John put it well: "In this is love, not that we loved God but that he loved us and sent his Son to be the expiation for our sins. Beloved, if God so loved us, we also ought to love one another" (1 John 4:10–11).

Holy Jesus, thank you for loving me, for that makes me love myself. Amen.

"Your hearts will rejoice, and no one will take your joy from you."

JOHN 16:22

A sign advertising an old-fashioned square dance said, "Don't come unless you plan to have a good time." What a wonderful invitation to our life of recovery! What an antidote to some sour-faced Christians we have known! Both recovery and Christianity should be fun. Why drag through life?

A great Christian teacher knew joy till the end. As he lay in what appeared to be a coma, his friends wondered if he was dead. Someone said, "Feel his feet. No one ever died with warm feet." The dying man opened one eye and said, "Joan of Arc did." Then he died, with a joke on his lips.

Most happy humans are busy with purposeful and enjoyable work. A well-known writer said, "If you observe a really happy man, you will find him building a boat, writing a symphony, educating his son, growing double dahlias in his garden, or looking for dinosaur eggs in the Gobi Desert. He will have become aware that he is happy in the course of living life fully."

No one has a "course of living" that offers a full life more than we have in recovery and in our Christian faith. In both we are set on a course, on a road with steps that lead to fullness and fulfillment. Not only are we blessed in the Twelve Steps with meaningful and enjoyable experiences, but with joy even in sorrow.

O Lord of joy and hope, keep my spirit joyful, as I keep my mind on you. Amen.

"And I will pray the Father, and he will give you another Counselor, to be with you for ever."

In the "Peanuts" comic strip, Snoopy, dressed in a flannel bathrobe and slippers, shared his great discovery. Looking sick and under the weather, he says, "I think I know why when you wake up at night and your head hurts and your stomach feels funny, the first thing you do is put on your bathrobe, then you drink a glass of water and take some pills and sit by yourself in the dark for a while until you're ready to go back to bed. But it's not the pills that make you feel better. It's the bathrobe."

For Linus, it's the blanket. Both symbolize warmth and comfort and safety. To snuggle into soft, warm fabric is to be calmed and soothed. Most of us have the same kind of feeling in our recovery in Christ. We enter into places of warmth and comfort. We are enveloped by friendly, accepting companions. We are safe, securely surrounded by a fabric of soft love. Dressed in our old familiar bathrobe—we don't even have to "dress up"—we are at home in comfortable slippers.

A church sign once said, "Welcome to All Who Have No Idea What in the World Is Going On." When we wake up sick and scared and confused, it's comforting to know that a meeting or a visit to church has the same soothing effect as our bathrobe. We don't need to know what's going on—we just need a friendly place to be safe.

Blessed Savior, hold me close and safe in your comforting arms when I'm scared and sick. Amen.

For we ourselves were once foolish, disobedient, led astray, slaves to various passions and pleasures, passing our days in malice and envy, hated by men and hating one another; but . . . the goodness and loving kindness of God our Savior appeared.

TITUS 3:3–4

This letter was written by a Dutch patriot just before his execution by a Nazi firing squad:

In a little while at five o'clock it is going to happen, and that is not so terrible . . . on the contrary, it is beautiful to be in God's strength. God has told us that He will not forsake us if only we pray to Him for support. I feel so strongly my nearness to God I am fully prepared to die. . . . I have confessed all my sins to Him and have become very quiet. Therefore do not mourn but trust in God and pray for strength. . . . Give me a firm handshake. God's will be done. . . . Greet everybody for the four of us . . . we are courageous. Be the same. They can only take our bodies. Our souls are in God's hands. . . . May God bless you all. Have no hate. I die without hatred. God rules everything.

Such a picture of total self-surrender is an inspiration to our recovery. The quietness of complete dependence on God, the lack of hatred or fear, the total confidence in the rule of God—all are the stuff of recovery. Our addictions and diseased dependencies were like firing squads. We faced our death sentences in our own sicknesses.

Yet we have gained a reprieve. The sentence is delayed. The execution has not yet been carried out, and the rescuer is no less than God himself. Whatever our circumstance, wherever we might be in our recovery or Christian pilgrimage, our rescuer is always God. The truth remains forever the same truth—Jesus saves. Our life is his. Our salvation belongs to him. No death sentence can overrule his pardon.

Blessed Savior, thank you for rescuing me. You are forever and always my only hope. Amen.

"Why then did you go out? To see a prophet? Yes, I tell you, and more than a prophet."

MATTHEW 11:9

During World War II, a young bride followed her husband to an army camp in the California desert. It wasn't long before she regretted her move. The dust and heat were terrible, and her new husband was too busy to spend much time with his bride. She grew lonely and bored. The only neighbors were native Americans who spoke little English. She wrote her mother that she was coming home. Her mother wrote back these words:

> Two men looked out from prison bars;
> One saw mud, the other saw stars.

The message was clear. The young woman decided to make the most of her situation. She learned the Indian tribal language. She studied the desert plants until she became a national authority on desert flora. She wrote a book about the beauty and wonder of the desert. Her contribution came from her choice "to see stars instead of mud."

We all have the same choice. Someone once said, "The world is a looking glass. Frown at it, and it will in turn look sourly upon you; laugh at it and with it, and it is a jolly, kind companion." This seems so simple, even trite—until we try it out ourselves. It's hard to take the responsibility for our own decision to see the good in the midst of evil.

Holy Jesus, give me your eyes to see with and help me choose to look up as well as within. Amen.

*To lead a life worthy of God, who calls you into his own
kingdom and glory.*

1 THESSALONIANS 2:12

A great Christian woman was asked how she prayed to
God. She said:

I pray as if I were to offer a petition to a monarch, of whose kindness
and wisdom I have the highest opinion. In such a case my language would
be: "I wish you to bestow on me such a favor; but your majesty knows
better than I if it would be agreeable to you or right to grant my desire.
I therefore content myself with humbly presenting my petition, and leave
the result of it entirely to you!"

This spirit is the essence of recovery. One prays expecting
kindness and wisdom from the King. Yet the prayer is
already answered in the privilege of praying. Contentment
comes from the asking itself. We are all like little children
who have a million requests to make to our heavenly Parent. As we clamor for this or that we have no real idea of
what is best for us. Yet we know we can always ask. That
freedom to request, that easy access to petition, is our
greatest favor and honor. We are never turned away in our
questioning, pleading—even crying—to God. If we trust him
we will also say we "leave the result of it entirely to you."
God's results are always good, always best, always right.

*O Christ, you know what is best for me. Thank you for always
hearing my requests and giving me what I need. Amen.*

Fret not yourself; it tends only to evil.

PSALM 37:8

A little boy was giving a friend a tour around his new house. "This is the living room; here is the kitchen; here is my bedroom; and here is the den. Do you have a den in your house?" "No we don't," his playmate replied, "my dad just growls all over the whole house." Maybe we should take note. If we do grumble, fret, and growl, perhaps it would be better to confine our noise to a den.

There is an interesting fact about the word *fret*. Not once in the Old Testament is fretting recommended. The New Testament ignores the word. The psalmist says fretting has evil tendencies. Today, however, we fret, worry, and complain constantly. Talk shows on radio and television prosper on the complaints and grumblings of countless people. A literal translation of the Hebrew for "fret not yourself" is "get not heated." A modern equivalent could be "cool it."

What is unhealthy about "fretting" is not only that it "gets us hot under the collar" but also that it does nothing else! If something is really unacceptable and wrong, something more than "fretting" should be done. That is what separates "zeal" from "fretting." Zeal takes action. A great Quaker expressed this two centuries ago:

I expect to pass through life but once. If therefore, there be any kindness I can show, or any good thing I can do to any fellow being, let me do it now, and not defer or neglect it, as I shall not pass this way again.

Fretting and complaining tends to "defer and neglect" action. As recovering Christians we could benefit by putting our strong feelings into productive action for ourselves and others and letting our "actions speak louder than our fretting."

Lord Jesus, save me from wasted words and constant complaining, and put my energies into our program of recovery and into action. Amen.

*It is the Spirit himself bearing witness with our spirit that
we are children of God.*

ROMANS 8:16

Many tribes in Africa place permanent marks on the
bodies of their members. These marks, usually cuts on the
face and chest, are identification signs. They reveal the
identity of the person and his or her tribe, and are proudly
worn as badges of honor and privilege. To be marked as
a tribal member is to be under that tribe's protection. A
weak tribe would not dare harm an isolated member of a
powerful clan; to do so would risk retaliation and blood
revenge. Similarly the mark of Cain in Genesis 4:15 was
placed on him to protect him.

As recovering Christians we are branded. We are signed
by the sign of the cross and marked as Christ's own forever. We belong to the tribe of Christ and live under his
powerful protection. Saint Paul describes our branding as
our "seal" of Christ's ownership. "But it is God who estab-
lishes us with you in Christ, and has commissioned us; he
has put his seal upon us and given us his Spirit in our hearts
as a guarantee" (2 Cor. 1:21–22).

*Jesus, I am proud and privileged to belong to you and to be marked
forever with your cross. Amen.*

But if we hope for what we do not see, we wait for it with patience.

ROMANS 8:25

Oysters are fascinating shellfish. Once in a while an irritating object, such as a grain of sand, gets under the shell of the oyster and works its way to the soft flesh inside. To relieve the irritation, the oyster secretes a smooth substance that coats the grain of sand. Layer upon layer of this coating is added until at last the bothersome speck becomes a pearl. Pearls, then, are simply victories over irritation.

What is true of a precious pearl can be true for us if we use the same method. We can all produce pearls in recovery. A series of smooth words and actions, a little here and a little there, offered with patience and love, work miracles. It comes in the form of the love and acceptance we always receive from the others in our fellowship. And when we offer our own patience and willingness to wait on God, we become more valuable to ourselves and others.

What could be a better example than the cross of Christ? Once a rough, hard wooden object of torture and death, that cross has become more valuable than any pearl or jeweled crown. Our Lord's cross is his sign of triumph and glory—and ours too. The old, rugged cross is our life and salvation.

Dear Lord, help me use limitations and rough spots as opportunities for your work of salvation in my life. Amen.

But now that you have been set free from sin and have become slaves of God, the return you get is sanctification and its end, eternal life.

ROMANS 6:22

Those of us who care would like to leave this world better than when we entered it. We would like to be remembered as benefactors to this earth. "There is only one way in which we can do this," Henry Van Dyke once said, "and that is by being taken up into the great plan of God. Then the fragments of broken glass glow with an immortal meaning in the design of his grand mosaic. Our work is then established, because it becomes a part of His work."

In our recovery, we seem to be mere fragments, little pieces and scraps without honor or worth. Yet our part may be "just right" and essential in God's grand pattern. If we make ourselves available and place the whole of our lives in his hands, God will use us in ways beyond our dreams. When we are willing to be a part of our recovery, of the Twelve Steps, and of each other's health, God will place us in the best of all possible places as he sees fit and fits us in.

Thank you for making me a part of your great plan, O Lord. I'm happy to be in your hands. Amen.

There is neither Jew nor Greek, there is neither slave nor free, there is neither male nor female; for you are all one in Christ Jesus.

When Napoleon's conqueror, the duke of Wellington, retired from military service, he returned to his hometown, where he attended the local parish church. One Sunday when the sacrament of Holy Communion was celebrated, as was the custom, the people went forward to the altar rail. When his turn came, the duke of Wellington stood up and moved to the center aisle, and just then an old soldier who had served under his command recognized him. He stood up and shouted, "Make way for His Grace, the Duke of Wellington!" The duke said, "No, not here. Here we are all alike."

In our Twelve-Step groups, we are "anonymous," which means that all members are equal; there are no superiors or inferiors. Everyone has equal importance. Our recovery depends on the absence of pride and distinction. We derive such humility from Christ himself. Our Lord had no suggestion of pride—no pride of rank, power, nation, or religion. He had no self-centeredness. He was other-centered. His shining secret and his sublime success was due to his complete dependence on God and his unfailing obedience to his Father's will. Our recovery comes from the same complete dependence on our Higher Power and our willingness to give our life and will over to God. When we surrender ourselves in allegiance to him, we are safely and serenely home at last.

Jesus, teach me to be at home with all persons as I come home to live in you. Amen.

These things I have spoken to you, that my joy may be in you, and that your joy may be full.

JOHN 15:11

A group of people go to an opera. One person uses the performance as an occasion to meet friends. One goes to see a famous performer. Another wants to get out of the house. Another goes under protest. Another goes for a change of pace and to unwind. But one goes simply to enjoy the music. She forgets herself, enters into the spirit of the performance, and falls in love with the music and the story. She alone fully receives the opera. Only she experiences what Jesus says, "that my joy may be in you, and that your joy may be full."

Our recovery in Christ can be the same. We can give ourselves to the program and live it, or we can treat it as incidental. We often hear of "working the program," "understanding the program," "accepting the program," but the real devotees truly "live the program" and "live the steps." Like the lover of opera, when we surrender ourselves to recovery in Christ, we become full of joy—joyful. We forget about side issues; we forget about other reasons or excuses; we forget ourselves. We enter into the spirit of our life in Christ and soak up the joy of being lost in his life and love.

An English newspaper asked once in a poll, Who are the happiest people on earth? The four prize-winning answers were: a craftsman whistling over a job well done; a child building a sand castle; a mother bathing a baby; and a Christian singing a hymn of praise. What seems important in each case is the absorbing enjoyment and pleasure of the activity itself. The act is its own reward. So is recovery in Christ.

Lord, give me no more reason to love you than to love you and be completely wrapped up in your life and in the recovery you give me. Amen.

In the beginning was the Word, and the Word was with God, and the Word was God.

JOHN 1:1

Who is Jesus? What significance does such a person have in our lives? An unknown writer wrote: "He who lives in the spirit of Jesus, becomes a human being."

Jesus has been called "God spelling himself out in language that humans can understand." The incarnation of God in Christ is the concrete demonstration of God "up close and personal" for us all. Jesus is the very image and likeness of God. To know Jesus is to know God. If we are to follow our yearning to know and experience our Higher Power firsthand, our best vantage point is knowing and experiencing Jesus Christ—in Scripture, sacrament, and prayer. Our voices join then with Richard, Bishop of Chichester, in his familiar prayer:

Thanks be to Thee, my Lord Jesus Christ,
For all the benefits which Thou hast given me.
For all the pains and insults which Thou hast borne for me.
O, most merciful Redeemer, Friend, and Brother,
For these three things I pray:
May I know Thee more clearly,
Love Thee more dearly.
And follow Thee more nearly,
Day by day.

Lord, in you, O Christ, I come face to face with God. May I ever seek you and you alone. Amen.

Immediately the father of the child cried out and said, "I believe; help my unbelief!"

MARK 9:24

We all know about "self-fulfilling" prophesies. When we believe something it usually takes place. A teacher was once congratulated for the incredible progress and grades her class was achieving. She replied that this success was no surprise, considering their high IQs, but the numbers the teacher took to be the children's IQs turned out to be the numbers on their storage lockers. She believed her students were exceptionally smart; she treated them that way; and they responded in kind.

Believing in someone, giving encouragement and support, works wonders. When Walt Whitman was just beginning to write, he found many obstacles. He could not find anyone to believe in his work. He was greatly discouraged. He almost gave up after publishing his first book. Then one day he received this letter: "Dear Sir, I am not blind to the worth of your wonderful gift of *Leaves of Grass*. I find it the most extraordinary piece of wit and wisdom that America has yet contributed. I greet you at the beginning of a great career." That letter was signed by the great Ralph Waldo Emerson. From that day Whitman never doubted his own ability, and from that day others began to believe in him, too.

God has the same encouragement for each of us. He believes in us. He cheers us on. He sees us as good and valued children. We can take heart and be encouraged by him. Recovery works the same way. The encouraging words of our friends and sponsors spark our own enthusiasm. In fact our Twelve-Step life becomes more than a recovery program; it becomes the center of our life and a fountain of faith.

Lord, because you believe in me, I can believe in myself. Amen.

> *"It is like a grain of mustard seed, which, when it is sown upon the ground, is the smallest of all the seeds on earth; yet when it is sown it grows up and becomes the greatest of all shrubs."*
>
> MARK 4:31

There was once a great master architect, who, while supervising the construction of a great cathedral, was constantly pestered by an apprentice with one request. The apprentice wanted to design and arrange the glass for just one of the cathedral windows. Even though the architect did not want to squelch his helper's enthusiasm, neither did he want to risk a novice wasting costly materials. Finally the boss allowed his apprentice to try his hand on one very small window, but he would have to provide his own materials. Thrilled with the chance, the helper collected all the bits and pieces of glass that had been cut and discarded, and with these remnants worked out a design of rare beauty. When the cathedral was opened for its dedication, people stood in awe and praise before the one small window designed by the apprentice.

In the eyes of Christ, each one of us can create beauty. We need not gain the applause or admiration of other people. Jesus applauds all who put their bits and pieces of time, effort, love, honesty, optimism, faith, and joy into their own little windows.

The winners we are urged to "stick with" are not always obvious. The winning may not be big, or noticed. The winners in our recovery groups are the ones who walk the program, not just talk the program. The listeners may just be more important than the speakers. The ones who are always at the meetings are winning by simply being there.

Dear Jesus, teach me to pick up whatever remnants I can find and arrange each bit into my recovery program. My life is often in pieces; help me include beautiful people to beautify your program design. Amen.

For all who are led by the Spirit of God are sons of God.
For you did not receive the spirit of slavery.

ROMANS 8:14–15

Waiting to board an airplane, on which he had a reserved seat, Gen. Theodore Roosevelt, Jr., overheard the urgent plea of a private soldier at the ticket counter: "I'm going overseas in three days. I want to see my mom before I go. I can only make the trip on time by plane." The agent sadly told the soldier that every seat was taken. The general stepped up and said, "I'll surrender my seat to him." The general's aide protested, "But this is a matter of rank." "That's right," replied General Roosevelt, "he outranks me. I'm only a general. He is a son!"

When we forget how important we are to God, we lose the high calling of our recovery. We are God's children. We stand as his precious sons and daughters. Nobody outranks us. We have the highest honor in creation. Our Twelve-Step program of recovery is tailor-made for God's valued children. We are not insignificant. We are extremely important —each one of us.

What we are involved in as we travel the road of recovery is the healing of God's family. We are God's princes and princesses, not lowly peasants or serfs. God shares his kingdom with us. We are nobility. All humanity is worthy and valuable. We are so precious that Christ died to save us. We may not feel or see our own value, but Jesus didn't suffer for nothing. Our value is set by God. We should respect what he honors.

How can I be so important to you, Jesus, when I feel so worthless? You must see something in me I can't. Amen.

And like living stones be yourselves built into a spiritual house, to be a holy priesthood, to offer spiritual sacrifices acceptable to God through Jesus Christ.

1 PETER 2:5

A woman traveling in Europe was an antique collector. She came upon a piece of great beauty and value, a Gobelin tapestry. The price was $25,000. She cabled her husband for his opinion and to ask if she could buy it. "No," he replied, "price too high." When she returned from Europe, she proudly displayed the tapestry. When her husband asked why she had disregarded his instructions, she said that she had followed his directions to the letter. She showed him the cable. It read, "NO PRICE TOO HIGH." Our salvation and our recovery was bought at a price—the highest price. Our lives cost God the sacrifice of his only son.

Sacrifice is offering, giving, presenting of love. In our struggle for health and recovery, we sometimes forget how high a price God paid in his son's sacrifice for our salvation. We also forget that that price does not have to be paid again—we are already sold, already purchased, and belong to God. We are his possession. We need only trust that he is exercising his ownership of us. We are his, and therefore we are safe. We also belong to a Twelve-Step group. However, we are not possessed by recovery. It's also the other way around. The Twelve Steps belong to us. We won them, and they own us. Recovery becomes our prized possession as we first give ourselves to it. That's the mystery of the Third Step.

Lord, I know I am yours. I also know you gave me the Twelve Steps. Thank you for being so generous. Amen.

Now to him who is able to keep you from falling and to present you without blemish before the presence of his glory with rejoicing.

JUDE 24

During the construction of the Golden Gate Bridge in San Francisco, no safety harnesses were used by the workers, yet none slipped and fell to their deaths. Why? A large safety net costing over $100,000 was installed. Nineteen men did fall but into the net, and were saved. They called themselves "The Halfway to Hell" club. Something else happened. Because the safety net was in place, 25 percent more work was accomplished. Safety also enhances production!

The great advantage that Christians have in recovery is that they are assured of safety. We have a safety net in Christ. He is with us always, as Deuteronomy 33:27 says: "The eternal God is your dwelling place, and underneath are the everlasting arms."

A dying man was asked what his religious affiliation was. He answered, "I am a Christian." His questioner said, "I mean, what particular persuasion are you part of?" "Persuasion?" said the dying man, looking up to heaven: "I am persuaded that 'neither death, nor life, nor angels, nor principalities, nor things present, nor things to come, nor powers,' shall 'be able to separate us from the love of God in Christ Jesus our Lord'" (Rom. 8:38). When we are persuaded of the same reality, we have a safety net that will never fail us.

Jesus, thank you for always being my safe harbor and rescuer. When I know you are with me, I am unafraid. Amen.

*"Truly, I say to you, today you will be with me in
Paradise."*

LUKE 23:43

There are times when we are burdened and tired. We
feel defeated and deflated. Our strength is gone. We are
desperate. A few years ago a woman went to the Mayo Clinic
for a routine checkup. After the examination, Dr. Charles
Mayo frightened her with this news: "You need an operation at once." The patient was overcome by fear and said,
"But I'll be all alone." Dr. Mayo gently laid his hand on her
shoulder and said, "No you won't; I'll be with you."

This very thing happened to Jesus. In the Garden of
Gethsemane he felt his father's gentle hand on his shoulder assuring him of his presence. We can have the same
reassurance. When we are burdened and down, when we
feel alone and weak, we can anchor our hopes on the
following three truths:

God believes in me; therefore, my situation is never hopeless.

God walks with me; therefore, I am never alone.

God is on my side; therefore, I cannot lose.

In fact, God has a special and secret gift of grace in the
midst of our trouble. Seek him in it. Someone has written:

> We are not here to play, to dream and drift,
> We have work to do and loads to lift,
> Shun not the struggle, face it, 'tis God's gift.

*Help me, Jesus, to believe in your presence with me always and
to face each trial with you at my side. Amen.*

He answered, "Whether he is a sinner, I do not know; one thing I know, that though I was blind, now I see."

JOHN 9:25

In recovery we are told "how it works." The process of sharing what happened, what it was like, and what it's like now helps provide a pattern for growth and awareness. Yet no explanation can really do justice to a mystery. The core remains mysterious and wonderful. An anonymous Christian expresses this wonder well:

> You asked me how I gave my heart to Christ
>   I do not know;
> There came a yearning for Him in my soul
>   So long ago;
> I found earth's flowers would fade and die,
>   I wept for something that would satisfy
> And then, and then, somehow I seemed
>   To dare
> To lift my broken heart to God in prayer
> I do not know, I cannot tell you how;
> I only know He is my Savior now.

The Christian in recovery finds out that "how it works" is not relevant. All the Christian knows is that Christ is the Savior still and will continue to be. Everything else fails; nothing else really works except the unspeakable, unfathomable work of Christ our Lord.

Jesus, you are my Savior, and you alone. Your work and how you work is beyond my understanding. Yet I don't need to know how—only who—and that's you. Amen.

Thanks be to God for his inexpressible gift!
2 CORINTHIANS 9:15

The motto for the recovering Christian is, "It's too late." Why? First of all, there is nothing we can do to save ourselves. Second, God does not require us to do anything to be saved. Third, Jesus Christ has already done it all. Therefore, it's too late for us to try to do a blessed thing. We might as well give up our struggle and our stirring and accept what has already been accomplished. We are not the pioneering trailblazers or the courageous ground breakers of salvation. We are immigrants traveling to a land already prepared and waiting.

So, it is into an already established and secure land of salvation and health that we enter when we begin the Twelve Steps. The victory is won. All we need do is take the gift that is offered. Our only response is thanksgiving and sharing. We are the recipients of a generous welfare program. We are the ones "on relief," dependent on the generosity of God. We can't "work" the program; we can only accept and live within the program's benefits. We are beneficiaries, not creators. It's too late to create. We can only thankfully receive.

To know it's too late for me to do anything, Lord, is a relief when I know you've taken care of everything. Amen.

The last state of that man becomes worse than the first.
LUKE 11:26

Jesus tells a little horror story about demons. The point is clear and vivid. It can apply to us and the dangers in recovery. It was about someone who was healed, cleansed from the power of one demon, and then:

When the unclean spirit has gone out of a man, he passes through waterless places seeking rest; and finding none, he says, 'I will return to my house from which I came.' And when he comes he finds it swept and put in order. Then he goes and brings seven other spirits more evil than himself, and they enter and dwell there; and the last state of that man becomes worse than the first. (Luke 11:24–26)

Recovery is impossible in a vacuum. Our compulsions to eat, drink, take drugs, work, gamble, or do whatever controls us are our demons. They possess us—until through the grace of God our demons are driven out. Where do they go? Are they really gone? Are we safe? We know the answers: they are near, waiting to return; they are never gone. We are only safe when we replace the old space with the ever-new life of God, "one day at a time."

Unless God truly takes over your house and mine, our evil spirit will come back with renewed strength and with more demons to torment us! Those of us who are trying to walk the recovery road can take Jesus' warning to heart. God's grace, like nature, abhors a vacuum. Our fellowship, the steps, our program of recovery, as well as our Christian faith, church communities and activities are "demon replacements." When our life is full of loving persons and healing programs that maintain fellowship with God in Christ, no demon, old or new, can find room to dwell.

To you, O Christ, I open my house. Enter in and bring your friends with you. Keep me filled with goodness, kindness, and love. Help me keep my demons outside by filling my inside with you. Amen.

PERFECTIONISM

King Oscar II of Sweden visited a village school one day, and he asked the pupils to tell him who the greatest kings of Sweden were. The answers were in unison: "The great King Gustavus Adolphus." The teacher whispered to a little boy, "and King Oscar," which he repeated out loud. "Is that right?" answered the King. "And what has he done that is so great?" The confused little boy softly stuttered, "I don't know." "Well, I don't have any idea either," laughed the King.

Humility is such a delightful and appealing virtue. We could use so much more of it. Where does it come from? Are we born with it? Perhaps. Yet for many, including myself, any humility I have came from God and hard knocks. Admitting to ourselves that we are inadequate, imperfect, and fallible human beings is so difficult. The doorway to such humility is *shame.*

I have come to appreciate shame. Not shamefulness. Just plain and simple shame. To me to have appropriate shame is to be honest, human, and transparently open. Living with a sense of modesty and claiming no superiority over our fellow humans is what I think is appropriate shame. Shamefulness, however, says that we are worthless, junk, disgusting, failures, rejects, and so on. Plain old shame says, I know I am not perfect and have so much farther to go, and God is not finished with me yet. Honesty compels us to be unassuming and unpretentious. Such modesty also is able to claim our value and worth as God-given, as well as our healthy shame. God did not create us as Angels or perfect beings, but rough-cut beings, who are in process, on a journey to God. We are incomplete and insufficient, seeking God's completion and sufficiency. There is no sense in pretending we are more than we are. Perfectionism is a pretentious disease that seems to go along with most addictions. Being delivered from "being perfect" as well as "being trash" is recovery.

Therefore, since we are justified by faith, we have peace with God through our Lord Jesus Christ.

ROMANS 5:1

A famous doctor, who was known for his kindness, met a dirty, ragged boy on the street. The boy boldly asked to be taken into the doctor's own home. The doctor said, "I know nothing about you, my boy. What have you to recommend yourself?" The little fellow pointed to his ragged clothes and said, "I thought these would be enough." The doctor gathered him into his arms and took him home.

Everything Jesus taught about our Father offers the same hope. We have nothing but our hunger, our weakness, and our tattered rags to recommend us, but that's enough. We are closest to God's compassion when we are weakest and most vulnerable. We can't claim anything for ourselves. No goodness, no intelligence, no beauty, no great work in any way can "recommend" us to God. Only our desperate need for help provides our "letter of recommendation." It is our pain and our need that impresses God. When we ask, he gathers us up in his arms and takes us home.

As we present our powerlessness and unmanageable lives to God, we get his attention. Jesus came for the sick and suffering, for the least and the lost. He came for us. He still comes for us and to us—in our weakness and need, not in our strength and self-sufficiency.

When I am in rags and my life is tattered and torn, Lord, please take me in. Amen.

Therefore, my beloved, shun the worship of idols.
1 CORINTHIANS 10:14

A well-known saying among preachers is, Every heart has in it a God-shaped vacuum. The obvious point is that we cannot be complete or full unless God lives in our hearts. Without God within our being we are empty and incomplete. Anthropological studies clearly demonstrate this need in all cultures to fill human life with "divine" beings. There is an instinct in us that yearns for God. Many tribal peoples create idols and totems that become religious responses to this yearning. They develop rituals and ceremonies to fill the vacuum.

Most of us know that we tried to fill our vacuum with drinking, eating, gambling, or some other action, or with some person. These became our idols. Yet the yearning for completeness and fulfillment is normal. Our urgent craving for relief and comfort was human and natural. The only mistake we made was the choice of our god. Our appetite was good. Our diet was wrong.

God is the only diet that will satisfy the vacuum shaped for him. Our recovery is a process of "replacement," replacing our old gods that enslaved us and addicted us with God who will face us and fill us with himself.

O God, come as Christ Jesus, the only true shape and substance that will satisfy. Come and live in my heart. Amen.

November 3

"But I say to you that hear, Love your enemies, do good to those who hate you."

LUKE 6:27

A Chinese proverb says, "The fire you kindle for your enemy often burns yourself more than him." A little five-year-old was being punished by being made to sit in his mother's closet. Strange sounds came from inside, then all was silent. The mother opened the closet and saw her son sitting in the middle of her clothes with a scowl. "Billy, what are you doing?" she asked. "I pulled all your clothes down; I spit all over them, I spit all over your shoes, and now I'm just sitting here waiting for more spit."

In real life spite and spit never really run dry. We all seem to have an endless supply of resentment. Our storehouse of blame is never really exhausted. Yet our hateful grudges stand directly in the way of our recovery. How can we win the war over our resentment? By taking the Third Step. When we give our life and will to God, we give him our bitterness—all our spit and spite. We don't need to get even or avenge ourselves. All such even-getting justice is in God's hands—he says "Vengeance is mine says the Lord. I will repay." (Romans 12:19)

Save me from the resentments of "other blame," Lord. Save me from bitterness. Amen.

And from his fulness have we all received, grace upon grace.

JOHN 1:16

A mother and her young daughter were making noodles, but somehow they had messed up the recipe. Reviewing the instructions, they discovered that the little girl had used sugar instead of salt. With a few substitutions and a lot of skill, the mother accomplished a miraculous feat—she made a sponge cake out of the ingredients!

God works like an experienced chef. He takes what seems to be a disaster and creates something better. Very few people appreciate this miracle of God's renewal as well as we do. Out of our addictions and compulsions we ran into disaster after disaster—until we gave all our wreckage over to God. Placed into his experienced and loving hands, our ingredients are combined to create our new lives of health and recovery. We are turning out much better than we ever dreamed!

The grace of God never runs out. His gift of salvation can turn any sour project, mistake, or failure into his victory. What is most wonderful is that he uses what we have "botched up" for the ingredients! He doesn't require us to introduce or import new stuff. He takes us the way we are—and then creates a miracle recipe that only his love and skill could accomplish. And he keeps on doing his culinary miracles as long as we stay in his kitchen.

Dear Christ, create in me your recipes. Use my mistakes and successes and combine them all for your outcome. Amen.

The grace of the Lord Jesus be with you.

1 CORINTHIANS 16:23

A legend tells of a poor woman who wanted a bunch of grapes from the king's garden for her sick child. She saved what money she could and tried to buy the grapes from the king's gardener, but was refused. She got more money. The gardener still said no. The king's daughter witnessed the second refusal and went to the poor woman and said, "Dear lady, you are mistaken in your attempts. My father is not a merchant, but a king. His business is not to sell, but to give." She then plucked the grapes from the vine and gently dropped them into the woman's apron.

Our life in Christ is the same, so is our walk in recovery. We can't buy our health and salvation. Our king does not sell, he gives. We are not shoppers. We can't purchase any aspect of our health. We live in "grace," which is just another word for "gift." The Twelve Steps are gifts; they are also grace and are therefore free, without any price tag at all. All our recovery costs is our willingness to ask for what we want. Jesus told us to "ask, seek, and knock" and we will receive. The fruit of recovery is available, in season, ripe, delicious, nutritious and always free. What's so hard to believe is that God is so generous. But he is.

Your generosity, Jesus, is hard to understand but wonderful to accept. Thank you for all your gifts to me. Amen.

"It is finished."

JOHN 19:30

A youngster did quite well making money mowing lawns for his neighbors after school. One afternoon his mother noticed he was taking his own sweet time getting started. When she asked why he was so slow, he said, "I'm waiting for them to start themselves. I'll wait awhile. Then I'll take over. I get most of my work from people who are halfway through."

In a sense, at least half of our recovery is "unfinished business." Getting well is never fully completed. Naturally, we like to finish all our tasks in one effort, or "one mowing." We also like to think we can do it all by ourselves. Recovery is doing and redoing, one day at a time, one job at a time. It never seems to end. Yet there is always someone there to help—and like the grass-cutting youngster, even take over for us and help us out. As we travel the road of recovery and salvation, we become aware that we are not only in motion most of the time, but we are traveling together with our friends. We are on a lifelong pilgrimage together. It may never seem to end, but we are also never alone and without helping companions.

Of course, we all need to rest. We have to take a breather now and then, at least every 24 hours. Each night's rest provides the energy and strength to begin each new day— one at a time, bit by bit, step by step. But as we "walk and cut," we need always remember we are pioneers, not settlers. We are workers and walkers. There are always new challenges. There are always road hazards and weeds. Yet at the end of each day we can say with Jesus, "It is finished."

One day done, Lord. Another on the way. With a little help from my friends it will get done too. Lord, keep me walking one day at a time. Amen.

*For now we see in a mirror dimly, but then face to face.
Now I know in part; then I shall understand fully, even as
I have been fully understood.*

1 CORINTHIANS 13:12

More often than we would like we are puzzled and per-
plexed by our troubles. So much of our difficulty seems
senseless. When our troubles don't make any sense, we can
remember these words:

Not till the loom is silent
And the shuttles cease to fly,
Shall God unroll the canvas
And explain the reason why.

When everything seems futile and senseless, we see from
our perspective, not God's. We can see only confusion. God
sees purpose and plan; he is in control and directing the
action. We can eliminate more confusion by relaxing and
trusting his supervision. He knows where he's going, and
he knows where he's going with us.

A woman experienced a sudden and apparently senseless tragedy. She was so crushed that she said in her sorrow, "I wish I'd never been made." Her friend said, "My
dear, you are not yet made. You're only being made. God
is not finished with you yet." We are all on God's loom. He
is weaving us. The rough and dark threads combine with
the smooth and light ones to produce what he has in mind.

*Thank you for all the threads of life, Lord. Weave them together
in my life as you will. Amen.*

*And he was in the wilderness forty days, tempted by
Satan; and he was with the wild beasts; and the angels
ministered to him.*

MARK 1:13

Temptation is not sin. It is an invitation to sin, an adver-
tisement to participate in evil. By itself, temptation is neither good nor evil. As Shakespeare said, "It is one thing
to be tempted, and another thing to fall." We can hear sin's
commercial; we don't have to buy. As the old hymn says:

> Yield not to temptation
>   For yielding is sin;
> Each victory will help you
>   Some other to win;
> Fight manfully onward,
>   Dark passions subdue;
> Look ever to Jesus
>   He'll carry you through.

All the things that tempt us away from our program and
back to our compulsive addictions will surely be strong.
Recovery is not easy. But if we follow the Twelve Steps and
Jesus we'll be carried through all our temptations. We cannot be distracted by attractive temptations if we "look ever
to Jesus." He will give us strength to prevail.

*Lord, help me refuse to buy what sin is selling. Keep me from the
temptations that attract me and call me to you instead. Amen.*

"No longer do I call you servants, for the servant does not know what his master is doing; but I have called you friends."

JOHN 15:15

In Aesop's fables we hear about two men who were traveling through a forest. Suddenly a huge bear crashed through the trees. One of the men, thinking only of his own safety, climbed a tree. The other, unable to fight the fearsome bear alone, threw himself down on the ground and played dead. He had heard that a bear would not touch a dead body. It must have been true. The bear sniffed at the man's head and then walked away. The man in the tree climbed down and said, "It looked like the bear whispered something in your ear. What did he say?" The other man said, "The bear said that it is not wise to keep company with a fellow who would desert his friend in a moment of danger."

When we look back at our struggle with addiction, who were the ones who "stuck with us"? Who are the ones who are still with us now? Who can we trust? Who is walking with us?

Our Twelve-Step groups are devoted to friendship and equality. Every meeting is a safe and secure place to meet friends who won't run out on you. Recovery is for companions who walk hand in hand together, not a "Do it yourself project" or "Everyone for himself." We are together for us all to get put back together.

Oh Christ, you are my best and dearest friend, keep me friendly and close to all your other friends. Amen.

"You are anxious and troubled about many things; one thing is needful."

LUKE 10:41–42

There was once an elderly shopkeeper who was on his deathbed, surrounded by his family. He feebly asked, "Is Sara here?" "Yes, I'm here," said his wife. "Is Ruth here?" he asked. "Yes, Daddy." "And Bill?" "Yes, Father." Then the old man sat up with terror in his eyes and yelled, "Then who's minding the store?"

Some of us are champion worriers. If we were placed in a tranquil and safe place, we would still find something to worry about. If we didn't worry and fret about it, it wouldn't get done. Worry is a tool we use to control and manage our life. Yet we know that when it comes to our addiction, we are out of control and are powerless to manage our lives. Why worry, then?

Most of us keep worrying out of habit, but habits can be broken. That's what the Twelve Steps are for. Through our meetings, meditations, phone calls, reading, and prayer we can replace our old worrisome ways of "white-knuckled" control with the habit of the peace and power of God-control. We can let him "mind the store" and *really* let him do the worrying from now on. That's not easy. We are so used to doing all the driving, it seems foolhardy to turn loose of the wheel. But God is a good driver. He'll do a good job, and he will even help us "turn loose" if we ask.

Lord, loosen my grip. Calm my fear and help me let go. Amen.

"So if the Son makes you free, you will be free indeed."
JOHN 8:36

A little girl was misbehaving and really giving her mother a hard time. Her mother told her to go sit in the corner until her father came home. The child went to the corner, but refused to sit. After a struggle, her mother physically forced her daughter to sit down. When her father saw her, he asked what she was doing. She said, "Well, on the outside I'm sitting down, but inside I'm standing up!"

We can't help but admire a strong will and do applaud perseverance and courage. Even childish rebellion and stubbornness are better than fearful and slavish obedience. We are not created to be slaves and to grovel in the dust; we are created to be free. Liberty is our lot.

But when our rebellion is against God, against love, against health, against goodness, against truth—even against life itself—what then? Who's free then? To remain stubbornly attached to our addiction is slavery, not freedom. To stay loyal to our illness is as far as we can get from liberty. To give up our proud perseverance in staying sick is not to become trapped but set loose! When we surrender to God, we are emancipated.

O Christ, in whose service is perfect freedom, free me from my own tenacious grip on my own sickness. Amen.

But now we are discharged from the law, dead to that which held us captive, so that we serve not under the old written code but in the new life of the Spirit.

ROMANS 7:6

A missionary was found lying exhausted and near death in the jungle. These people took pity on him and nursed him back to health. He stayed with them, and his gentle, loving ways attracted them to him. He taught them a few new skills and preached to them of Jesus and God the Father. Finally, he had to leave. They begged him to leave them something to remember him by. So he built them a sundial and told them how it could tell of the sun's progress from morning to evening. The natives were enthralled and grateful. The missionary left. The people grieved over his departure. The chief said, "We must preserve forever our dear friend's gift." So they built a canopy over the sundial to protect it from the sun.

Our life in recovery is often like that. We think we can preserve our progress, so we enshrine our old triumphs and rest on our past accomplishments. Recovery cannot be kept under a canopy. It must be allowed to be open to the light and freshness of each new day. We always have more to learn. We always need to go to meetings. We always need to walk the Twelve Steps. Nothing can be a shrine. Everything needs new, fresh starts each day, "one day at a time."

Lord Jesus, keep me looking up and looking forward to new discoveries and new challenges. Keep me from building shrines to my past. Amen.

He took the bread and blessed, and broke it, and gave it to them. And their eyes were opened and they recognized him.

LUKE 24:30–31

The word *companion* is rich and meaningful. It comes from two words: *com*, which means "with," and *pan*, which means "bread." A companion is someone with whom we share bread. In ancient days to invite someone to partake of your food was an invitation to friendship. Companionship is freely offered and freely chosen. We cannot choose our family, our relatives, or our neighbors, but we are, as Emerson said, "the architects of our own friendships."

Nothing is more important to recovery than "the company we keep." Our companions have more influence on us than any other people. All of us have heard of "peer pressure"; the power of our associates and friends is enormous. One of the best pieces of advice in recovery is "to change your playmates and your playgrounds." It makes no sense in recovery to subject ourselves to the power of other sick people. "Stick with winners" is a good slogan and will help us stay sober, serene, abstinent, and healthy.

The best friend we have, of course, is Jesus. He is our "divine Companion," the one we break bread with in Holy Communion and also the one who gives us other companions called Christians to stay healthy with.

Dear Lord, help me stick to playmates and playgrounds I need for health and recovery. May I choose companions who follow you. Amen.

*Jesus went about all the cities and villages, teaching
in their synagogues and preaching the gospel of the
kingdom, and healing every disease.*

MATTHEW 9:35

The great supporter of Alcoholics Anonymous Carl Jung
once wrote:

Among all my patients in the second half of life—that is to say, over
35—there has not been one whose problem in the last resort was not that
of finding a religious outlook on life. It is safe to say that every one of
them fell ill because he had lost that which the living religions of every
age have given their followers, and none of them has been really healed
who did not regain his religious outlook.

Over two thousand years ago, Plato wrote, "If the head
and the body are to be well, you must begin with the soul;
that is the first thing." It is gratifying to see that today science and medicine are recognizing Plato's wisdom. Almost
every treatment center today that is succeeding in treating
addictive diseases saturates the therapy with spiritual healing and the Twelve Steps. Our best medical people are following Louis Pasteur's words: "A little science estranges
men from God; much science leads them back to him."

Perhaps medicine will realize that it owes its greatest debt
to Jesus of Nazareth, "the great Physician." The spirit of
Jesus founded hospitals and gave healing its love and therefore its power. The healing hands of Christ bring the true
health and wholeness of complete salvation—body, mind,
and soul. Jesus healed whole persons not just bodies. Our
Twelve Steps depend 100 percent on Jesus and on no other.

*O Lord of health and salvation, keep me close to your healing heart
and hands. Amen.*

"The seed should sprout and grow, he knows not how."
MARK 4:27

An old radio program began each day with these words: "Look to this day, for it is life, and in its brief course lie all the realities of your existence—the bliss of growth, the glory of action, the splendor of beauty. Look well, therefore, to this day." Each thought is an inspiration, but none as exciting as "the bliss of growth." Not only do we want to grow from birth, we *need* to grow. We must grow or we die.

Everything alive is growing, constantly becoming, always in process. To be alive is to be in motion. Growth cannot occur independently, either. Nothing grows totally from the inside out; something from the outside must be integrated. Recovery is therefore, by necessity, growth that takes in nutrients.

Someone has divided people into "trees" and "posts." A tree put into the ground begins to grow. A post stuck in the ground begins to rot. In recovery in the church, it's a joy to see trees grow and a sorrow to watch a post rot.

Lord of life, keep me rooted in the Twelve Steps and keep me planted in faith, so that I continue to grow. Amen.

And when he drew near and saw the city he wept over it.
LUKE 19:41

At the beginning of a class in college, a professor asked about a missing student. He was told that the absent student's mother had just died. When the professor asked for a show of hands of those who had lost a parent, several hands went up. The professor said, "You students please write notes of comfort; you know what it's all about." Loss must be experienced in order to be shared, and it must be shared in order to be healed.

A little boy made a special Christmas ornament for his parents. On the way out of school with his gift, he dropped it and it shattered on the pavement. He immediately screamed with grief at his loss. His father rushed to his side and said, "Hush, Son, be quiet. It's all right. It doesn't matter. It doesn't matter." But his mother, more acquainted with such deep moments, took the sobbing boy in her arms and said, "Oh, it does matter, it matters a great deal." And she wept for her son's loss and added her tears to his.

Grief is a profound part of recovery and new life. Tears of regret, remorse, and despair water the roots of love and of life itself. To deny and avoid the hurt and pain of life's losses is to negate life's importance. To fail to cry is to fail to live. Saint Paul said, "Weep with those who weep" (Rom. 12:15).

Blessed Jesus, join me to those in sorrow, and let my tears show my love. Amen.

For "every one who calls upon the name of the Lord will be saved."

ROMANS 10:13

A story is told about a Mr. Kline. He was a sad, sorrowful sort who felt that no one, especially God, cared for him. One Sunday he walked by a church and heard the words to an old hymn:

> Saved by grace alone,
> This is all my plea
> Jesus died for all mankind,
> And Jesus died for me.

When he heard the third line, "Jesus died for all mankind," he thought he heard, "Jesus died for old man Kline." He shouted, "Why, that's me!" Stopping in his tracks, he went into the church, accepted Christ's special invitation and love, and became a Christian.

Whenever we feel a special and personalized call or prompting from God, it is no mistake. Individuals are brought to salvation one by one, and each encounters and then embraces Christ. Mr. Kline heard correctly. Jesus died for each unique individual. His love is reserved for each of us. Our recovery from addiction depends on believing that our Lord truly loves us, each one, with a special kind of attention that fixes on us — as if we were all that mattered.

When you notice me, Lord, and call me by name, I am so blessed and grateful. Thank you for choosing me. Amen.

For in this hope we were saved. Now hope that is seen is not hope. For who hopes for what he sees?

ROMANS 8:24

An old skeptic was finally persuaded to read the Bible. He resolved to read for an hour each day the very book he scorned. "Wife," he said after one week's reading, "if this book is right, we are all wrong!" After another week he said, "Wife, if this book is right, we are lost!" As he went on reading, he exclaimed, "Wife! If this book is right, we may be saved!" The skeptic and his wife accepted God's salvation, and when they did, they left all their "ifs" behind them.

When we read the Bible, and when we read the Big Book and our Twelve-Step literature, we are all eventually led to realize that "we may be saved." That is a wonderful and blessed discovery.

There was an artist who portrayed our struggle with evil and death as a chess game. In a portrait hanging in a great art gallery he shows Satan playing chess with a young man, who is checkmated by the devil. This picture obviously shows evil's triumph. One day a great chess master came to view the picture. He studied the chess board and the young man's situation, which was thought to be lost. The chess master suddenly shouted to the picture as if it were real, "Young man, don't give up! You still have a move!" So do we. We always have a move. That move is prayer and surrender to Jesus Christ. He will help us see our next move.

Lord, you always have a place for me to move. I know you will show me. Amen.

Beloved, never avenge yourselves, but leave it to the wrath of God; for it is written, "Vengeance is mine, I will repay, says the Lord."

ROMANS 12:19

Just about everyone has said, "I feel like I'm butting my head against a stone wall." Even more frustrating is that we continue to hurl ourselves against such walls, in endless futility. What is most tragic, however, is that most of the walls we bang into we built ourselves! We erect most of our own barriers.

The wall of resentment is a good example. Resentment is our decision to blame someone else. We decide that our hurt is due to the wrongs of another, inflicted on us. We retreat into our own bitterness and isolation. As our wall goes up, our wounds continue to bleed. Yet the blood we shed is a corrosive acid that eats away our soul.

Resentment does the greatest harm to the one who hoards it and nurses it. The antidote to resentment is forgiveness. We must forgive to live. We must take down our stone wall and use each stone as a stepping stone to reconciliation and peace. Christ will supervise the demolition if we ask him to let us out of our self-constructed prison.

Dearest Lord, keep me from building walls of blame that trap me in a prison of resentment. Free me with forgiveness and love. Amen.

But let it be the hidden person of the heart with the imperishable jewel of a gentle and quiet spirit, which in God's sight is very precious.

1 PETER 3:4

As we open ourselves to the "priceless gift of serenity" nothing is more pleasurable than contentment. Horace wrote that "you can traverse the world in search of happiness, which is already in reach of every man: a contented mind confers it on all." We are all here for a short time so why trouble ourselves and wear out our souls with anxious thoughts? Our hearts need to be at rest.

Contentment is accepting ourselves and our situation. It is the grateful use of what we have—little or much. It is to drink the cup of providence as we trust in the Lord. Not to drink is to reject our present situation and self. When we like what we have, we can do as we like.

Each step in our recovery, every one of the Twelve Steps, has contentment within it. Being content is like being full of a good meal. We are satisfied and thankful. Yet we get hungry again, and satisfaction passes. But, like three good meals a day, it repeats and repeats its need and its opportunity day after day.

Lord, keep me open to little satisfactions. Please save me from discontentment. Help me accept the blessings of each day. Amen.

No man has ever seen God; if we love one another, God abides in us and his love is perfected in us.

1 JOHN 4:12

When Saint John was in his "twilight years," the story goes, he would sit with his younger disciples and teach them. One day one of his disciples complained: "John, you always talk about love, about God's love for us and about our love for each other. Why don't you ever tell us about something besides love?" The aging apostle looked at his young disciple, and with love in his eyes, he said, "Because there is nothing else, just love, love, love."

Love, which is salvation, moves life from inside out; it directs our energy from self to others. It is giving not taking, accepting not rejecting. If we seek our own happiness and fulfillment, we will never find them; but if happiness and fulfillment *are* found, it will be because we have forgotten our own search for happiness and fulfillment by helping others find theirs. The pattern for this other-directed life is Christ, who is also the power we need to love his way. God is love. "There is nothing else, just love, love, love."

The word *religion* is derived from the Latin word *religare*, which means to "bind back." When we practice our religion, we bind ourselves back to God, who is our origin and our destiny, our beginning and end. What accomplishes this binding is love.

Lord, grow and increase in my heart, so that my love will grow from the inside out. Amen.

*Let the word of Christ dwell in you richly, as you teach
and admonish one another in all wisdom, and as you
sing psalms and hymns and spiritual songs with thankfulness in your hearts to God.*

COLOSSIANS 3:16

As children we experienced the dizziness of being twirled
and whirled round and round until we fell down. Knowing
how fast we can lose our equilibrium, it is amazing to watch
a dancer do endless twirling pirouettes without falling or
stumbling. What keeps a dancer's head clear in such long
whirls is a technique call "spotting." Concentrating on one
spot with each spin enables a dancer to remain steady and
balanced.

Sometimes life doesn't let us dance – or even move. One
such immobilized person said this:

I have an island in the palm of my hand, shaped like an almond. My
island represents my life inside, which is full and free and lovely. I treasure my island. When I look in my hand, I see what my old freedom
was like when I could move my body, and that is beautiful to remember.
But I also see the new and strange freedom I am finding in my mind and
soul. When I look at my island I see everything right. I see God.

While strapped helpless to her bed this woman allowed her
experience to make her, not crush her. Why? Because she
found God in her island. She found God deep inside her
soul – ever with her. The "spot" she saw was a spotlight to
God within. Whenever we get dizzy or fall down or have
to stay down, we can look for our spot, our light within to
guide, guard, and greet us. That place is God's dwelling
place inside.

*My Lord, please help me always look for you and see you in all
circumstances. Amen.*

"So, every sound tree bears good fruit, but the bad tree bears evil fruit."

MATTHEW 7:17

The ancient philosophy that a person becomes what a person thinks is as old as the Hindus and the Hebrews. Over three thousand years ago in the Hindu Upanishads we read: "Man becomes that of which he thinks." We read in Proverbs 23:7: "As he thinketh in his heart, so is he." The same idea is found in Buddha, Marcus Aurelius, Confucius, Mohammed, Aristotle, Socrates, and hundreds of others. It must be true.

We live from the inside out. Both are important. Yet the truth that the inner world of the mind shapes our lives is hard to deny. Perhaps the loveliest passage on the power of thought is by John Ruskin:

Make yourselves nests of pleasant thoughts. None of us yet know, for none of us have been taught in early youth what fairy palaces we may build of beautiful thought. Bright fancies, satisfied memories, noble histories, faithful sayings, treasure houses of precious and restful thoughts, which care cannot disturb, nor pain make gloomy, nor poverty take away—houses built without hands, for our souls to live in.

Two places to find such treasures are the Big Book and the Bible. The best way to avoid "stinking thinking" is to live in both books.

Jesus, keep me immersed in the Big Book and the Bible before I try out too many others. Amen.

Beloved, we are God's children now; it does not yet appear what we shall be, but we know that when he appears we shall be like him, for we shall see him as he is.

1 JOHN 3:2

An old widow was living in poverty. A young man, hearing of her condition, went to visit her and see if he could minister to her. The old woman complained bitterly of her situation but said her son in Australia was doing quite well. The visitor asked, "Doesn't your son do anything to help you?" She replied, "No, nothing. He writes me each month, but he sends me only some little pictures with his letters." The young man asked to see the pictures. To his amazement, he found each picture to be currency, each worth about a hundred dollars! The poor woman had no idea of the value of this foreign money and saw only pictures. She could have lived in luxury.

We may think such ignorance is foolish. Yet we make the same mistakes. We overlook treasures at every meeting. We fail to see the worth in each step. We often live as poor, poverty-stricken souls when we could live like kings and queens. We don't see the wealth surrounding us that God sends us every day. Saint Paul calls us "to have all the riches of assured understanding and the knowledge of God's mystery, of Christ, in whom are hid all the treasures of wisdom and knowledge" (Col. 2:2–3).

Jesus, I know I am rich in you. Keep me aware of the treasure you are. Amen.

And he took a cup, and when he had given thanks he gave it to them, and they all drank of it.

MARK 14:23

William Law asked the question, "Who is the greatest saint in the world?" He answered his own question this way:

The greatest saint is not he who prays most or fasts most; it is not he who gives alms, or is most eminent for temperance, chastity, or justice; but it is he who is always thankful to God, who receives everything as an instance of God's goodness and has a heart always ready to praise God for it.

Perhaps the secret to being "always thankful to God" is to be "thankful for small favors." We tend to set our sights too high. We want to cheer and applaud our success only when it is great. Why not give thanks for food, sleep, air, water, breath, color, texture, smells, sights, sounds, and little details of life? Why not give thanks for our Twelve Steps, our meetings, our sponsors, our sobriety, and our birthdays in recovery?

In the Old Testament the thankful saints are found in most abundance in the Psalms. Typical of such thankful response is Psalm 103:

Bless the Lord, O my soul; and all that is within me,
  bless his holy name!
Bless the Lord, O my soul, and forget not all his benefits,
who forgives all your iniquity, who heals all your diseases,
who redeems your life from the Pit, who crowns you with
  steadfast love and mercy,
who satisfies you with good as long as you live.

Thank you, O Jesus, for all the goodness and healing you bring me each day. Amen.

He took the seven loaves, and [gave] thanks.

MARK 8:6

A farmer invited his sophisticated cousin from the city to his farm for supper. Before the meal the host thanked God for the food. The visitor said with a jeer: "That is so old-fashioned; nobody with an education prays and thanks God anymore." The farmer admitted that there were some on his farm who never gave thanks to God. Much pleased, the relative said, "So there are some intelligent and sensible beings here. Who are they?" The farmer answered, "They are my pigs."

This farmer instinctively knew what a Department of Agriculture study revealed. A crop of 100 bushels of corn from one acre of land, in addition to a farmer's labor, requires: 4 million pounds of water, 6,800 pounds of oxygen, 5,000 pounds of carbon, 160 pounds of nitrogen, 125 pounds of potassium, 75 pounds of sulfur, and other elements too numerous to list. In addition to these ingredients, rain and sunshine at the right time are essential. The report concluded that only 5 percent of the produce on a farm is due to the efforts of the farmer.

When we walk the Twelve Steps and enter into our recovery, it is like joining a farm. We can work day and night and only give 5 percent of what it takes—at least 95 percent comes either from what was there before we came or from what God supplies. Recovery is a gift, grace freely given. We don't do it alone, thank God.

Dear Christ, your grace is more than I can ever repay. Keep my heart full of thanks. Amen.

"Father, I thank thee."

JOHN 11:41

Forest fires are fearsome. To be caught in one would be a ghastly death. Only one thought would occupy the mind: escape. Once, while stopped by a river, an explorer watched a forest fire raging toward his party. The fire was on the opposite bank. He was safe. Before the flames fled foxes, rabbits, wolves, deer, bears, mountain lions, squirrels, and finally several men and women. They all stood together on the bank, and then swam to safety on the other side. When they reached the safe shore, all the animals stopped and stood watching the destruction of their forest home on the other side. No one harmed another living thing. Men and beasts had forgotten their natural enemies in the face of the common peril.

Each time a desperate soul enters a Twelve-Step meeting, the same thing happens. Everyone faces a common need to survive the fire, to escape a mutual fear. We seek out each other for one reason: survival.

But there is life beyond survival. The pilgrims at the first Thanksgiving knew about the joy and relief of survival, but they also gave thanks for more. That more is salvation. We survive, yes, but we must also thrive. Thanksgiving is also for the blessings of life in all its abundance. The Twelve Steps are just like that. They are our safe shore across from the consuming fire, but they also satisfy as well as save. Thank God, we don't have to be in danger to benefit from our program. Thank God we always have countless opportunities to celebrate Thanksgiving to God for all he has done for us.

Thank you, Lord, for everything. Most of all thank you for my own gratitude. Amen.

Then said Jesus, "Were not ten cleansed? Where are the nine? Was no one found to return and give praise to God except this foreigner?"

LUKE 17:17–18

What good are "thank-you" notes? Aren't they just a polite custom? One professor answers by telling how one Thanksgiving he was thinking of his blessings and remembered his old English teacher. He wrote a letter thanking her for her inspiration and influence in his life. She wrote back in these words:

My dear Willie,

I cannot tell you how much your note meant to me. I am in my eighties, living alone in a small room, cooking my own meals, lonely, and, like the last leaf of autumn, lingering behind. You will be interested to know that I taught school for fifty years and yours is the first note of appreciation I ever received. It came on a blue, cold morning and cheered me as nothing has in many years.

The professor sat down and cried, a power of "love let loose" stirred within him, and he sat down immediately and wrote another "thank-you" note to an old friend. He received this reply:

My dear Will,

Your letter was so beautiful, so real, that as I sat reading it in my study, tears fell from my eyes; tears of gratitude. Then, before I realized what I was doing, I rose from my chair and called her name to show your letter to her—forgetting for a moment that she was gone. You will never know how much your letter has warmed my spirit. I have been walking about in the glow of it all day long.

What good are "thank-you" notes? All the good in the world, that's all. When we set some love loose in the world we are the very closest to Christ.

O Christ, teach me thankfulness and move me to thank others and show my appreciation. Amen.

"For out of the abundance of the heart the mouth speaks."
MATTHEW 12:34

The story is told of a man sitting on a crowded subway, reading his paper. He noticed an elderly woman standing above him, stood up, tipped his hat, and offered her his seat. The woman dropped her packages, her eyes widened, and then suddenly closed as she fainted on the spot. When she was revived, she looked up into the face of the kind man who had offered his seat and said, "Thank you." Then the man fainted.

A philosopher once said, "God has two dwellings: one in heaven and the other in a thankful heart." If there is any one element essential to recovery it is "an attitude of gratitude."

Millions of Christians hear these words as they receive Holy Communion: "The Body and Blood of our Lord Jesus Christ which was given for you, take, eat and drink in remembrance that Christ died for you—and be thankful."

When I think of all you have given me, O Christ, I am so thankful. Amen.

And his disciples answered him, "How can one feed these men with bread here in the desert?"

MARK 8:4

In Shakespeare's *King Henry VI* are these words:

My crown is in my heart, not my head,
Not decked with diamonds and Indian stones, not seen;
My crown is called content.
A crown kings seldom wear.

A recent self-help book lists the marks of a satisfied person. To be satisfied and serene a person has meaning and direction in life, rarely feels cheated or disappointed, has attained several major goals, is in love and gives love, has many friends, is cheerful, is not sensitive to criticism, and has faith rather than fear.

Another word for satisfaction is "acceptance." Recovery is built around being able to absorb and accept life with all its pains and pleasures, and the Twelve Steps teach us how.

One of the best ways to learn satisfaction is to begin appreciating little things, giving thanks for little favors, and developing an "attitude of gratitude." The more we demand, grab for, complain about, worry over, the less we can value, cherish, savor, enjoy, and accept. To look for the many little blessings is a choice we all can make.

Dear Lord, open my heart to receive each moment as a blessing and help me to relax and be satisfied. Amen.

Ambrose Bierce said, "an acquaintance is a person whom we know well enough to borrow from but not well enough to lend to." Calgary Bob Edwards said, "the difference between a friend and an acquaintance is that a friend helps; an acquaintance merely advises." Both quotations have wisdom. It is amazing how we can use people, and the less we know about them, the more we tend to make them instruments or agents or even depersonalize them. The waiter, delivery man, mail carrier, and clerk in the store are all there to gain something from. An acquaintance is similar. We can borrow from them but not lend. Maybe we don't borrow money, but thoughts, opinions, and ideas but may hold back any of our wisdom or personal disclosures until we know them well enough to be trusted as friends. We need more friends and less acquaintances. Friends do help and those who call themselves friends and merely advise are really acquaintances.

Most of my time in recovery, I depended on friends. We are blessed by friends. We know friends. The best sponsors I had were friends who shared their own "experience, strength, and hope" and did not offer advice or tell me what to do or how to do it. What helped me the most was a friend being vulnerable enough to share his walk and from that experience I gained strength and hope. Praise God for helping-friends and deliver us from mere advice-givers.

I am impressed by how little advice Jesus gave. His knowledge was way above mere advice. He showed the way. He walked the talk and invited us to follow him. All his teachings were down-to-earth, practical, workable instructions from his own life and witness. He gave us his life. He gives us his spirit. He allows us to find our own way with his gentle guidings.

December 1

I can do all things in him who strengthens me.
PHILIPPIANS 4:13

A frog found himself caught in a very deep rut on a country road; his friends tried to help him get out, but their efforts were in vain. At last they left him in great sadness. The very next day one of these friends was hopping along that country road, and whom did he meet but the same frog who the day before had been hopelessly stuck in the rut: "I thought you were stuck for good, and couldn't get out," said the friend. "That's right, I couldn't," the freed frog said, "but a truck came along down that rut, and I *had* to get out!"

Didn't we jump into recovery the same way? We thought we were stuck, hooked, hopelessly caught in our addiction, until we *had* to get out.

We can do what seems impossible when we really have to. Our instinct for survival is a powerful force. The impossible sometimes becomes possible when the situation is drastic. Jesus said, "All things are possible to him who believes" (Mark 9:23). When Jesus said this, the father of the child who lay sick said, "I believe; help my unbelief!" (Mark 9:24). This can be our same response when we are stuck in a rut, or have hurdles to jump that seem impossible. We may not leap out all at once with one bound, but God has a way of helping us, step by step, to get out of our sticky places.

Lord, when I'm stuck I know you will help me get free eventually if I keep believing in you. Amen.

"To give light to those who sit in darkness and in the shadow of death, to guide our feet into the way of peace."
LUKE 1:79

In the deserts of Arabia there is a guide who never loses his way. He is called the Dove Man. He carries a homing pigeon with a fine cord attached to its legs. The other end is tied to the guide's wrist. When in doubt as to what direction to take, the guide throws the bird in the air. The bird quickly strains at the cord in the instinctive direction of home, and with this knowledge the guide is back on track.

We too have such a guidance system; we call it the Twelve Steps. Every step acts like a homing pigeon to point the way. Frequently, we are surprised, yet the steps are always accurate and true. Our own instincts and urges are not reliable; only the Twelve Steps are on track.

Guidance and direction for recovery is never a solo search in a lonely desert. Recovery is a rich experience, filled with people, program, and promise, in which we are surrounded and immersed in relationships. We get better and find our way in groups, not all by ourselves. In fact, the guidance is enhanced in a community of caring persons who rely on God's guidance, confirmed by many.

Teach me, O Christ, to trust the guidance of the Twelve Steps, my sponsor, and my group. Amen.

"Unless a grain of wheat falls into the earth and dies, it remains alone; but if it dies, it bears much fruit."

JOHN 12:24

A woman came back from a Christian retreat, and a friend asked what it was like. She answered, "I died!" "What do you mean?" her friend responded. "This weekend I discovered that I had spent my whole life hiding. I had never been honest with anyone: my family, my friends, myself, or God. The worst part was, I wasn't even in touch with my own dishonesty and distortions. This past weekend all my lies died; my old hiding places collapsed. I am so glad I went through this death experience in order to become the new person that God is creating. Now I know what a 'born again' Christian is."

As strange as this sounds to some, this "death experience" is exactly what happens in the Third Step. This "surrender step" is death. It is death to our old wills and lives as we turn them over to God. An ancient saint said, "God has to hollow us out before he can fill us up with life and love." All our old debris of self-centeredness, self-pity, and self-control has to die. As Saint Paul wrote:

Do you not know that all of us who have been baptized into Christ Jesus were baptized into his death? We were buried therefore with him by baptism into death, so that as Christ was raised from the dead by the glory of the Father, we too might walk in newness of life. (Rom. 6:3–4)

Now, that's a Third Step! For Christians in recovery, what could be truer and more hopeful?

Dear Christ, I give myself to you. Take me as I die to my old selfish ways and live in you and your love. Amen.

"I can do nothing on my own authority; as I hear, I judge; and my judgment is just, because I seek not my own will but the will of him who sent me."

JOHN 5:30

The Frank Sinatra song "I Did It My Way" is the theme song for lots of people. Its message is that whatever I've done, for better or worse, I did my way—and that is wonderful.

What Jesus says is exactly the opposite. He says we cannot fulfill our lives doing it *our* way. It is God's way and his will that is truly wonderful. For every person who can applaud his or her own success and selfish gain, there are thousands more who are led to destruction and death through their self-conceit. "I Did It My Way" is the supreme blasphemy, the original sin of Adam and Eve. To celebrate such a song is to sing the song of slavery.

Addicted persons who sing these lyrics remain forever lost and out of control, enslaved by their disease. Only by hearing and receiving the words of Christ, who is our way, truth, and life, can we find our true selfhood. We need no more songs of self-worship or self-pity. We need the good news of Christ's love and companionship—Christ who in his weakness "turned his will and life over to the care" of his father.

Gracious Savior, may I live in your life of complete dependence on the Father. Shatter my pride and give me my true respect and honor as your disciple and child. Amen.

December 5

Besides this you know what hour it is, how it is full time now for you to wake from sleep. For salvation is nearer to us now than when we first believed.

ROMANS 13:11

Thoreau once said, "Only that day dawns to which we are awake." When we were caught in the clutches of our addiction, it was like a bad dream about a bad person. We lived like sleepwalkers, not knowing what we were doing, driven by voices other than our own.

Now we are awake. Now we can dream good dreams in the daytime—about the good person we are and can become. If we advance confidently in our good dream's direction, what we imagine for ourselves will come true. We can be free and happy. We can be alert and unafraid. We can listen to our true selves, not what others may say or want. We can listen to what God speaks in our heart. Then we can join the unknown poet who said:

> The foolish fears of what may pass,
> I cast them all away
> Among the clover-scented grass,
> Among the new-mown hay;
> Among the hushing of the corn
> Where drowsy poppies nod,
> Where ill thoughts die and good are born,
> Out in the fields with God.

Our life in recovery is like being in God's beautiful pasture, free in his lush meadow, surrounded by nature's beauty and life. This is a dream that is coming true.

Oh Christ, I praise you for waking me up to the good dreams and visions of life and love around me. Amen.

"Therefore I tell you, whatever you ask in prayer, believe that you receive it, and you will."

MARK 11:24

John Wesley, the founder of the Methodist church, was once aboard a sailing ship caught in a storm. He was terrified, while others on the ship remained quite calm. Wesley was impressed by their confident courage and yearned for the same quiet bravery and trust. When he asked for their secret, he was told, "Act as if you do have such faith and courage, and in time how you act will take hold of you." The great psychologist William James called this the "as if" principle. He said, "If you want to have a quality, act as if you already had it." In recovery we encourage this when we say, "Fake it till you make it."

Behavioral scientists base their theories upon the "as if" principle. Actions, deeds, and behavior contain the power of life. The same belief governs Holy Scripture and the Twelve Steps. The Bible and recovery both call us "to do," "to follow," "to admit," and "to give." Acts are prior to attitudes. We are abstinent, sober, and immersed in a program through actions: meetings, steps, reading, praying, talking, listening. Recovery is busy. Behavior is active.

Like a person who puts on a uniform, we soon become like the persons that uniform represents. We behave "as if" we were actually what we seem. As Tennyson said, "I must lose myself in action, lest I wither in despair."

Lord, get me going and get me doing. I'm better when in action. Amen.

*For he says, "At the acceptable time I have listened to you,
and helped you on the day of salvation." Behold, now is
the acceptable time; behold, now is the day of salvation.*

2 CORINTHIANS 6:2

As Dr. Frederic Loomis lay dying, he remembered
George Eliot's words: "It's but little good you'll do, water-
ing last year's crops." He knew he was dying. He wanted
to leave a final thought for his loved ones. He reached for
his pen and wrote:

Moaning over what cannot be helped is a confession of futility and fear
and of emotional stagnation. The best way to break this vicious, morbid
circle is to stop thinking about yourself, and start thinking about other
people. You can lighten your own load by doing an outward, unselfish
act for someone today. This will keep you from morbid worry and fear.
It is the best medicine.

Happiness is only possible without worry, and the way to
cease worry is to accept each day's possibilities and to reject
its impossibilities. When we leave what is beyond our power
to God, we stop worrying. The past is beyond our reach.

When we fill our lives with God's presence and love, we
will be cleared each day from past regrets and future fears.
Our health lies in building fences of trust around today and
filling it with loving works that please God, which can't help
but give us pleasure too. Then we are grateful for the good
we find in the here and now.

*Dear Jesus, when I think of you my worrying stops. You gave me
this day, keep me in it. Amen.*

"Nevertheless do not rejoice in this, that the spirits are subject to you; but rejoice that your names are written in heaven."

LUKE 10:20

We love to label each other. We divide up humanity into classes and categories according to race, nationality, creed, career, sex, politics, income, size, and appearance. Our descriptive labels are endless. Yet despite all of our interesting and external names, we are one person. We are an inner self. No matter what uniform or costume we wear, we are the special human being we are within—our "self."

Someone once asked Socrates about one of his friends, who was always sad, even though he was wise and a world traveler. Socrates explained, "He is unhappy because wherever he goes he takes himself with him." Whatever label or identity we cling to, we still have our selves with us. An old proverb reads: "Though you sail the seven seas, you cannot escape yourself." Yet it is yourself that God loves and for whom Christ died.

Lord, save me from clinging to my label. Keep me open to you in the depth of my soul—my self. Amen.

December 9

And the peace of God, which passes all understanding,
will keep your hearts and your minds in Christ Jesus.

PHILIPPIANS 4:7

A rich industrialist from the North was horrified to find a Southern fisherman lying lazily beside his boat smoking a pipe. "Why aren't you out fishing?" asked the industrialist. "Because I have caught enough fish for the day," said the fisherman. "Why don't you catch more than you need?" asked the industrialist. "What would I do with it?" asked the fisherman. "You could earn more money," was the reply. "With what you sell your extra fish for you could get a better motor and boat; you could go into deeper waters and catch more fish. You could buy nylon nets. You could catch more fish and make more money. Soon you could have two boats, then a fleet of boats, employees, and a real business. Then you would be rich like me." The fisherman asked, "Then what would I do?" The industrialist said, "Then you could sit down and enjoy life." The fisherman said, "What do you think I'm doing now?"

When is enough enough? Where do we find satisfaction and contentment? Can we project our success always to the future, or be content with today's success? Often we strive and work until we drop. We fail to take time to relax and enjoy simple rest and peace. If we don't take time each day for ease, we may stay in dis-ease. Every day is not a burden or a frantic series of jobs to do. Every twenty-four hours should include some time for prayer, meditation, and rest—even if we take only a few breaks away from the grind. If we don't take a break, we may wind up broken.

Jesus, you rested and found times to relax. Please help me save times and spaces in each day to enjoy some peace with you. Amen

For God is at work in you both to will and to work for his good pleasure.

PHILIPPIANS 2:13

Two elderly Irish women were sitting on a park bench. One was weeping. She sobbed, "Why, after all my years of obedience and prayer, hasn't God touched me? Why is he so far away?" She buried her head and wept on. Suddenly she raised her head and shouted, "He touched me! He touched me! I felt his hand! Praise God!" Then she looked at her friend and saw that her companion had her hand on hers. "Oh no, Mary, it's only your hand, and I thought it was God's!" Mary answered, "Indeed it was my hand. What did you think God would be doing? Do you think he would make a long arm reaching out of heaven to reach you? He just took the hand nearest to you and used that!"

Every time we are touched by the hand of friendship, every time we are supported by the hand of help, every time we are directed by the hand of guidance—these are the hands of God. Human hands helping God's hands of heaven. Mother Teresa said that God has only our hands with which to bless the world. We hold, we help, we feed, we greet, we caress, we applaud, we support, we console—all with our hands. Yet in every action of such love, God's hand is involved. God is love, and when love is present, so is he. He hands us his love to handle with our hands.

Recovery is God's world. He populates his world with people. He acts, heals, directs, and saves through his people. We are his tools and instruments—his hands. Shall we let him use them? He will if we let him.

Lord Christ, when you took my hand, you gave me your hands to use as mine. Amen.

> *"And he who does not take his cross and follow me is not worthy of me. He who finds his life will lose it, and he who loses his life for my sake will find it."*
>
> MATTHEW 10:38–39

There is a story told of a mental patient who was certain that he was dead, completely convinced that he was a corpse. The doctors tried to reason with him. Finally, they succeeded in getting him to agree that corpses do not bleed. The man agreed to test that out. He allowed the doctors to prick his finger, causing the blood to flow. The patient looked at his bleeding finger, then said, "What do you know! Corpses do bleed!"

There are many of us like that around. We may not be in mental hospitals, but our thinking somehow is not quite right at times. We call this "stinking thinking," rationalizing, excusing, and denial. Most of us in Twelve-Step recovery are infected with false ideas and delusions. Truth and honesty are hard to find and even harder to accept.

By far the most prevalent mistake made in recovery in Christ is believing that we can live a "partial program" or be less than fully committed to Christ. It takes all Twelve Steps; it takes the complete and full gospel. *Heretic* comes from the Greek word meaning "choosy ones." Fullness of recovery and salvation are not for picking and choosing. But we keep deceiving ourselves by thinking we can give so much and then no more. We hold back; we are unwilling to risk total commitment. Impossible? How do we know until we try? Surrender is a full-time job. When we risk it, we find freedom, but not until we give our "lives and wills over to the care of God" will we go beyond a "partial program."

O Christ, keep my thinking straight, headed straight toward the risk of surrender to your will and not my denials and excuses. Amen.

"No longer do I call you servants, for the servant does not know what his master is doing; but I have called you friends."

JOHN 15:15

> Tis better to have loved and lost,
> Than never to have loved at all.

When Tennyson wrote these familiar words, he obviously believed that love is a success no matter what the results. All love is worth it. Longfellow echoed Tennyson when he said,

> Talk not of wasted affection,
> Affection never was wasted . . .
> That which the fountain sends forth
> Returns again to the fountain.

When the great pianist Paderewski was touring the United States, several gifted children were to play before him. One little girl played beautifully until she missed a note and made the piano sound like rusty bed springs. She began to cry. Paderewski at once came over and kissed her on the forehead—which was a kiss she never would have received if she had played it right. The great maestro was not indifferent to music, but he was more tuned into love. No one's kiss could have meant as much to that child.

As recovering Christians we have an even better love story. It is about one who was the greatest Lover. All the discordant notes of humanity's misery and sin were hardly matters of indifference to him. That is why his gracious love means so much. If a kiss on the forehead is important, what kind of love did the cross provide? He is the fountain and source of all love. None of it is wasted. All of it flows from him and back to him, bringing forth springtime in winter, Easter in December. His love flows into all twelve months, and also into all Twelve Steps. Alleluia!

Dear Christ, your love makes all love last. Thank you for loving me. Help me love myself and others more. Amen.

December 13

All have sinned and fall short of the glory of God.

ROMANS 3:23

A minister once posed this question to a class of children: "If all the good people were black and all the bad people were white, what color would you be?" Little Suzie answered, "I'd be streaky!"

A man was looking for a good church to join, and he was shopping around. One Sunday he entered a church as the people and minister were reading from their prayer book. They were saying, "We have left undone those things which we ought to have done, and we have done those things which we ought not to have done." The man sighed with relief and said to himself, "At last I've found my kind of people."

Both little Suzie and the church-shopper discovered the reality of sin and its complete and pervasive presence. No one is either good or bad—but both. People are like skunks and zebras. Our stripes identify us. We are streaked. We are both evil and holy. We cannot pretend to be without sin, or without goodness. It's a relief to know we are not perfect. But for recovering Christians, who tend to think too badly of themselves, it's more of a relief to know we have "good streaks" in us. We are a mixed bag. But we can increase our good streaks even though our bad ones will always remain to keep us honest and humble.

Dear Christ, thank you for being so accepting of me. I have so many faults; help me see my good points too. Amen.

Conduct yourselves wisely toward outsiders, making the most of the time.

COLOSSIANS 4:5

An ancient story tells of a monarch who was constantly worried and harassed. He called his wise men together and asked them to invent a motto that would help in times of distress. It must be brief enough to be engraved on a ring and be appropriate for all situations — good or bad. They studied and prayed. The wise men came up with this motto: This, too, shall pass away. These words have become a part of our inner consciousness. Whenever we hear them, we are blessed. Robert Louis Stevenson, as his suffering grew worse, was inspired to continue writing when he remembered these five words. Lincoln was able to endure hatred and great opposition when he recalled them. Nothing lasts forever, a fact that may keep us from despair and greed, from cockiness and carelessness. Time passes. Life goes on. Each day is fresh and new. There is always more. There is always God.

Lord Christ, keep me from hanging on too tight. Let me be open to the flow of life as time passes. Amen.

And how can men preach unless they are sent? As it is written, "How beautiful are the feet of those who preach good news!"

ROMANS 10:15

For twenty years the great French artist Renoir was in great pain and misery. Rheumatism had wracked his body and crippled his fingers. Sometimes, as he held his brush between his thumb and forefinger and slowly and painfully applied his paints to the canvas, great beads of perspiration broke out on his forehead. His suffering often was so great that he cried out in pain as he painted. He could not stand up to paint, so he was placed in a chair that was raised up and down to give him access to the upper and lower parts of his canvas. Sometimes a doctor gave him sedatives, but the suffering was hardly touched. Yet Renoir persisted, painting in pain great masterpieces of beauty and enchantment. One day his disciple Matisse pleaded with him, "Master, why do you do more? Why torture yourself?" Gazing at one of his favorite canvasses, Renoir replied, "The pain passes, but the beauty remains."

What a grand motto this is for our recovery! We have gone through great pain and suffering, but it has passed; it is over and gone. Yet the beauty, the victory, remains. So much of what we have yet to do will be painful, but the results will last. Or pain can energize us and stimulate us to move on and move away from our suffering. Whatever it does, our pain indicates that we are alive and sensitive, not numb and senseless—or dead.

O Christ, keep me painting, doing, working, living in spite of the pain I suffer. Amen.

"Therefore do not be anxious about tomorrow, for tomorrow will be anxious for itself. Let the day's own trouble be sufficient for the day."

MATTHEW 6:34

The great Greek philosopher Pythagoras lived five hundred years before Jesus. One of his most famous sayings was, "Leave not the mark of the pot upon the ashes!" In other words: Wipe out the past; forget it; start the day fresh. The way to escape from worry is to focus on the present. The past cannot be undone. The future is out of reach.

When we give ourselves to each day and let the present absorb all our interest, energy, and enthusiasm, our tomorrows will be secure and our yesterdays satisfying. Seneca said:

Some there are that torment themselves afresh with the memory of what is past; others, again, afflict themselves with the fear of evils to come; and very ridiculously both—for the one does not now concern us, and the other not yet. . . . One should count each day a separate life.

Our recovery is built upon "one day at a time." We cannot carry the load of yesterday and the fear of tomorrow. Someone wise said, "Our main business is not to see what lies dimly at a distance, but to do what lies clear at hand." Clearly, our present day, this day, is at hand and is all we can handle.

Lord, keep me focused on this day. Inspire me to give my energy and thoughts to what lies at hand. Amen.

"Nor will they say, 'Lo, here it is!' or 'There!' for behold, the kingdom of God is in the midst of you."

LUKE 17:21

Through the centuries we have searched for happiness. The pursuit, in fact, is a constitutional right. Though we find happiness in many things—work, love, family, friends, possessions, honors, sports, physical pleasure, and religion—the common denominator is that it must occur *within*. Without an inner dimension all outward conditions mean nothing.

A wise man once identified one inner condition of happiness as so common, so near at hand, so plentiful, and so overlooked that we are surprised when we are told what it is: work, satisfying work. The best promoter of health is something to do that you like, and what you like depends on an inward decision. Happiness is having an ongoing activity that we have in our hearts. As Michelangelo said, "It is only well with me when I have a chisel in my hand."

Recovery and the life in Christ all offer such happiness. Recovering people and Christians are busy. It goes with the territory. Thank God every morning we have something to do, another step to take, another verse to read, another sacrifice to make, another prayer to pray, another deed to do. To live is to act, and to act with purpose and meaning is happiness.

Lord of life and work, give me energy and vitality to like what I do. Amen.

And the disciples were filled with joy and with the Holy Spirit.

ACTS 13:52

Self-acceptance is regarded as being essential for recovery. It is also necessary to happiness. Another description of self-acceptance would be contentment. David Grayson said:

All the discontented people I know are trying to be someone they are not. Contentment comes as the result of acceptance—of surrendering ourselves to the fullness of life—of letting life flow through us.

This is the heart of recovery and salvation. When we surrender to the life-flowing spirit, we become filled like the disciples. Then our self-acceptance simply means receiving and accepting the Holy Spirit of God. We become content. We are full of joy. Why? Not by accepting who we are, but by receiving the gift of God.

What is so wonderful about this gift is that we can do nothing to get it except surrender to it. To surrender to him is hard. We want to earn or work our way to him. Unfortunately, that's wasted effort. He is ours already just waiting to be received, accepted, and celebrated. When we relax and give up our need to save ourselves, we will find our genuine selves.

All yearning and striving ceases. Christ is enough. When we allow Jesus to enter our lives, we are flooded with his peace and contentment, just because he is with us. We desire nothing more; there is nothing more worth wanting. We begin our program of recovery seeking our own self-acceptance and discover that what we seek comes only by receiving Christ. We start out trying to find ourselves and wind up finding him—and find it all!

Lord, I yearn to find you. Help me to yearn only for you and find myself. Amen.

Therefore encourage one another and build one another up, just as you are doing.

THESSALONIANS 5:11

In the many words written describing happiness, these words of Beran Wolfe are among the best:

To find happiness we must seek for it in a focus outside ourselves. That is, if you live only for yourself you are always in immediate danger of being *bored to death* with the repetition of your own views and interests. No one has learned the meaning of living until he has surrendered his ego to the service of his fellow men.

Recovery is saturated with such thought. We recover as we surrender our egos to the service of our Higher Power and of others. As we gather with our fellow sufferers, we cannot help but think of them; that is, *if* we have surrendered to God. Jesus was known as "the man for others." His life gained its intense brilliance not by self-declaration but by living and dying for others—for you and me. When we reach out in Christ with the same spirit, we are lifted out of our own pain. We forget our bruises as we minister to the hurts of our companions.

All of our recovery programs must have this element of self-forgetfulness. Also, when we follow the words of Saint Paul and "encourage and build one another up" we gain a precious surprise: we are saved from our own boredom! What can be more of a tedious drag than our own egos? True joy is being lifted beyond our own selves, which someone once called "solid lumps of ego weighing a ton." Self-centeredness is not only boring, it's heavy.

Jesus takes care of both. He energizes and lifts us out of boredom and heaviness when he says, "Whoever loses his life for my sake will find it" (Matthew 16:25) and "My yoke is easy and my burden is light" (Matthew 11:30).

Jesus, you are my power of love that pulls me out of myself to others. Keep tugging at me. Don't let me stay weighed down in my own boredom. Amen.

The Lord stood by me and gave me strength.

2 TIMOTHY 4:17

So much of our life in recovery is difficult. Much of our wholeness and health is achieved through sheer endurance. We are called to "hang in there" and move from one day to the next, taking what comes each day. Somehow we manage. Sometimes we wonder how. Often we wonder why. The Chinese sage Confucius gave us his best guess: "The gem cannot be polished without friction, nor men perfected without trials." Perhaps the rough edges of life and the tough times of recovery have a purpose.

Failure and disappointment (even slips and relapses) can have the purpose of creating strength. Very few people enjoy exercising to the point of pain, yet the greatest athletes know that pain is the price they pay for success. A wise physician once said:

Just as we can immunize ourselves against bodily diseases by taking graduated doses of toxin into our bodies, so we can immunize ourselves against adversity by meeting and facing the unavoidable sorrows of life as they occur.

The real failure of our past was in *not* "meeting and facing" our difficulties. We tried to avoid the unavoidable. We went to great lengths to keep from meeting any pain. Our addictions all started out as ways to avoid the unpleasant and painful. We took the easy way.

Now, however, we know that what lasts the longest sometimes hurts the most. Now we realize that each day's pain can be met and faced with our program and our power. Jesus Christ will "stand by us and give us strength," day by day and bit by bit.

Great Physician, give me your medicine. With you I can endure. Thank you for your daily dose of love and health. Amen.

And after you have suffered a little while, the God of all grace, who has called you to his eternal glory in Christ, will himself restore, establish, and strengthen you.

1 PETER 5:10

Acceptance bears us up. It is like buoyant water to a swimmer. The more we trust what we are immersed in, the better we float, the more progress we make to the shore. The word *amen* means "so be it; it is accepted." Recovery is the willingness to have it as it is. Accepting what has already happened is our first step to overcoming our sickness. Helen Keller demonstrated this when she said, "I thank God for my handicaps, for, through them, I have found myself, my work, and my God."

As Christians we must never forget that we follow the way of the cross, the way of suffering and pain, the path of humble obedience. Through his love Christ empowers us to embrace pain and submit to suffering, absorbing it in a sea of love. Whatever evil may befall us, we can see good and God in the midst of our darkness. When we no longer struggle and resist, we can find a reservoir of strength inside that God provides for us to draw on. The greatest power we are provided is the patience to wait.

When we wait for God's word and will, we can notice much more than when we are impatiently and frantically struggling, using up energy that could be healing and strengthening us.

Lord, teach me to accept the inevitable, to embrace my situation and you at the same time, and wait. Amen.

"Every one when he is fully taught will be like his teacher."
LUKE 6:40

A little boy timidly approached a lingerie clerk in a department store. It was Christmas Eve day. He shyly whispered, "I would like to buy my mother a slip for Christmas." "Very nice," the clerk answered, "but first I need to know more about your mother. Is she short or tall?" The little boy said proudly, "Why she's perfect!" With that information, the clerk wrapped up a size thirty-six for him. A few days later his mother returned her slip and exchanged it for a larger size!

When, Jesus says in Luke, we are fully taught, we will become like our teachers. He means something more than just physical likeness. We all follow role models. We want to be like those we admire. Our teachers, preachers, coaches, sports heroes, and above all, our parents provide patterns for us to imitate. In fact, one of our mottos in recovery recognizes this power of imitation with "Stick with the winners." During treatment we are also urged to "Change our playmates and our playgrounds."

But what about the little boy and the clerk? Who was closest to Jesus? We know that the clerk was shallow and incorrect. The clerk was wrong, but so is almost everyone else in our culture! We live in a world that is obsessed with externals. The little boy was profoundly right. He was yet untouched by our worship of slenderness. His mother was "perfect" to him. She was "just right" because she was loved and therefore seen in her true light. The little boy knew what Jesus knew: love sees inside. It is the inward and spiritual beauty of Christ that we yearn to copy and become. What he creates within will live with him forever in a beauty beyond perfection.

Dear Lord and master, may I become more and more like you, as you teach me your way of inner beauty and love. Amen.

The shepherds returned, glorifying and praising God for all they had heard and seen.

LUKE 2:20

An American writer described one Christmas Eve he spent with his wife in a drab little cafe in Paris. Everyone was eating in stony silence. An old flower woman came through the door. She went from table to table. No sales. She sat down to a bowl of soup. Into this sad scene a young sailor rose from his table where he had been smiling and writing a letter. He went to the flower lady's table. "Happy Christmas," he said, as he picked up two corsages. "How much are they?" "Two francs, monsieur." He pressed one of the small corsages flat and put it into his letter with a kiss, and handed the woman a twenty-franc note. "I don't have change, monsieur, I'll get some from the waiter," she said. "No, ma'am," said the sailor, leaning over and kissing her ancient cheek. "This is my Christmas present to you." The sailor then went to the writer's table: "May I have permission to present these flowers to your beautiful daughter?" he asked. In one quick motion he gave her the corsage, wished them a Holy Christmas, and departed. Everyone had stopped eating to watch the sailor. When he left there was a deep silence. Then suddenly Christmas exploded throughout the restaurant like a bomb.

A letter, a smile, flowers, a kiss, a gift, a compliment, a greeting—all from one person to transform a dull, drab place into a glowing and joyful place. Because of Jesus and his joy in one heart, "Christmas can explode like a bomb" in other hearts. All it takes is love and the risk of showing that love by giving it to others.

O holy Jesus, be in my heart like an explosive power of joy and glory. May I light my own fuse. Amen.

"For to you is born this day in the city of David a Savior, who is Christ the Lord."

LUKE 2:11

In 1863 Henry Wadsworth Longfellow was listening to the Christmas bells only six months after the Battle of Gettysburg. As the nation mourned its dead, he ached with the pain of his wounded son, and as he listened, the bells inspired these words:

> I heard the bells on Christmas Day
> Their old, familiar carols play,
> And wild and sweet
> The words repeat
> Of peace on earth, good-will to men!
>
> And thought how, as the day had come,
> The belfries of all Christendom,
> Had rolled along
> The unbroken song
> Of peace on earth, good-will to men!
>
> And in despair I bowed my head;
> "There is no peace on earth," I said,
> "For hate is strong
> And mocks the song
> Of peace on earth, good-will to men!"
>
> Then pealed the bells more loud and deep,
> God is not dead, nor doth he sleep.
> The Wrong shall fail,
> The Right prevail,
> With peace on earth, good-will to men!

These words are as true now as ever. Christmas is news each year. News happens whether we know it or not, and Christmas will keep on happening, with us or without us, in triumph or tragedy. Christ never fails. The message is still as clear today as on the hills of Bethlehem. "Glory to God in the highest—the Savior is born!"

Dearest Jesus, release the joy in my heart in your coming, so that I may sing with the angels. Amen.

*And going into the house they saw the child with Mary his
mother, and they fell down and worshiped him.*

MATTHEW 2:11

Each Christmas the recovering Christian has the opportunity to find and to witness the greatest of all joys—the birth
of Jesus, our Savior. In the past, we might have indulged
ourselves to the limit in a festival of eating, drinking, and
partying. We might have wound up tired, if not exhausted,
and finished the Christmas season in depression and sadness. This Christmas we have a chance to capture the true
joy and exuberance of the shepherds, the angels, the Wise
Men, and the Holy Family.

Perhaps we can devote ourselves to a "Holy" Christmas
instead of a "Merry" one. What other way can we meet the
Holy one, except with holiness and awe? We need not grieve
over what we have given up; we can praise God for our
deliverance from such shallowness and thank him for his
love and join our voices with angels and archangels who
forever sing this hymn to the glory of his name:

> Holy, Holy, Holy, Lord God of Hosts
> Heaven and earth are full of thy glory,
> Glory be to thee, O Lord most high.
> Blessed is He who cometh in the name of the Lord
> Hosanna in the highest. Amen.

*O holy Christ, give me a renewed spirit of love and reverence for
your name. May I ever fall down and worship you. Amen.*

"Behold, I am the handmaid of the Lord."

LUKE 1:38

Mary's faith began (as all faith begins) in simple, humble trust in the grace of God, not in any great effort or work. Mary's faith began with childlike wonder, receptivity, and openness to the angel's message. Mary is our supreme example of the grace of receiving, not giving or doing. She inspires us to acceptance, to the welcoming of God's embrace, to submission to God's initiative. Mary calls us to see God as active and energetic. As God moves, he has the right of way. As God speaks, we listen. As God pitches, we catch. As God directs, we yield.

The highway sign Yield is a motto for everyone in recovery. It expresses what we mean by "Let go and let God." It is the essence of surrender. We yield when we stand aside, when we give way to another, when we submit to the first move, when we wait, accept, and receive.

It is impossible to yield when we are afraid, angry, or selfish. When we are threatened, we give way to nothing; we yield to no one. When we keep on standing alone, steadfast, stubborn, and insistent on others yielding to us, we become so selfishly petrified that we cannot grow or give life to any seed. We are inpenetrable.

Yet if we drop our defenses, soften ourselves, open our lives, we become like freshly plowed and cultivated soil—soft, yielding, and ready to embrace with tenderness and warmth the holy gospel of love. When we yield to God's seeds, they take root in our lives.

Jesus, please loosen and break up my hard, stubborn ground. Plow me up, and make my soil soft and yielding to your love. Amen.

"His name shall be called Emmanuel" (which means, God with us).

MATTHEW 1:23

About a hundred years before the birth of Jesus, a Greek mathematician wrote about the seven wonders of the world. His list was: the Great Pyramid of Egypt, the lighthouse at Alexandria, the Hanging Gardens of Babylon, the Colossus of Rhodes, the Tomb of Mausolus, the Statue of Zeus at Olympia, and the Temple of Diana at Ephesus. Today we might list many more buildings, towers, and temples.

As grand as any of civilization's wonders have been and will be, none are as grand as God's forests, oceans, mountains, his cosmic universe. Yet more wonderful still is that the mightiest of the mighty—our God and creator of the universe—loves you and me as his own children! He lives and dwells in us. He came to us as Jesus, Emmanuel ("God with us"), to save us from sin and death and to lift us to joy and glory.

Dag Hammarskjöld once wrote that:

We die on the day when our lives cease to be illumined by the steady radiance, renewed daily, of a wonder, the source of which is beyond all reason.

That "steady radiance" streams from the face of Jesus, born in a stable, who shines into our hearts, giving light and life to us all—not just at Christmas but "renewed daily." There is no "wonder of the world" like him.

O child of Bethlehem, let me gaze in wonder and love at your shining face again and again and rejoice. Amen.

"Behold, I bring you good news of a great joy which will come to all the people."

LUKE 2:10

When a baby gets to be two months old, its first smile usually appears. By the fourth month the infant explodes into what we call laughter. What would life be without the delight of laughter? It relieves tension, attracts friends, and helps us withstand life's pain. Scientists have studied the benefits of laughter for years. Apparently when we laugh, we aid every organ in the body. Laughter relaxes, exercises, and calms us. He who laughs, lasts.

A special kind of laughter is called joy. Joy has been called "the gigantic secret of the Christian." To rejoice is more than to laugh—joy comes from within and carries with it grace and gratitude for all life. A joyful person may seldom laugh out loud but always carries a smile within the heart. Where does this joy come from? The angels announced it at Bethlehem: "Joy to the world, the Savior is born." Our joy is our response to Jesus, our salvation.

Recovery that has no joy is not recovery. When we walk the way of the Twelve Steps, we tread on joyful ground. When we enter into our fellowship of new life, of addiction healing, we enter into the land of joy. What is this joy like? It's more than happy, more than laughter; it is a peace and serenity that passes all understanding, it is life with God.

My joy in your birth is always fresh each Christmas, Lord. Make every day your birthday in me. Amen.

> *"But whoever drinks of the water that I shall give him will never thirst."*
>
> JOHN 4:14

Saint Augustine once wrote, "Our hearts are restless, Oh Lord, until they rest in Thee." For centuries we have known that there is within each human being an emptiness that cries out to be filled by God. Unfortunately, our instinct for God is often confused with other desires, and we try to fill God's space with lesser deities. Alcohol, food, and drugs, activities and other persons are welcomed into our "God-space," yet they never fit or fill us. They may control us and may dominate us, but they never satisfy our longing. Only God can fill that longing we have for him.

God is not only our destination and our true home; he is also the very life and heart of our being. He is our home; we are his home. To be at home with God is to make a home for him in our hearts. Step Three is the beginning of "setting up our home" in God. Each Christmas time we sing a carol that issues a fresh invitation to Christ, our God, to fill our special space reserved just for him:

> O Holy child of Bethlehem!
> Descend to us, we pray;
> Cast out our sin, and enter in:
> Be born in us today. Amen.

Dear Christ, come fill me with your life. Only you can fit the empty space in my heart. Amen.

From his fulness have we all received, grace upon grace.
JOHN 1:16

Almost everyone who has entered into Twelve-Step recovery programs can look back and remember when we thought we didn't need any help. What did we care about "grace"? Then after a time we remember our despair, our endless sorrow and our constant ache for such "grace". Nothing seemed to happen. Where was this God, this "higher power"?

In Samuel Beckett's play, *Waiting for Godot*, we are presented a picture of such "pre-recovery" days. The author tells the story of two tramps who wait in vain for someone named "Godot." This name is an obvious symbol for God. God equals Godot. Through the entire play the characters keep looking forward to Godot's arrival. But the curtain falls. We never see him come. We know that he will never come. The author plainly believes that God will never come for anyone — ever.

We know better. As recovering Christians, we know him in our Twelve-Step healing and we know him in Jesus Christ. We "have all received grace upon grace." In fact, that's how we found him, through grace. We stopped trying and stopped looking and gave up. We "let go and let God." We discovered that we didn't have to wait. Godot was with us all along. We realized that it is vain to wait when love has already arrived and lives in our hearts. At this time of year, when we have just re-celebrated his birthday, we can pray for his coming afresh and anew all of next year. Hear the words of St. John:

And the Word became flesh and dwelt among us, full of grace and truth; we beheld his glory. (John 1:14)

We still do.

Jesus, why do I wait for you, when you are already here with me? Why do I look for you as if you were absent? Thank you for your presence in the Twelve Steps and in your Church. Amen.

> *"I am the Alpha and the Omega, the first and the last, the beginning and the end."*
>
> REVELATION 22:13

The Italians have a marvelous custom at the end of the year. As midnight on New Year's Eve approaches, the streets are deserted. There is no traffic. There are no pedestrians. Even the policemen take cover and clear out. Then at the stroke of midnight, the windows of the houses fly open. To the sound of laughter, music, and fireworks, each member of the family pitches out old crockery and dishes, detested ornaments, hated furniture, and a whole batch of personal possessions that remind them of something in the past year they are determined to wipe out of their minds.

As we wind up our year, we too can wipe out the past. The year is completed, over, finished. Another fresh new year lies ahead. What was bad is gone; what is good will stay with us to enrich us. Was Christ with us this past year? Of course. Can we expect his presence in the new? Certainly. What a comfort is his presence.

We cannot know what the New Year will bring. We will have pleasure and pain, satisfaction and disappointment, success and failure. How much of which, we cannot tell. Yet we know that Christ our Lord will be with us every day of the year, come what may.

Lord, as I cast away my past mistakes I look forward to another year, another chance to grow and be with you. Amen.

Prayers for the Recovering Person

For the Presence of Christ

O living Christ, make us conscious now of your healing nearness. Touch our eyes that we may see you; open our ears that we may hear your voice; enter our hearts that we may know your love. Overshadow our souls and bodies with your presence, that we may partake of your strength, your love, and your healing life. Amen.

For Self-dedication

Into your hands, O Lord, we commit ourselves this day. Give to each one of us a watchful, humble, and diligent spirit, that we may seek in all things to know your will, and when we know it may perform it gladly, to the honor and glory of your name; through Jesus Christ our Lord. Amen.

For Self-surrender

O God, who has taught us that we are most truly free when we find our wills in yours, help us to gain this liberty by continual surrender unto you, that we may walk in the way which you have ordained for us and in doing your will may find our life; through Jesus Christ our Lord. Amen.

For Victory over Temptation

Grant us, O Lord, to pass this day in gladness and peace, without stumbling and without stain; that, reaching the evening victorious over all temptation, we may praise you, the eternal God, who is blessed, and who governs all things. Amen.

For a Right Attitude toward Pain

We ask you not, O Lord, to rid us of pain; but grant in your mercy that our pain may be unfettered by rebellion against your will, unsoiled by thought of ourselves, purified by love of our kind, and ennobled by devotion to your kingdom; through the merits of your only Son our Lord. Amen.

For a Confident Spirit

Almighty God, who is the only source of health and healing, the spirit of calm and the central peace of the universe, grant to us your children, such a consciousness of your indwelling presence as may give us utter confidence in you. In all pain and weariness may we throw ourselves upon your care; that knowing ourselves fenced about by your love, we may permit you to give us health and strength and peace. Amen.

For Brave Sufferers

We thank thee, O Father, for all who hallow suffering: for those who in their thoughts for others leave no room for pity for themselves; for those whose patience inspires others to hold on. And grant, O loving Father, to all who are bound in the mysterious fellowship of suffering the sense of comradeship with others and the knowledge of your love, and give them your peace which passes all understanding. Amen.

At Night

O Lord, who has pity for all our weakness, put from us worry and all misgiving, that having done our best while it was day, we may, when night comes, commit ourselves, our tasks, and all we love into your keeping; through Jesus Christ our Savior. Amen.

An Approach to Christ

To think of you, O Christ, is to rest. To know you is eternal life. To see you is the end of all we desire. To serve you is perfect freedom and everlasting joy. Therefore we come to you. Amen.

For Rest in the Lord

Grant, O Father, that as your blessed Son did turn from much business to quiet communion with you, so we in life's strain and stress may find in you our strength and peace; through Jesus Christ our Lord. Amen.

For Those in Need

O Lord Jesus, grant us in loneliness to realize your continual presence; in deafness, the sweetness of your voice; in blindness, the sufficiency of your light; in reproach, the satisfaction of your sympathy; in poverty, the riches of your love. Amen.

For Control of Speech

O God, who knows how often we sin against you with our tongues; keep us free from all untrue and unkind words; consecrate our speech to your service; and keep us often silent, that our hearts may speak to you and may listen for your voice; through Jesus Christ our Lord. Amen.

For the Will to Share

O God, who to save us did give your only-begotten Son, stir us with such love toward you that we may gladly share whatever you have entrusted to us of life and strength, influence and love, money and time, for the relief of the world's sorrow and the coming of your Kingdom. Amen.

God in Everyday Life

We thank you, O God, for the revelation of yourself in the common ways of life, and in special times and things and places. Help us to be ever watchful for new knowledge of you, so that in the temporal we may discern that which is eternal; through Jesus Christ our Lord. Amen.

For Kindness

Grant, O Lord, that in all the joy of life I may never forget to be kind. Help me to be unselfish in friendship, thoughtful of those less happy than myself, and eager to bear the burdens of others; through Jesus Christ our Savior. Amen.

For Humility

O Lord, open our minds to see ourselves as you see us, and save us from all unwillingness to know our infirmities; for the sake of Jesus Christ our Savior. Amen.

For Perseverance

O God, who has called us to your service; show us your purpose for our lives; though it be hard, make us long to follow it. Give us courage to persevere till, at the last, we reach the goal which you have set for us; through Jesus Christ our Lord. Amen.

In Time of Weariness

O God, the strength of those who labor and the rest of the weary, grant us when we are tired with our work to be recreated by your Spirit; that being renewed for the service of your kingdom, we may serve you gladly in freshness of body and mind; through Jesus Christ our Lord. Amen.

For Christian Gladness

O God, author of the world's joy, bearer of the world's pain; at the heart of all our trouble and sorrow let unconquerable gladness dwell; through our Lord and Savior Jesus Christ. Amen.

For God's Help

Grant us, O Lord, in all our duties your help, in all our perplexities your counsel, in all dangers your protection, and in all our sorrows your peace; for the sake of Jesus Christ our Savior. Amen.

Benedictions

May the God of all grace who has called us unto his eternal glory by Christ Jesus, after that we have suffered awhile, make us perfect, establish, strengthen us. To him be glory and dominion for ever and ever. Amen.

May God be within us to refresh us, around us to protect us, before us to guide us, above us to bless us, beneath us to hold us up; who lives and reigns, one God, world without end. Amen.

For Serenity

God grant me the Serenity to accept the things I cannot change; Courage to change the things I can; and the Wisdom to know the difference.

Living one day at a time; accepting hardship as a pathway to peace; taking, as Jesus did, this sinful world as it is, not as I would have it: Trusting that you will make all things right if I surrender to your will; that I may be reasonably happy in this life and supremely happy with you forever in the next. Amen.

Slogans & Sayings

	Jan.	Feb.	March	April	May	June	July	Aug.	Sept.	Oct.	Nov.	Dec.
But For The Grace of God	28	16	22	20	17	23	15	27	24	20	17	30
Easy Does It	2	15	10	17	29	24	22	19	11	16	5	19
Expect A Miracle	14	26	27	11	13	22	9	30	26	8	4	23
First Things First	29	2	11	13	20	16	26	28	22	25	25	27
If Nothing Changes	31	17	31	11	18	14	19	8	8	7	4	1
Keep An Open Mind	14	27	31	14	3	30	13	2	28	14	7	26
Keep It Simple/Think	19	20	13	30	25	29	2	14	25	22	26	26
Let Go and Let God	13	14	19	19	10	15	28	16	23	17	2	11
Listen & Learn	30	7	24	25	28	17	27	17	30	24	12	22
Live & Let Live	23	17	14	28	9	30	29	13	22	11	27	29
One Day At A Time	9	13	20	24	20	10	21	20	10	31	6	16

Steps and Slogans Index

The Twelve Steps

	Jan.	Feb.	March	April	May	June	July	Aug.	Sept.	Oct.	Nov.	Dec.
1. Our Weakness—*Romans 7:15-24*	3	1	1	1	1	1	1	1	1	1	1	1
2. God's Power—*Mark 10:51-52*	4	2	2	2	2	2	2	2	2	2	2	2
3. Our Collapse—*Romans 12:1*	5	3	2	2	3	3	3	3	3	3	3	3
4. Our Examination—*Psalm 139*	6	4	3	4	4	3	3	3	3	3	3	3
5. Our Confession—*James 5:16*	7	5	4	5	5	15	5	4	4	4	4	5
6. Our Readiness—*Isaiah 30:13*	9	5	5	6	10	5	6	5	5	5	5	6
7. Our Request—*I John 1:9*	10	24	6	6	7	5	6	5	5	5	5	6
8. Our Damage List—*Psalm 19:12-14*	8	6	5	7	6	6	7	6	6	5	5	6
9. Our Repair Job—*Matthew 5:23-25*	8	10	6	7	6	6	7	6	6	20	5	7
10. Our Vigilance—*I Corinthians 10:12*	26	19	7	8	30	7	8	4	7	1	16	7
11. Our God-Search—*Psalm 63:1-7*	10	12	8	9	7	8	9	8	8	7	9	8
12. Our Responsibility—*Galatians 6:1-9*	11	8	9	10	8	9	10	9	9	9	9	19

Subject Index

	Jan.	Feb.	March	April	May	June	July	Aug.	Sept.	Oct.	Nov.	Dec.
Acceptance	25	18	12	17	23	30	14	24	1	4	20	13
Action	1	20	28	10	27	11	30	11	7	11	28	17
Awareness	30	29	16	18	30	25	13	10	14	21	23	10
Choice	16	14	15	27	19	21	25	5	29	14	13	6
Crucifixion/Holy Week	20	9	17	10	2	4	31	15	28	26	17	21
Faith	21	7	18	20	22	12	23	12	27	23	14	14
Fear	12	9	4	29	2	28	18	26	12	28	10	5
Higher Power	2	11	24	16	18	16	23	30	26	29	29	20
Hope	14	26	30	3	13	26	6	30	28	21	18	31
Love	11	8	17	21	16	21	20	14	28	10	21	12
Resentment	27	6	6	7	11	7	12	6	29	6	19	7
Resurrection/Easter	1	13	26	15	14	19	24	31	19	27	14	25
Salvation	18	25	25	22	15	27	24	25	16	12	15	28
Security	6	28	23	26	21	24	3	21	15	13	29	21
Serenity	15	13	21	9	31	20	17	22	13	9	10	24
Service	22	8	26	23	26	6	7	18	18	4	24	21
Shame & Guilt	8	24	11	14	24	15	7	7	4	7	17	4
Sin	17	22	24	11	4	13	31	29	20	18	16	15
Suffering	20	1	29	1	12	13	13	20	18	15	16	15
Surrender	24	21	13	12	3	19	20	15	17	17	15	18